TONY PÉREZ

TONY
PÉREZ

From Cuba to Cooperstown

JOHN ERARDI

To Tom, the
Big Dog of
Running—
From Milford to
Cooperstown, & Hell
of Farrer for
a Luke!,

John Erardi

ORANGE *frazer* PRESS

Wilmington, Ohio

ISBN 978-1939710-758
Copyright©2018 John Erardi and Orange Frazer Press

Orange Frazer Press
P.O. Box 214
Wilmington, OH 45177
Telephone: 937.382.3196 for price and shipping information.
Website: www.orangefrazer.com

Book and cover design: Alyson Rua and Orange Frazer Press

Cover photograph courtesy of Focus on Sport/Getty Images

Interior photographs courtesy of Arturo Pardavila III: page 258; Author's collection: pages xi, xiii, and 8; (Bill) Renken Photographic Services, Cincinnati: page ix; Cam Bonifay: pages 92 and 101; CEI Sports: page 75; Chuck Agonito: page 84; Chuck Davis: page 70; The *Cincinnati Enquirer*: pages 2, 72, 124, 126, 131, 177, 181, 184, 201, 205, 206, 217, 224, 239, 240, 244, 253, and 256; Dave Bristol: page 106; Gina Nicole Erardi: page 38; Greg Rhodes: pages xiv and 246; Jim Bunning: page 16; Larry Phillips: pages 186 and 196; Martín Dihigo Sr. Museum, Cruces, Cuba: page 26; National Baseball Hall of Fame and Library: pages 20, 32, and 60; Reds Hall of Fame, Jack Klumpe collection: pages 35, 63, 82, 103, 111, 112, 114, 123, 127, 133, 144, 153, 165, and 166; Tim VonderBrink: pages 12, 30, 48, 54 and 58.

Library of Congress Cataloging-in-Publication Data

Names: Erardi, John G., author.
Title: Tony Pérez : from Cuba to Cooperstown / John Erardi.
Description: Wilmington, Ohio : Orange Frazer Press, [2018] | Includes index.
Identifiers: LCCN 2017053060 | ISBN 9781939710758
Subjects: LCSH: Pérez, Tony, 1942- | Baseball players--Cuba--Biography. | Baseball players--United States--Biography.
Classification: LCC GV865.P466 E73 2018 | DDC 796.357092 [B] --dc23
LC record available at https://lccn.loc.gov/2017053060

First Printing

Contents

Author's Note

Little Havana—Going back to the source now, to the forerunner of Pérez, Ruiz, and Cardenas; back to Oliva, Versalles, Valdespino, and Pascual, to what got me started and years later drew me to do this book: I turned thirteen the day the 1965 World Series opened in Minnesota. There was nothing I loved more than baseball when I was twelve and thirteen. I was intrigued by the Twins' Cuban players and the zest with which they played the game. Beyond that, I didn't put much together, except that I was aware that these men with the mellifluous first and last names had come from the same island-country where, three Octobers earlier, nuclear missiles had been aimed at us.

Ten years after that World Series on TV, I took my dad, one of my brothers, one of my sisters, and a college buddy to Games Three, Four, and Five of the 1975 World Series in Cincinnati, the first such Fall Classics for any of us. At home in Syracuse were our younger brother and sister and our tea-drinking Irish-American "mither" with her love of words and baseball players of style and substance, leading to her nightly 11 o'clock declaration, "Put the Tiant, ('tea on'), Luis." Needless to say, she was pulling for you-know-who in Game Four, while the Erardis in attendance were pulling for Pérez & Company. By Game Five, even Mary Jane Gannon was pulling for the Big Dog to break out of his 0-for-15.

I was back for the 1976 World Series, this time in Standing Room Only with brother Greg (who one autumn later was in the major leagues himself) and another college buddy who stood baseball-kibitzing with Kevin "Crockah!"

Dobson of TV *Kojak* fame as Pérez drove in Ken Griffey Sr. for the walk-off victory against Catfish Hunter in Game Two to set up the sweep three days later at Yankee Stadium. (The Sweep began, for real, the comparisons with the '27 Yankees of Ruth and Gehrig for "Greatest Team of All-Time." I'll always love what '27 Yankees pitcher Waite Hoyt-turned-Reds-broadcaster told Pete Rose: "You guys catch it better.")

Not until I began doing this biography did I learn that Tony's parents and two brothers and three sisters had never gotten to see him play in person as a professional, not even in the World Series. Until I talked with the Cuban-born Tiant at the 2015 All-Star Game in Cincinnati, I had no knowledge of the fact that he had brought *his* mother and father to the States in 1975 (after being separated from them for fourteen years), when they saw him pitch in the major leagues for the first time.

So, in that sense, I hadn't wised up much in the ten years between Oliva-Versalles and Pérez-Tiant.

But by the time the 2017 World Series hit center stage—it would be the first time two Cubans hit home runs in the same World Series since Oliva and Versalles in 1965—I had wised-up a lot: I knew exactly what I was watching in Yuli Gurriel and Yasiel Puig, who each hit two home runs in the Series. I knew context and transformation: 2017 was the first time in six decades that the World Series would be broadcast in Cuba since Castro had taken over on New Year's Day, 1959.

Subconsciously, if not overtly, I went into this project thinking that somehow the Cuban game was a stepchild of the American game—a watered-down, wanna-but-never-will-be, pale-ale version of our great national pastime. The Cubans, my thinking went, had ripped off our game and called it their own.

I've wised-up a whole lot since.

One trip to Cuba—followed by a whole lot of reading of Roberto González Echevarria and Peter Bjarkman—opened my eyes to reality. I was soon disabused of my Ugly American notion. In actuality, my assumption had been rooted in the same longstanding prejudice that helped create the Cuba that was the breeding ground for the late Fidel Castro's *Revolución*; I had assumed too much.

Author interviews Tony after the second-to-last game of the Big Dog's 2,777-game major-league career. The forty-four-year-old Cuban had just tied his friend, Puerto Rican Orlando Cepeda, for most career home runs by a Latino (379), October 4, 1986.

(Caveat: Just so you know—This book was never meant to be about Castro, nor is it now that he has passed. This book was, and is, meant to be about the essence of Tony Pérez—*El Perro Grande*, the Big Dog—and the environment that created *him*. A pox on the house of any activist in South Florida who reads into it any more than that. I have been told that the Cuba Lobby and some Cuban voices in South Florida will twist anything that so much as mentions Castro into a screed. Let this be my preemptive strike: I have presented Castro in no way other than historical fact. If you take it any other way than that, shame on you. But if you have to blame it on somebody, blame it on me, not Tony Pérez.)

After all this book-work, here's what I know: The American and the Cuban national pastimes are *different*, neither better than the other. And the cross-pollination can only help both. I love the precision of the American game played on the highest level possible. I love the stylishness and creativity and spontaneity of the Cuban game, and how the fans get into it with their cheers and jeers, willing themselves into the game as a vital and vibrant part of it. And they don't need drama to get into it; long before the first pitch, they've made themselves part of the show. I love that the Cubans integrated their game two generations before we did ours.

To me, what best exemplifies the differences in our games are the Cuban pitchers. Almost to a man, they have "it"—the art for the game. Even the power pitchers, including Aroldis Chapman and the late José Fernandez, have and had it. The American game is mostly power; there is more creativity among the Cubans.

This quality is refined in the Reds' Raisel Iglesias, possessed of a very good fastball but best distinguished by his "pitchability"—his wile and guile and creativity. I love watching this balance of head and arm outsmart the hitters—and then blow them away.

The infusion of more Cubans into our game will benefit it tremendously, because the game is going to become more artful. Why is that? *What* is that? In 1975, I had seen it up close in Cincinnati with Tiant; two years later, I saw it up close in Chicago with Diego Seguí. I would see it again in the next Cuban wave— the New York Yankees' Orlando "El Duque" Hernández in the late 1990s and early 2000s, and on into the Reds' Iglesias.

Is it something about the culture? I think so. Cuba is famous for its boxers and its ballet dancers; I'd seen incredible balance from women on their boyfriends' bicycle fenders throughout my travels in Cuba. I know firsthand that "me mither to be" loved the spontaneity of the Cuban people when she visited the island (in 1948) at twenty-three. I asked my brother if that spontaneity and creativity applied to the art of pitching; he had pitched with Seguí in Seattle in September of '77.

"Diego was very creative, as was El Duque, in that they changed speeds on all their pitches, changed their windups. And threw their pitches from a variety of arm slots," Greg said. "You never really knew what they were going to do next. They seemed fearless when it came to experimenting in game situations. I don't know where that came from, but to attribute it to cultural influences is as good a theory as any other that I could imagine."

I talked a lot about this "Cuba mystique" with the amazing eighty-year-old Gabriel Iglesias (no relation to Raisel) of Domino Park in Little Havana, Miami, in February 2016. Iglesias told me story after story of the Cuban players of his youth, of how many came out of the poverty. "That alone is going to make you resourceful because you have to eat. When baseball gives you a chance, you make the most of it. You play your heart out."

He said Saturnino Orestes Arrieta—major-league name "Minnie Miñoso"—is the patron saint of Cuban baseball work ethic. When the sugar plantation owner outside Havana wouldn't field a baseball team, fourteen-year-old Orestes did it all, finding the players and managing the team. At twenty—an age when Tony Pérez was in his third pro season—Miñoso was still playing baseball for $2 a game and working in a Havana garage.

Gabriel Iglesias, "The Oracle of Domino Park, Little Havana."

"You have to understand: The major leagues weren't scouting for black players in Cuba or anywhere else," Iglesias explains. "That was four years before Jackie Robinson. Miñoso was still in the Negro Leagues in 1948. When he had his first real chance in the majors—Cleveland, 1951—he was twenty-five; hit thirty-four doubles, fourteen triples, ten home runs, and stole thirty-one bases! You don' think he wasn't hungry? In 1960—my last full year in Cuba—Miñoso was still great! Hit .311, twenty home runs, led the league in hits and games played. Still hungry! Thirty-four years old! Cuba in the blood!"

I tell Iglesias, "If I were on the Hall of Fame's veterans' committee, I'd vote for Miñoso."

Iglesias shakes his head no.

"Lifetime .298," he says, citing the sub-.300 batting average. "Not enough."

But a .389 on-base percentage, I say, googling Miñoso on my phone; .459 slugging percentage. Mighty good. Pérez was .341 on-base, .463 slugging.

"Okay, maybe," says Iglesias, smiling.

Love it. Octogenarian with an open mind.

Oh, and how about this one, Oracle? (By this time in the conversation, I am addressing Iglesias as "Oracle.")

"Tony Pérez had one of the greatest age forty-three seasons by a hitter in baseball history," I say. (I'm guessing at that, but I later find out it is true.)

"How can you tell that?" he asks me.

"You've heard of On Base Plus Slugging Percentage?"

"Yes."

"Well, 'OPS+' adjusts for park and league effects. You can compare players from different eras. An OPS+ of 100 is league average. Pérez's '138' in 1985 was 38 percent above league average! At forty-three! I don't know if there's ever been another forty-three-year-old to go that high. His slash line was .316/.396/.470."

"Wow," says Iglesias.

Wow is right. My numbers' analyst, Greg Gajus, confirms it for me when I get back to Cincinnati. He tells me Pérez's 1985 season (minimum two hundred plate appearances) is the best offensive season by a forty-three-year-old in baseball history. The second-best age forty-three season is Carl Yastrzemski

(437 plate appearances) in 1983 with 106, six points above league average—but not in the same league as Pérez's 138.

I wished I'd known all this when I was talking with Iglesias. I especially wished I'd known it in 2000 in Cooperstown when I was talking with Hall of Fame classmates Carlton Fisk and Pérez. They are two of the truest, purest lovers of the game I'd ever met. They are also No. 1 and No. 2—1.9 to 1.7, respectively—for greatest "WAR" seasons ever by a forty-three-year-old.

Luis Zayas, former Sugar King living in La Habana, Cuba.

"One more story," says Oracle, his eyes beginning to glaze over.

"Shoot," I say.

"Miñoso loved his Cadillacs," he recalls. "Lived with his sister on Seventy-Second Avenue in Havana. Parked his Cadillac on the corner. I know. I had to go by that car almost every day; I made deliveries to the store on the corner."

"Amazing."

I had one conversation that tops it—with the old Havana Sugar King, Luis Zayas, in a Havana restaurant in December 2015. Second baseman Zayas played with fellow Cubans Mike Cuellar, Elio Chacón, and Tony González, and Puerto Rican Niño Escalera for the 1958 Cincinnati Reds' Triple-A affiliate at Gran Stadium in "Habana," managed by Nap Reyes and Tony Pacheco, the man who signed Tony Pérez.

And why had my conversation with Zayas topped my conversation with Iglesias? Because Iglesias spoke good English. Zayas barely spoke any English, and I barely spoke any Spanish. But for a full ten-minute stretch, with just names and baseball terms and hand and foot motions—one moment, we were standing up in the restaurant converting a phantom double play (our table was second base)—we "talked" without needing our interpreter, Sergio.

Then, realizing we weren't using him, we simultaneously turned to include him in the conversation. We saw the bewilderment on his face. Sergio is a Havanan like Luis, but Sergio isn't a baseball fan. He hadn't understood a phrase or a name or pantomime we had used.

Luis and I burst out laughing.

"To baseball," said Luis, raising his glass.

"*Viva el beisbol*," said I, clinking his glass.

Yes, *viva el beisbol*—and *viva El Perro Grande.* ◆

Streetscape, Old Havana, 2015.

* Editor's note: The name of Tony Pérez's wife of 50-plus years—the vivacious Pituka, who is almost as iconic as her husband in Cincinnati—is spelled "Pituca" in Spanish. We have chosen to use the familiar spelling throughout, however, because that is how Pituka is known in America, and what she goes by. Otherwise, we have been as true as possible to Cuban/*Español* spellings throughout.

TONY PÉREZ

Tony Pérez, about whom teammate Johnny Bench said: "Can we really know what he accomplished and overcame (to become a Hall of Famer), without having walked in his shoes?"

PROLOGUE
One of a Kind

"Need a ride?" asked the middle-aged man in the white guayabera shirt.

"Sure," I said, struck that there was no queue for taxicabs outside José Marti Airport in Havana, and no one to direct them. Just a solidly built man with jet-black hair and a pack of cookies in his left hand.

"Cookie?" he asked, holding forth the cookie pack.

I had eaten at the airport in Mexico and was still full, so I declined—a minor mistake as it turned out. "How was it?" I later asked Ron, one of my two traveling companions. "Good," he said. "Kind of like a Lorna Doone with lemon filling. You should have taken one."

Riding the expressway toward downtown Havana, we noticed right away the relatively light traffic, something one would never see in an American city of two million people, especially in a capital city on a weekday mid-morning.

After exchanging pleasantries—yes, Daniel was a baseball fan; he had two sons, and they frequently attended *Industriales* games on Sundays at *Estadio Latinoamericano* in the heart of Havana—I got right to the point.

"I'm in Cuba to do a book about Tony Pérez."

"Who?" responded Daniel.

"Tani PEER-ez," I answered, figuring the proper Spanish pronunciation would solve everything.

"Never heard of him," said Daniel. "Baseball player?"

"Yes," I said, a bit flummoxed. "He played for Cincinnati's Big Red Machine, the great American baseball powerhouse back in the 1970s. He's your—well,

Cuba's—only native-born son who played in the American major leagues and is enshrined in our National Baseball Hall of Fame."

"Well, you've got to understand," said Daniel, apologetically. "I was born in 1972. We never learned about Tony Pérez in school. But I can tell you about Martín Dihigo and Dolf Luque." (Both played in the 1920s and 1930s; Dihigo, actually, into the 1940s. He even managed pro winter-league teams well into the 1950s, when Daniel's father would have been born. Luque was a second-year pitcher for the 1919 World Champion Reds.)

I tell him I've heard of Dihigo, "Cuba's black Babe Ruth." Dihigo is in the National Baseball Hall of Fame, too—even though he never played in the major leagues. Like Ruth, who almost certainly would have been enshrined as a pitcher had he not switched to playing outfield to concentrate on his hitting, Dihigo did both. Everybody who saw Dihigo play said he was the best player on the field at every position, no matter which one he played—and he played them often, except for rare opportunities at catcher. There were years in Cuba and Mexico when he won the earned run average title and batting title in the same season.

Daniel nodded. "I can tell you about Yoenis Céspedes and Kendrys Morales in the World Series," he said. "I can tell you about El Duque (Orlando Hernández, who defected from Cuba on Christmas Day 1997 and helped pitch the New York Yankees to world championships in 1998, 1999 and 2000). They all played for my favorite team, the *Industriales*.

"Tell me about Tony Pérez."

"Heart and soul of the Big Red Machine," I said. "Actually, Pete Rose was the heart. You've heard of Pete Rose?"

Daniel nodded. "Most hits, right?"

"Yes, most hits," I said. "Tony was the soul," I continued. "There's a big mural of the Big Red Machine inside Great American Ball Park in Cincinnati, and Tony is out front. That is how his teammates regarded him. He was the leader in the clubhouse. He kept everybody in line by saying just the right thing at just the right time. Pete and Joe Morgan and Johnny Bench had the bigger egos, you know, the bigger heads.

"You've heard of Johnny Bench? Joe Morgan?"

Yes, Daniel nodded, telling me that Bench was famous as a catcher, Morgan the same as a second basemen. Somehow, he had heard of them.

I went on to explain that the Reds had erected a statue of Pérez at Great American Ball Park three months earlier, to go with Bench's and Morgan's.

"Pete Rose?" Daniel asked. "No statue?"

"Coming," I answered.

"Tell me more about Tony Pérez."

"Thirtieth on the all-time RBI list."

"How many?" Daniel asked.

"One-thousand six hundred and fifty-two," I said.

Daniel whistled. "Lot of RBI," he said. "Babe Ruth, how many?"

"Over 2,000," I said. "Willie Mays, over 1,900. Ted Williams, over 1,800. Honus Wagner, over 1,700." (I knew the greats and their RBI numbers, practically had them memorized, because I had been writing about Pérez in 1985 and 1986 when he was still accumulating RBI, and was still writing about him every year for nine years after that while he was on the Hall of Fame ballot waiting for 75 percent of the writers' votes that would finally bring immortality—in 2000, much to the relief of his fans.)

"More RBI than Ernie Banks, George Brett, Mike Schmidt, and Willie Stargell," I said. "One hundred more than the great DiMaggio."

Daniel had heard of DiMaggio.

"Big Red Machine, lots of runners on base," said Daniel, grasping the modern analytics that hold that RBI are largely a function of opportunities. Still, that's a lot of RBI.

"More," said Daniel, meaning about Pérez.

"His statue is a re-creation of his swing from Game Seven of the 1975 World Series. Two-run homer off Boston Red Sox left-hander Bill Lee, off what they called the 'eephus' pitch, to cut the Boston lead from 3–0 to 3–2. Most important hit in Cincinnati Reds history. Without that hit, there is no Big Red Machine. Nineteen-seventy-five, same World Series that Luis Tiant pitched in; beat the Reds twice. The Reds had already lost two World Series, 1970 and 1972. Three strikes, you're out. They won it all again in 1976. Swept the New York Yankees."

5

"I know about Tiant. His father was a great pitcher here. And then what for Pérez after 1976?"

"Then the Reds traded him to Montreal, and the Big Red Machine was gone. Later, he played for Boston; Philadelphia—where he was reunited with Rose and Morgan and they went to the World Series again in 1983; and then back to Cincinnati to play for Rose. Oldest player to hit a grand slam. His last home run was in 1986, No. 379, to tie the Latin-American record, with Orlando Cepeda. Elected to the Baseball Hall of Fame in 2000, with his manager Sparky Anderson and the Boston Red Sox catcher, Carlton Fisk, who hit a famous home run, off the foul pole, in Game Six."

"Great player," said Daniel, shaking his head. "Cuban. Wow."

That's what I was thinking, too. I'm in Cuba to begin work on a book about Tony Pérez, and the first Cuban I meet, a dyed-in-the-wool baseball fan, doesn't know who Tony Pérez is?

I asked myself how had I gotten to this point. What had made me think I could find Tony Pérez on a Communist island that had purged the name of Atanacio Rigal Pérez from the collective memory in a place that reveres baseball like no other? ◆

Tony in his first full season as a twenty-three-year-old rookie in 1965 at Forbes Field. The future Big Dog was a Little Dog. Newlywed wife, Pituka hadn't yet had a chance to fill him out with rib-sticking Cuban cuisine.

CHAPTER 1
"Cooba"

Ten thousand feet below, we see it. But we soon realize it isn't the mainland, because we can see a bigger island just beyond. We—my two traveling companions, Tim and Ron, from my days at the *Cincinnati Enquirer,* and I—are flying into "Cooba" from the west, from Cancún, Mexico, our least expensive way in. There were no commercial flights from Miami.

The smaller island, I knew from my early research, is *Isla de la Juventud,* where Fidel Castro was imprisoned from 1953–1955 before he exiled himself to Mexico City to plan for *La Revolución.* And, most important to Cincinnati Reds fans in 2016, *Isla de la Juventud* is where the Reds' young pitcher Raisel Iglesias was born and raised and where he played for the Grapefruit Croppers in the highest level of the Cuba amateur league before defecting in November of 2013.

But my mind isn't on *Isla de la Juventud* when we fly over the smaller island. It is on the big island beyond, the mainland of Cuba, because that is where my story is: the story of Tony Pérez, who doesn't want his story told.

I'd thought about the big island since I was a ten-year-old watching the black-and-white TV in our living room in Liverpool, New York.

It is October 1962, and I am watching the American president, John F. Kennedy, address the nation, the young president who was such a favorite of my Irish-American, Roman Catholic mother. Even at ten, I know that what he is saying is a very big deal, something about Russian missiles being trained on our country from Cuba, and that our president is attempting to face down the Soviet premier, Nikita Khrushchev, to get him to remove them. My parents are nervous, the first time I recall sensing that emotion from them.

Only a few days earlier, I had watched on that same black-and-white TV as the San Francisco Giants' Willie McCovey scorched a pitch at what seemed like a million miles per hour toward New York Yankee second baseman Bobby Richardson, who gloved it cleanly to end the 1962 World Series. It is my first memory of seeing a baseball game on TV.

Three Octobers later came my favorite World Series. By then, we had a color TV, and I remember watching a marvelous blend of exotic talent that included shortstop Zoilo Versalles, right fielder Tony Oliva, and rookie outfielder Sandy Valdespino. I recall hearing that they were Cuban—or Cooban, as they say in Cooba—and I vaguely recall making the connection that they were from the country where the missiles had been aimed at us. I did not know that Versalles, Oliva, Valdespino, and their teammate and countryman Camilo Pascual, the pitcher, could not go home to Cooba, even though they were baseball heroes.

I did not know until I was halfway through writing this book that several years after his team had won the American League and was headed for the 1965 World Series, Versalles said this:

"I stand in front of my locker with Tony, Camilo and Sandy, and we don't say nothing. Tony cries. I think this is the biggest moment I ever have in my life and I can't go home and tell about it. I have nothing to do with politics. The trouble between Castro and the United States should not cause things like this."

That same year—1965—I also knew the name of Tony Pérez, because I followed baseball closely in *The Sporting News*, which my dad had delivered to our house. I knew that Pérez had just played his first full season with the Reds. (His statistics that year were nothing that hinted at his eventual greatness: 104 games, 307 plate appearances, 12 homers, 46 RBI and a .260 batting average.) I knew that Pérez was from Cooba, but I didn't put two-and-two together: I didn't know that Pérez, twenty-three, couldn't go home to share his baseball stories with his family.

It never occurred to me that they couldn't come watch him play.

I have gotten to know Tony well since his return as a Reds player in 1984, and have quoted him often in published stories since then. I even consider him and his wife, Pituka, to be my friends. Tony, however, was not willing to cooperate with me for this biography. He is too modest and humble for that. And I know for a fact it would have opened old wounds for him to talk about certain aspects of his life, particularly leaving his mother and father and sisters and brothers behind in Cuba to pursue his baseball dream.

I understand. And yet, I couldn't forsake this project. I had been watching the Big Red Machine since 1974, and personally covered Pérez and Pete Rose and Davey Concepción as players in 1985 and 1986, and I had gotten to know them well, along with rest of the Big Red Machine in their post-baseball lives, especially Joe Morgan and Johnny Bench, through my work on commemorative newspaper sections for uniform number retirements, Hall of Fame inductions, and statue unveilings. All have unique life stories, and Rose, Morgan, and Bench have been the subjects of multiple books. But I believe Pérez has the best story of all, and nobody has ever written it.

I knew his story, but I wanted to flesh it out in greater detail. I wanted to respect Tony's privacy, but I believed his story was too good to leave to the historians after he's gone. By then, many if not most of the principals will be gone, too. There is an upside for me. Writing a biography without Tony's collaboration freed me to visit the places and talk to the people that collectively could provide me with the greater detail I sought, allowing me to better tell the story not only of Tony himself but also of his homeland—and the political, cultural and baseball climates that produced him.

That is why I had to visit Cuba—as well as visit the American cities with minor league ballparks that Tony played in—and Little Havana and southern Florida, where so many Cuban exiles live. In alienation and separation, Tony is like them, cut off from their families and country for so many years. No matter the depth of rapprochement after almost sixty years of enmity between the two countries, there is no fully recovering from that loss.

Had Tony Pérez collaborated with me on this book, I know from past experience he would not have wanted the names of Fidel Castro or Che Guevara in it.

And yet how can they not be, when the Revolution they led has affected Pérez's life—and the lives of millions of others—so profoundly?

By October of 1956, U.S.-backed Cuba president Fulgencio Batista had been back in office for five years, having re-ascended to the top spot in the government. Batista pushed tourism to diversify the sugar-based economy but also to enrich himself and his compatriots. On the government payroll he put mobster Meyer Lansky, who had more than the muscle needed to clean up the games of chance and reassure American tourists that Havana was every bit as safe and secure as Las Vegas. The American tourists, by and large, came for the beaches and the floor shows and to interact with the handsome Cubanos; many also came for the gambling and sex shows. In 1955, Batista had ginned up the stakes and

Hotel Nacional stands sentinel above the Malecón in the Vedado area of Havana as a 1957 Buick LeSabre passes by; 1957 was the year the Marianao Tigres, led by pitcher Jim Bunning and left fielder Minnie Miñoso (Tony followed Minnie's exploits closely) won the Caribbean Series.

applied his own muscle—known as "Hotel Law 2074"—to provide government loans and tax breaks for Lansky, his fellow mobsters, and American corporations seeking investment. It was a true Gold Rush: In 1955 and 1956 alone, ground was broken on four major hotel-casinos—the Hilton, Deauville, Capri and, Lansky's pride-and-joy, the Riviera.

Political assassinations rarely happened in the United States, not even in New York City, which had its share of mob hits. But in Havana, in 1956, such violence was a way of life. It began at Lansky's swanky Montmarte Night Club in late October of that year.

Two gunmen, one armed with a submachine gun, the other with an automatic pistol—each man sharing the goals but not the blessing of the exiled, self-avowed revolutionary Fidel Castro—rode the elevator to the third floor of the art deco building on the corner of Twenty-Third and P streets, two blocks from the Hotel Nacional in downtown Havana. They knew what nightclub to hit because Montmartre was a favorite watering hole for President Batista's top brass.

Cuba's military intelligence chief, Blanco Rico, had dropped by Montmartre late in the evening for a nightcap, after celebrating the wedding anniversary of Batista's minister of finance. Rico's party had just left the room after a final round of drinks and small talk following headliner Mario Lanza's encore performance of "Arrivederci Roma." As the party waited for the elevator, the gunmen—realizing that their top mark, Santiago Rey, Batista's minister of the interior, was not at the club—spotted Rico, chief of the *Servicio Inteligencia de Militar* (SIM), and sprayed the foyer with twenty to thirty bullets within a few seconds, hitting Rico eight times, all in the back.

Rico, who was not armed, had tried to flee, as did the others; two people ran headlong into a full-length mirror. Rico lay dying. Two other officers and their wives were wounded, two seriously. The walls were splattered in blood, the floor was covered in shattered glass. People were screaming and crying for help as the gunmen fled down the back stairs.

It was a brazen political hit at a mob-owned venue, greatly offending both Batista and Lansky, each of whom regarded it as bad for business. The hit on Rico brought the inevitable reaction from the government, which beefed up its already formidable military presence in Havana just as the winter league baseball season was beginning. *Revolución* was in the air. As described in the book *Havana Nocturne*: "Police and soldiers stood guard at public buildings and strategic points, bridges, the harbor tunnel, and entrances to the city. Agents of SIM (the secret police that Rico had headed) patrolled the city day and night, and began a roundup of all revolutionary elements. Mostly the show of force was just that—a show."

Yes, the sporadic violence in the city—the "hits" and the explosions—were more annoyance than anything, all of it aimed at the government, little against tourists or average citizens, and none, of course, directly aimed at the mobsters, because the mobsters themselves weren't the rebels' main concern. The mobsters built and owned the hotels and casinos and nightclubs and therefore provided many jobs to working Cubanos. And rarely did anything happen around the ballpark, in part because of the security presence, but more so because no self-respecting Cubano, not even a *revolucionario*, dared mess with *beisbol*. That was a sure way to lose public support. And mobsters never hit other mobsters in Havana: Lansky had outgrown internecine warfare—it brought too much attention from law enforcement and fed negative stereotypes. For Lansky, hits were the stuff of the Cosa Nostra of the 1920s and 1930s. Lansky's philosophy was that the fruit of vice in Havana was low-hanging and rich. No need for fighting; just line the pockets of Batista and be assured of his protection.

But the terrorists and revolutionaries played by their own rules. At 1:30 a.m. on New Year's Day, 1957, a blast rocked the popular Tropicana Night Club in Marianao, twenty minutes outside Havana, shattering glass, toppling chairs, and blowing off the arm of a seventeen-year-old girl. At the time, nobody suspected her of setting off the bomb, but several months later the Tropicana owner, Martin Fox, concluded she was the likely perpetrator.

Several revolutionary groups were wreaking havoc in Cuba against the government. Most notable among them was the *Directorio Revolucionario Estudiantil*, whose leader, José Antonio Echevarría, had flown to Mexico City in late August to meet with the twenty-nine-year-old Castro, who had exiled himself from Cuba a few months earlier, vowing in so many words to return one day to overthrow the U.S.-backed Batista. "As a follower of Jose Marti," Fidel had said, "I believe the hour has come to take rights, and not to beg for them, (but) to fight instead of pleading for them. From trips such as this (Castro's to Mexico), one does not return, or else one returns with the tyranny beheaded at one's feet." In Mexico, Castro and Echevarría vowed their mutual commitment to the struggle against Batista, and agreed to advise one another ahead of time before taking any action, and to coordinate their efforts once Castro landed in Cuba.

Nonetheless, it was Echevarría's *Directorio Revolucionario* that had taken out Blanco Rico in late October of 1956, an assassination that Castro condemned, while criticizing the repression of the Cuban people by Batista's regime. "I do not know who carried out the assault on Blanco Rico," Castro told a reporter in the Cuban underground press, "but I believe that from a political and revolutionary standpoint, the assassination was not justified, because Blanco Rico was not an executioner."

At the Havana ballpark, word was that the boss man wouldn't take the hit lying down, that he would strike back quickly. The Cuban players knew how things worked in Havana. They informed their American teammates—six gringos allowed per club in the winter league—of Batista's "eye for an eye" justice. Sure enough, the very next day, Cuban officers surrounded the Haitian embassy in Havana, where several Cubans were known to have sought asylum, raising police suspicions.

The police, who had staked out all the foreign embassies, said they had seen four men scale the walls of the Haitian embassy earlier that Monday morning, October 29. By lunchtime, the police sent in an assault team. Its approach was highly questionable. When Cuban police chief Rafael Salas Canizares arrived at the embassy's front door with his chief of detectives, the *pop-pop-pop* of gunfire burst from the second floor. Salas was hit six times in the torso and once in the head. Police on the street opened up and didn't stop until all the shooting from the second floor had ended. Chief Salas and nine civilians lay dead. Rico's killers were said to be among them, but it was later refuted.

Less than a mile away, visiting pitcher Jim Bunning was just sitting down to lunch at the Hotel Presidente. ◆

This is one of the teams from Havana that fourteen-year-old Tani Pérez would have followed on radio at home in Central Violeta. (Left to right) First row: Witty Quintana*, Minnie Miñoso, Roldofo Arias*, Julio Becquer*, Juan Izaquirre, Nap Reyes (Manager), Jose Maria Fernandez (coach), Fred Hahn, Asdrubal Baro*. Second row: Felix Manuel (trainer), Hal Bevan*, Mike Fornieles, Juan Delis*, Aldo Salvent, Alberto Alvarez*, Al Federoff, Jim Bunning, Jose Valdivieso, Lazaro Zarza, non-uniformed man (unknown). Top row: Bill Werle, Hal Smith, Solly Drake, Orlando Leroux, Connie Marrero*, Enrique Maroto*, Reynaldo Alfonso, Rene Friol*, Vicente Lopez.*

*Played one, two or three seasons for the Cincinnati Reds' Triple-A affiliate, Havana Sugar Kings (spring/summer, 1954–1960).

CHAPTER 2

Cuando Miñoso Batea:
"La Pelota Baila el Cha-cha"

The atmosphere outside Gran Stadium in Havana was festive and exhilarating for twenty-five-year-old Jim Bunning as he remembered it, refreshed by memories evoked by the wonderful description in Roberto González Echevarría's *The Pride of Havana: A History of Cuban Baseball*. *Carnita*—pork—was roasting on open fires for *pan con lechon*, a dish redolent with garlic and sizzling fat. Vendors sold a sparkling array of baubles, pennants, and scarves. Through this colorful, aromatic scene came a bouncing beat of rumba, salsa, and *son cubano* from guitars, bongos, and maracas. It matched the sounds coming from the Buena Vista Social Club of overpopulated Marianao, a few miles southwest of old Havana, home of the Oriental Park Racetrack, the famous Tropicana night club, and the wily ol' lefthander, Luis Tiant Sr.

The scene was more party-like and aromatic than anything Bunning had been accustomed to in his two partial seasons in the majors and five in the minors. Not even the machine gun nests on the way to the ballpark and the soldiers armed with machine guns on the stadium roof could detract from it.

If Gran Stadium of the 1956–1957 Cuban Winter League could be compared to one American major league stadium at the time, it would be Wrigley Field in Chicago, because Gran held about thirty-one thousand fans and featured a roof that covered the entire grandstand, foul pole to foul pole. The field itself was maintained by Alfredo "Pajara" Cabrera—"a tallish, gaunt figure in denim uniform, with a cigar stuck in the middle of his mouth and a rake in his gnarled hands," as described in *The Pride of Havana*. The ancient former major league

17

shortstop (one game, St. Louis Cardinals) was born in the Canary Islands, sailed to Cuba as a nineteen-year-old, and began his pro career in 1902, four years after Cuba achieved its independence in the Spanish-American War.

The undisputed star of the Marianao Tigres—Bunning's team, the one with the orange and black piping on its uniforms—was Orestes "Minnie" Miñoso. Most Valuable Player of the 1952–1953 Winter League. He was the idol of fourteen-year-old Tani Pérez in the sugar-plantation company town of Central Violeta, three hundred miles away.

Central Violeta is located in the dead-center of the island, halfway between Havana and the Sierra Maestre Mountains on the eastern end. Tani identified with Miñoso not only because Minnie was such a great player but also because Minnie had grown up in a sugar plantation town and worked in a sugar mill, as Tani was doing in Central Violeta. Tani had begun work at the mill that fall. His father, José Manuel, worked next to him; and before that, José Manuel's father, Tani's grand-father, had worked there, too. It's what most Central Violetans did. The name of the town was taken from the refinery, which honored the owner's eldest daughter, Violeta. "Central," pronounced "Sen-TROWEL," was the prefix for every sugar company town in Cuba.

Tani's job was to stamp and load the bags of white gold onto trucks bound for the Cuban ports, and ultimately Miami, two hundred miles away. And although Tani by far preferred playing baseball for the mill team, he knew the process of sugar-making, because it supported his family and sustained his village. In the surrounding fields, straw-hatted men in coarse linen and armed with machetes—*cortadores de caña* or *macheteros* (cane cutters)—set fire to the crop from January to June, the dry season. The fire burned the long and sharp leaves, shaped like curved swords, right off the nine-foot-high stalks. The *macheteros* would then begin cutting, close to the ground where the su-crose is concentrated and the leafy top can be lopped off, more than four tons of cane on a good day. After that, the dead leaves were stripped and the stems loaded onto wagons and pulled by horse to the sugar mill to be shredded and crushed between huge rollers that squeezed out the juice. The liquid—boiled, filtered, evaporated, and spun—left raw brown sugar crystals, and the residue from those processes was used to make fertilizer, rum, cattle feed, and fuel for the mill's giant boilers.

Tani Pérez was ten when Minnie Miñoso won the Cuban League MVP the first time. Miñoso had been playing for Marianao every season since he was a nineteen-year-old in 1946–1947, when Tani was a toddler. For as long as Tani could remember, Minnie Miñoso was a household name in Central Violeta.

By fifteen, Tani was the starting shortstop for the Central Violeta mill team, and his prowess soon captured the attention of a local bird dog. Tani had little of Miñoso's speed, but he was skinnier than a stalk of sugarcane and routinely stretched doubles into triples. Despite his sinewy frame, he was already showing surprising power, mostly to center field and right-center. Tani's father was *un grand fanático*—a huge fan—of Miñoso, and passed that love on to his son. They would listen to the games of the Cuban Winter League on the radio, and pull for Miñoso of the Marianao Tigres.

In Miñoso's first six years in the major leagues (1951–1956), three times he led the American League in baseball's most exciting play, the triple, a whopping eighteen in his fourth season (even though he was already thirty-one years old) and, in the season just completed, eleven. In each of his first three seasons in the AL he had also led the loop in stolen bases. Even in late October of 1956, a month shy of his thirty-fourth birthday—long in the tooth for most major leaguers—Miñoso was still one of the game's most exciting players, equally renowned in Cuba as in the States. Tani Pérez grew up wanting to *be* Minnie Miñoso.

Tani also knew about the Cincinnati Reds, because Tani's father had told him that Miñoso's first Marianao manager was Armando Marsans, who was Cuba's first big-time American major leaguer when he broke in with the Reds in 1911. (Marsans played four seasons with Cincinnati, then all or parts of four more seasons with the St. Louis Browns and New York Yankees.) And Tani knew well that Miñoso's manager for three straight seasons in the Cuban Winter League (1950–1953) was former Cincinnati pitcher Dolf Luque, who

Said "Tani" Pérez to his crying mother on the day he left for the United States in March, 1960: "Don't worry, Mama. You see Minnie Miñoso? I am going to be better than him." Replied his mother: "You love to dream, Tani. You cannot dream that way."

had won twenty-seven games for the Reds in 1923. José Manuel told Tani stories of Luque, who hadn't pitched in the majors since 1935 and was only five months shy of his fiftieth birthday when he pitched creditably for a couple of innings against the visiting 1940 Cincinnati Reds during their visit to Havana that spring for a tuneup. (The '40 Reds, led by sluggers Ernie Lombardi and

Frank McCormick and star pitchers Paul Derringer and Bucky Walters, went on to win the World Series that year, beating the Detroit Tigers.) Relieving Luque on that March day in Havana was left-handed Luis Tiant Sr., who continued the Americans' exasperation for seven additional innings into extra frames.

And, of course, Tani knew that Cincinnati was the major league affiliate of the Havana Sugar Kings, the Reds' top-level minor league team. The Sugar Kings, beginning in 1954, went head-to-head with the Washington Senators for Cuban talent.

But it was Miñoso, a member of the Chicago White Sox, who was the player at the center of Tani's dreams. The song that fueled Tani's dream—"Cuando Miñoso Batea"—played on radios throughout Cuba, including in Central Violeta:

El balón sale y va y va
Vaya por delante, que es un jonrón!
Lo que es un gran éxito.
Una tremenda emoción!
Cuando Miñoso batea en serio, la pelota baila el cha -cha
Cuando Miñoso batea en serio, la pelota baila el cha -cha
Cuando Miñoso batea en serio, la pelota baila el cha -cha
¡Carrera! Miñoso jonrón!
Es Miñoso, la gente, y este dispara fuera del parque!

The ball goes and goes and goes
Go ahead, it's a home run!
What a great hit!
A tremendous emotion!
When Miñoso bats in earnest, the ball dances the cha-cha
When Miñoso bats in earnest, the ball dances the cha-cha
When Miñoso bats in earnest, the ball dances the cha-cha.
Home run! Miñoso home run!
It's Miñoso, people, who hit it out of the park!

Fifty-four years later, at the Minnie Miñoso Hall of Fame Forum in Chicago, Tani Pérez recalled his experience as a baby Sugar King watching Miñoso in a winter-league game in Havana. The Cuban Winter League ran late October through February; the Sugar Kings played mid-April through September, also at Gran Stadium, in the Triple-A International League. Pérez saw Miñoso again after his first season of pro ball in 1960, when Tani was still going home to Cuba after playing in the States. Pérez was invited onto the field in uniform during batting practice of the Marianao Tigres at Gran Stadium in what turned out to be Miñoso's last season in Cuba. (Miñoso left Cuba for good in February 1961.)

"I watched him practice," recalled Pérez, choking up. "I shagged his fly balls. For me, that was great. I was there in the same clubhouse as him. The only thing that could be better is if his plaque was in the same room as mine in Cooperstown."

It was Miñoso's name that Reds signee Tani invoked to his mother, Teodora, in March of 1960 when she told him she didn't want him to leave for the States to pursue his baseball dream. She would miss him too much.

No se preocupe, Mamá. Ves Minnie Miñoso? Voy a ser mejor que él!—"Don't worry, Mama. You see Minnie Miñoso? I am going to be *better* than him!"

Jim Bunning was a young, struggling right-handed pitcher from Southgate, Kentucky, in search of a third pitch and a starter's role in the American major leagues when he joined the Marianao Tigres and their nonpareil star, Minnie Miñoso, in Cuban winter ball in late October, 1956. Bunning had been in Havana only eight days when the assassination of Blanco Rico occurred. The Hotel Presidente was four blocks from the crime scene. The right-hander learned about the rampage later that morning before the traditional Sunday doubleheader played by Havana's four professional teams at Gran Stadium.

Bunning's Cuban-born Tigres teammates—shortstop José Valdivielso and first baseman Julio Becquer, a couple of other struggling young players trying to establish themselves in the American majors—weren't shocked by the bloody assassination at Montmartre. They said the murderers wouldn't have dared act if any professional ballplayers were present, out of respect. And they weren't kidding. It's how the best of the best—*el máximo monstruo*—were regarded in Cuba. Bunning had already seen it and felt it; if you were a ballplayer, you were treated like a king, unable to buy a drink or a meal once you left your hotel.

Seven weeks after the bloody assassination of the head of Cuban military intelligence, Bunning and his wife, Mary, took that same elevator to the third floor on Montmartre, walked through that same foyer and entered the club. Mary was in town to celebrate the Bunning's fifth wedding anniversary. The pitcher was already in a great mood because he had found that third pitch so he could get out left-handed batters. And not only had Bunning found it—thanks to Marianao's pitcher-pitching coach, the uncannily canny Connie Marrero, who stood only 5-foot-5—he was dominating with it.

"I had come to Cuba to learn how to pitch, not to goof around," explained the late Bunning sixty years later. "I had four kids and bills to pay. If you apply yourself, you're going to get a lot of great input from the Cuban coaches and players. Connie was great for me. He taught me the slider that jammed left-handed batters *hard*. Because of Connie, I won twenty games that next season in Detroit, pitched another fifteen years in the big leagues, and made the National Baseball Hall of Fame. Thank you, Connie Marrero."

But wasn't Bunning concerned that rebels might hit the Montmartre Night Club again?

"Not with Nat King Cole performing, I didn't!" Bunning chirped. "He was as big as it got back then. It was great because when Nat heard we were in the audience—he was a big baseball fan—he dedicated the whole show to us. He sang and played all his hits." Among them were "Straighten Up and Fly Right," "Mona Lisa," and "Unforgettable;" the instrumentals—he was a piano virtuoso—"Tea for Two," "April in Paris" and "If I Could Be with You (One Hour Tonight);" and his latest album, an instrumental, *The Piano Style of Nat King Cole,* had been in the record stores for months now.

Cole was thinking about recording an album in Spanish—which he would do next year—so for the Bunnings he sang "Quizas, Quizas, Quizas" ("Maybe,

Maybe, Maybe"). The pitcher understood most of the words, given his four years of Spanish classes at St. Xavier High School and two more at Xavier University.

Three hundred miles away, Tani Pérez, a Cubano of color, had no familiarity with what Cole, an African-American, had to endure in the States. Tani played side-by-side on the Central Violeta sugar mill with light-skinned Cubans and mulattoes. Nobody on the team was discriminated against when they went from town to town to play their sport. Nobody refused to house or feed Pérez because he was dark-skinned. He knew nothing of the worst of it in the States. Cole knew from personal experience—and Bunning knew from growing up in Kentucky—that Cuba was much more enlightened on matters of race than anywhere in the States. Only two months earlier, Cole's first network TV variety show, *The Nat King Cole Show*, aired—without commercial sponsorship. While Cole was performing at the Montmartre Club, NBC was weighing a plan to expand the show from fifteen minutes to thirty on the summer schedule, and seek a national sponsor. The show happened, but despite all the eager, popular white and black singers and comedians coming on Cole's show at union minimum, the national sponsor never surfaced. Neither Cole nor Bunning could accept this lack of equal opportunity for persons of color. Nor could Cuba. Cuba integrated its baseball leagues two generations before Jackie Robinson.

"Madison Avenue is afraid of the dark," Cole remarked.

The Cuba of Pérez's youth was blissfully enlightened compared to what was going on in the States. It would be another five years before Pérez would come face to face with racism. And he'd have to go to the American South—Rocky Mount, North Carolina, and Macon, Georgia—to find it.

Bunning paid close attention to current events, especially in Cuba. It had been six weeks since the rebel leader Fidel Castro and his men had landed—"more a shipwreck than a landing," Che Guevara described it—at the eastern end of the island.

"Batista says the army cut Castro to shreds and that he is dead," Bunning said to Mary, "but if they cut them to shreds, how come the soldiers are still patrolling that part of the island?"

On the day after Valentine's Day, 1957, Bunning was packing up at the Hotel Presidente to return to Kentucky. His team's 5–1 record in the Havana-based round robin tournament hosting Panama, Venezuela, and Puerto Rico had led the Marianao Tigres to the Caribbean World Series Championship. "I had to go out of the country to win my only ring," recalled Bunning sixty years later, with great delight.

A few blocks away, real intrigue was unfolding. Three of Fidel Castro's rebels picked up *New York Times'* special correspondent Herbert Matthews at the Sevilla Biltmore Hotel and drove him six hundred miles into the Sierra Maestre Mountains for a secret meeting with *El Comandante*. A three-part series in the *Times* a few days later—with photos of the reporter with Castro—clearly showed Castro alive and well, quoting him as being hell-bent on toppling the Batista regime. The series blew the lid off things in Cuba, even as Batista and everybody else in the government denounced the report as fictitious. For two-and-a-half months, Batista and his top brass had been insisting the army had killed Fidel when he and his boatful of revolutionaries had come ashore. The *Times'* report said otherwise.

By the time Bunning had returned to the States, he knew what most people on the street in Cuba didn't, because the bundles of *New York Times* that had been flown to Cuba were censored by scissors-wielding *governistas* who literally went through every paper, clipping out Matthews' report. But within a matter of days, it was all for naught, because sympathizers arranged for three thousand copies to be shipped individually to the homes of the cognoscenti and the intelligentsia in Cuba, thereby spilling the news and unclothing Batista.

It was that report—and ultimately the Bay of Pigs Invasion in 1961 and the fallout from the Cuban Missile Crisis in 1962—that ultimately conspired to keep Tani Pérez from going home to Cuba again for ten more years, and only then to visit his ailing father. ◆

The great Martín Dihigo, circa 1939, of the Cienfuegos Elephants, is Cuba's greatest player. His legend is as big on the island—and as well-deserved—as Babe Ruth's in the U.S.

CHAPTER 3
The Sugar Mill Trinity

CRUCES—Under a Popsicle-blue, cotton-swabbed sky, we approach a lovely town square in central Cuba, sixty-five miles inland from the Bay of Pigs (*Bahia de Cochinos*). We see three middle-aged men passing the time on a sturdy concrete bench. As we draw closer, one of them notices the wishbone "C" on one of our caps, smiles, and asks where we're headed.

"The Martín Dihigo Museum," says our Spanish-speaking guide.

It looses a torrent from the bench-warmers.

"You have come to the right place!" and "Dihigo is the best!" and "Cincinnati—the Sugar Kings!" We have been on the island for only three days, and already we have learned that while not everyone in Cuba is a baseball fan, those who are, are *apasionado*, passionate, never at a loss for telling us what they think. It is always—*always*—worth hearing, because it is usually wisdom passed down through the ages. The Sugar Kings line is a reference to the Cincinnati Reds being the major-league affiliate of the Triple-A Havana Sugar Kings of the International League, 1954 to 1960.

Of the three greatest Cuban players—Martín Dihigo, Minnie Miñoso, and Tony Pérez—Dihigo was the best. Cuba regards him as the best player that it ever produced, and a good case could be made that he was the best player of all-time *anywhere*. Not only could he slug and run, he easily played each of the infield and outfield positions when he wasn't pitching, where he was dominant. He was Babe Ruth without the big stage, Satchel Paige without the self-promotion.

But because Dihigo Sr. was dark-skinned, he couldn't play in the American majors, an injustice that the great New York Giants manager John McGraw both trumpeted and lamented, calling Dihigo the best player he ever saw.

On September 5, 1938, in an integrated Mexican League game in Veracruz, Dihigo matched Paige (the league's first African-American) pitch-for-pitch in a 1–1 game through eight innings, then hit a walk-off home run over the center-field wall off Paige's reliever to win 2–1. Dihigo led the league that season with what is still the lowest earned run average in league history, 0.92, and also won the league batting title with a .387 average. When Paige, the greatest pitcher in the Negro Leagues, was inducted to the National Baseball Hall of Fame in 1971, he said, "I'm not the best, Martín Dihigo is." Six years later, Dihigo was enshrined in Cooperstown.

Dihigo, Miñoso, and Pérez are the Sugar Mill Trinity of Cuban baseball players. All were born in sugar mill towns. Among the many things that Cuban baseball has that the American major leagues doesn't, is a single, clear, undisputed, intimate line of *grande entre los grandes*—greatest of the greats. Martín Dihigo begat Minnie Miñoso, who begat Pérez. Dihigo and Pérez are in America's National Baseball Hall of Fame in Cooperstown, and Miñoso surely should be. Not only did each know his predecessor, all knew one another. When the future greats met the already-greats, the "conversation" always ended with the eldest saying, *Pásalo*—Pass it on.

The young Minnie saw Dihigo play; he even faced him once in a game. Miñoso's best memory of Dihigo, though, came as a boy. Minnie told his story in a 2008 *Newsday* newspaper article: "I lived sixty, eighty miles from Havana, so I used to buy this newspaper to see what Martín Dihigo did the day before. I used to spend one penny to buy a sweet coconut, one penny for salt crackers—that was my lunch—and the other (three) pennies to buy the newspaper to see what happened with Martín. Some people try to include me in that group (with Dihigo). I said, 'No way you will ever hear me put myself together with this guy.'"

So, too, with Pérez, not wanting to put himself with Miñoso. Pérez saw Miñoso play and talked with him. He also talked with Dihigo Sr.; well, actually, he more listened than talked. In the off-season after Pérez's first year of pro ball in Geneva, New York, where Pérez played with Martín Dihigo Jr., the great one's son, the two young men were playing in a pickup game at *Estadio Latinoamericano* (Latin America Stadium) with no obvious adult supervision, at least none sufficiently acquainted with the young men. It was 1960—the year before Castro expunged professional baseball from Cuba. Dihigo Sr. watched from the stands as his son and Pérez shared a cigarette in a place they thought was out-of-view.

"I thought maybe a locomotive was coming through the ballpark with all the smoke coming out of the dugout," Dihigo Sr. told the boys, letting them know that was no way to make the big leagues. "Be careful what you put in your body."

Martín Dihigo Jr. tells us the story with relish, cementing his connection with his father and himself with Pérez.

Pásalo.

"Pass it on."

It is happening again in Cuba-U.S. baseball relations, in a time-warp sort of way—like everything else here.

Before we arrived in Cruces, all we knew—and the reason why we were so eager to talk with Martín Dihigo Jr.—was that he is the son of *"El Inmortal"*—the words on Dihigo Sr.'s gravestone and on his bust at *Estadio Latinoamericano.*

We have no appointment and no idea if Dihigo Jr. is home. It takes only one stop at the museum, where a docent calls him. A big man wearing a brick-red T-shirt touting a grunge/hip-hop/metal clothing line, with a dachshund at his feet, greets us at the front door.

"*Hola!* Cin-cee-nah-tee? Si, si! Come right in!"

We don't know Dihigo Jr. from his manager in Geneva, New York—Jack "Scat" Cassini—but Dihigo Jr. is as warm and welcoming as can be.

"Come in, come in!" he says, pulling up four chairs.

He is a fuller-faced version of his papa, whom we had seen only in photos. When Dihigo Sr. was at the height of his fame in the late 1920s through the early 1940s, pedestrian sports writers rarely captured a player's personality. But we cannot imagine the father's personality being any brighter than that of the warm, ebullient, effervescent son. He jostles, he jousts, he brings you in; laughing for Dihigo Jr. comes as naturally as breathing.

"How is life in Cin-cee-nah-tee? What are the prospects for *Los Rojos*? And who is this 'Tony Perez' you are asking me about? You mean 'Tani PEER-ez?' " asks Dihigo Jr., mischievously, putting the accent on the first syllable of the last name where it belongs. "Nobody in Cuba will know who you are talking about if you ask them about 'Tony Perez'." And, actually, even then, Pérez's name pronounced either way will have meaning to baseball fans in Cuba only if they have some awareness of baseball in the States, particularly forty-year-old American baseball that includes the Big Red Machine. But, we quickly learned, any baseball fan over age fifty in Cuba has heard of the Big Red Machine.

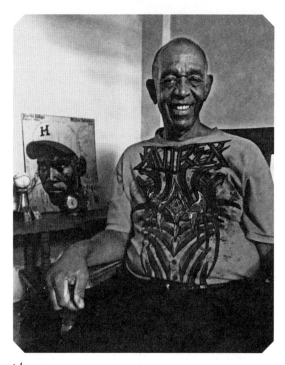

Martín Dihigo Jr., son of "The Immortal," at his home in Cruces, Cuba. He and Tani Pérez played minor-league ball together in the States.

On the wall behind a small TV in Dihigo Jr.'s home are photos of his famous father and framed, single-page testimonials; baseballs mounted in trophy cups sit on small tables that go back decades. It is a delicately presented shrine to "El Maestro" and "El Inmortal," Dihigo Sr.'s monikers, the only player enshrined in the baseball Halls of Fame of four countries: Cuba, Mexico, Venezuela, and the United States.

Behind Dihigo Jr. is a long dark hallway, where we count at least five doors, all to the right, five separate rooms housing what are probably four separate families and a bathroom. In Cuba, you see these conditions everywhere. It is the life that Dihigo Jr. chose—actually had chosen *for* him—when he came home from the States to stay after the 1962 season, his fourth in the pros. After spending 1959 in Geneva, New York/Palatka, Florida; 1960 with rookies Pérez and Pete Rose in Geneva; 1961 in Topeka, Kansas; and 1962 in Geneva/Macon, Georgia, Dihigo Jr. came home because his famous father was finally back home. Dihigo Sr. had spent most of 1952 through 1958 in Mexico, where he went to manage baseball teams, both to make a living and to protest the corruption of the Batista regime.

In a letter from Mexico City dated July 15, 1958, Dihigo Sr. lays it all out for his son, first chastising him gently for not writing to him in Mexico, and then, more harshly, for not writing to his mother, Dihigo Sr.'s wife, in Cruces.

El hijo que olvida a sus padres, va por el mal camino, y quiero hacerte una parte de mi historial como jugador de baseball, begins Dihigo Sr.—"The son who forgets his parents is going down a wrong road. And I want to make you a part of my history as a baseball player."

Unbeknownst to anybody in Cuba at the time—except the soldiers on either side of the fight in the Sierra Maestre Mountains, four hundred miles from Cruces—the date of that letter, July 15, 1958, marked a turning point in *La Revolución*. It was then, at Jigue, that the forces of Fidel and Raul Castro, and Che Guevara, seized the upper hand. At the time, Dihigo Jr. was playing for the instructional team of the Havana Sugar Kings. He would begin his pro career in the States the next season.

Dihigo Sr. wrote the letter to his son in the same week that Castro wrote to a former classmate who commanded the opposing troops at the critical battle of Jigue. Castro urged the classmate to surrender and come join the rebels. Dihigo's letter gives the impression that he has had to parent his son from afar for a number of years. Dihigo Sr. was away from home a lot, managing teams throughout Latin America. The younger Dihigo was already showing promise as a ballplayer, having been scouted in Cruces by the Sugar Kings and transported to Havana to attend a baseball school, just as Pérez would do a few months later.

Dihigo Sr. was not only a great pitcher and hitter, he was one of the most in-demand managers in Cuba and Mexico. He caught his son and Tani smoking, and told them it was no way to fulfill their aspirations of being professional ballplayers.

"In 1923, when I first left Cuba for the United States, I was one year older than you—sixteen years old," Dihigo Sr. wrote his son. "Your father played twenty-five years in baseball. Never have I not written, not just to my family, but to my friends and even acquaintances, because in doing this, it makes my life easier...I live in an environment of true family."

Also unbeknownst to most Cubans, and certainly to Dihigo Jr., *El Inmortal* was giving financial support and succor to Castro and his rebels, who were training and plotting in Mexico from July 1955 through November 1956.

As was Dihigo Sr.'s way since the 1930s, he summered in Mexico City, where the money was good for a player and manager of his stature, and wintered in Cuba, where he also played and managed. Fidel Castro, Che Guevara, and Dihigo were in Mexico City simultaneously in the summers of 1955 and 1956. At the time, Castro was viewed as a possible savior for Cuba, somebody who could rip the grip from Batista.

It is entirely plausible that Dihigo Sr. visited with Castro and Guevara in Mexico City, separately or together. There are a lot of unsubstantiated reports that Dihigo had previously met Guevara, "a smiling man in a Prussian blue suit," a recollection that was widely referred to in profiles of Dihigo, usually timed to 1952. But Guevara wasn't in Mexico in 1952; he was on a motorcycle trip through South America, concluding that autumn with a flight to the U.S. before heading home in November to study for his medical exams. Most likely, Dihigo first met Guevara in July or August of 1955, when Dihigo was fifty and Guevara twenty-seven. They were probably introduced by Castro, then twenty-nine, who had played baseball as a young man and would have known Dihigo, a national icon since the early 1930s.

The summer of 1956 seems a little late in the history of the rebels for a meeting with Dihigo Sr. The rebels were pretty far along by then. Castro and his followers, including Guevara, were arrested in Mexico City in late June 1956 and charged with plotting the assassination of Batista. They spent varying amounts of time in jail, the longest going to Che, who logged fifty-seven days. In September, Fidel slipped across the border into Texas to meet with his former enemy and ex-Cuban president, Carlos Prio Socarras, and left with at least fifty thousand dollars for the attempted overthrow. (According to a former KGB agent, the money was not Prio's, it was the CIA's. If that's true, as Jon Lee Anderson writes in his definitive work, *Che*, "it would lend weight to reports that the American intelligence agency had tried early to win over Castro, just in case he succeeded in his war against the increasingly embattled Batista." Fidel's biographer, Ted Szulc, said the CIA *did* funnel money to Castro in 1957 and 1958, via an agent attached to the American consul's office in Santiago, Cuba.)

In other words, Dihigo Sr. was hardly being "anti-Cuban" or "anti-American" in backing Castro/Guevara in 1955–1959. Despite Dihigo Sr.'s consorting with these revolutionaries, he advised his son in writing to steer clear of various rebel groups operating all over Cuba, especially in Havana, in 1958.

"Be aware of those little revolutionary groups, because that doesn't take you anywhere," Dihigo Sr. counseled. "Baseball players are outside, totally outside, of the political environment."

The flow of high-end Cuban baseball talent that began defecting to the United States in the mid-1990s, and the warming of relations between the American and Cuban governments beginning in December 2014, has generated articles in the Cuban sporting press about *El Puñado,* "The Handful": Pérez and Tony Oliva and Bert Campaneris and a few others, Cuban-born stars in the American majors in the 1960s and 1970s who were too young to play anything more than developmental ball in Cuba. They hadn't been forgotten back home; they weren't known at all. Only the scouts were aware of them. The Cuban government didn't allow publicity about those they regarded as defectors.

Baseball fans in the States are just learning about famous Cuban players of yesteryear—people like Dihigo Sr., Cristóbal Torriente, and José Mendez—in the

Tony's smile, too, rates right up there with Minnie Miñoso's, fellow member of the Sugar Mill Trinity.

context of newcomers like Yoenis Céspedes, Jose Abreu, and Aroldis Chapman. That Yasiel Puig lit up not only Los Angeles but the whole baseball world in the spring and summer of 2013, allowed the great Dodgers announcer Vin Scully to wax eloquently about Dihigo Sr. to millions of listeners in the West. That Cuban pitcher Raisel Iglesias started Opening Day 2016 for the Cincinnati Reds allowed Cincinnati scribes to recall Reds star Dolf Luque, who had done the same thing in 1921 and 1928, and went on to become an all-time great. Luque is the only player besides Dihigo Sr. to have a bust at *Estadio Latinamericano*, the former Gran Stadium, where Jim Bunning won the Caribbean World Series in 1957. Castro changed the name of *Gran* to *Latinoamericano*, just as he did almost everything else after taking control in 1959.

In the letter to his son, Dihigo Sr. tells the young Martín, in so many words, to be humble no matter how great might be his baseball success. It is as though Dihigo Sr. was whispering in Tani Pérez's ear, too. Tani knew the legacy of Dihigo Sr. long before he met the son.

Of all the great Cuban players over the years, it is Dihigo Sr. whom Pérez most mirrors: Unselfish, unflappable, joyous—an excellent teammate who always took in the younger players, especially the Latinos.

Dihigo Jr. had the humility of his father, but not the talent. A fleet-footed and sure-handed center fielder, he probably couldn't have made it much higher than he did—a step-and-a-half from the majors. But had he been able to visualize the majors from Macon, Georgia, it would have made for an interesting decision for *El Inmortal's* son. By October 1962, his famous father was well-entrenched as Minister of Sports for Castro. Dihigo Jr.'s decision to come home was made easier by his performance. He hit only .190 at Macon. Among Dihigo Jr.'s teammates at Macon in 1962 was Pete Rose, who made the jump to Cincinnati for Opening Day in 1963 and never looked back. Prospects do what Rose, Tommy Helms, and Art Shamsky did in Macon: Respectively, they hit .330, .340 and .284 with 16 home runs.

Considering that Dihigo Jr. was two years younger than Rose and Helms, and a year younger than Shamsky, perhaps he had a puncher's chance at "turning things around" had he stayed in pro ball. Either way, he appears untroubled by his decision.

"Family first," he says. "I learned that from my father. I loved him, and my mother and grandmother, and so I came home. No regrets. I did not like the racism in Macon. We did not, and we do not, have as deep a racism here. It was difficult for me."

Except for the racism observations, Dihigo Jr. does not talk of politics, only baseball, during our hour-long visit. He says he still dreams of making acrobatic catches in center field, and running fast around the bases, and that his only wish when he thinks of the two countries—the one in which he was born and the one in which he played with Rose and Pérez—is that "when we play you on the field, that it be fair, a good game, with lots of fans in the stands. And that we *beat* you! Then, we all shake hands." At that, he smiled widely and stood up.

Dihigo Jr. has been so gracious with his time that when we finally bid him good-bye, we are getting a late start—five-thirty in the afternoon—for the expected three-and-a-half-hour trip to Ciego de Ávila. There we will spend the night and then head for Pérez's hometown in the morning. It means we are going to be driving three hours in the dark, something we had been warned not to do in rural Cuba. ◆

CHAPTER 4
Zero Dark Thirty

ON THE ROAD TO CIEGO de ÁVILA—By the time we reach Highway 1, the *Autopista Nacional*, which is the main highway from Havana to Sancti Spíritus in the middle of the island, I understand why our driver-guide was so fidgety as the interview in Cruces wore on.

It is 6:30 p.m., almost at the end of what the special operations people refer to as "evening nautical twilight," when one can see only vague outlines of animals moving across the landscape without the use of artificial light. As we come upon the intersection of the first road to Santa Clara, birthplace and playground of the St. Louis Cardinals' Aledmys Díaz, a hot rookie during the 2016 season, I think, *A half hour from now, what's that donkey cart going to look like in the slow lane without a rear reflector?* Coming upon the second Santa Clara road intersection fifteen minutes later, we find out. Breaking hard, our driver suddenly swerves to the left to avoid clipping another donkey cart carrying two couples and the driver—all oblivious to our presence.

For the next two hours of zero dark thirty—no light stanchions on a four-lane highway, two lanes either way and a first-quarter moon no help at all—we pass a near-steady stream of carts, horses, donkeys, bicycles, mopeds, and pedestrians, drawn right from an episode of the *Twilight Zone*, or better, a Fellini movie. We see (or, more like it, don't quite see) every conveyance known to mankind in pre-Spanish independence Cuba, some in the slow lane, some on the shoulder, and not a candle's worth of light among them, save for the burning end of an occasional cigar.

This is most definitely *not* the Cuba that Tani Pérez left behind in March 1960—not even the Cuba he returned to in 1972 to visit his ailing father after a ten-year absence because of the estrangement between the United States and Cuba. There were more cars then. Now there are at least twenty bicycles for every car; even the horses and donkeys outnumber the cars probably five- or ten-to-one. The bicyclists and donkey-riders have no reason to think they don't own the roads, because they do. Cars out here are as rare as Cuban women who don't think they're beautiful. (Although most are right.)

The presence of cars began to wane in the 1990s during the "Special Period," when the Soviet Union broke apart. And there went Cuba's economic support, and with it so many of its consumer goods, including automobiles.

Six months after that nighttime trip past Díaz's hometown, I reminisce with him in the visitor's dugout at Great American Ball Park in Cincinnati. I show him the little map that I had drawn on a Post-it note. My map shows the route my two friends and I had taken from Cienfuegos to Cruces to Ciego de Ávila, past Santa Clara, a quiet city of 250,000, and yet a place of considerable historical note.

Santa Clara is where Che Guevara is buried. On October 8, 1967, he was cornered and wounded in battle in the Yuro Ravine in southeast Bolivia in an operation conducted by Green Beret-trained Bolivian soldiers of the Second Ranger Battalion. He was held overnight in a dirt-floored schoolhouse in the small hamlet of La Higuera in Vallegrande province, then executed the next day by a Bolivian sergeant. Cuban-American CIA operative Felix Rodriguez, code name "Felix Ramos," passed along the order from the Bolivian High Command to execute Guevara, telling the soldier to be sure not to shoot him in the head, so that it would appear his wounds came in battle. Che's body was then airlifted by helicopter to a nearby desolate dirt airstrip on the edge of town and buried with several comrades.

Twenty-eight years later, his remains were exhumed and returned to Cuba, the country he had sought to liberate. He was re-buried with full military honors in a mausoleum beneath a twenty-two-foot-tall statue. The year was 1997—the year Díaz turned seven and the eldest of Tony Pérez's three sisters died in Cuba. Santa Clara is Guevara's final resting place because it is here that he had led the final major battle of the Cuban Revolution. It occurred in late December 1958, the battle that convinced President Batista it was time to go. (Batista and his family flew from Havana, bound for the Dominican Republic, at two o'clock in the morning on New Year's Day 1959, sitting atop a fortune of $300 million he had amassed while in office.)

Santa Clara is also the birthplace of revolutionary Olga Rodríguez, who was raised in a peasant family and the first woman to join the Revolution in the Escambray Mountains of south-central Cuba. It was there she met and married American William Morgan, the famed "Yankee Comandante" from Toledo, Ohio, who rose from foot soldier to lead the second front in Castro's Revolution. When Morgan learned that the intent of the Supreme Leader was not to free the Cuban people but to transform the Pearl of the Antilles into a Communist state, Morgan turned on Castro, and began recruiting soldiers to overthrow him. Castro learned of this through his spies and had Morgan arrested.

On March 11, 1961—just as Tani Pérez was leaving for Tampa, Florida, and his second professional spring training—Morgan was executed by firing squad. It took place, said *The New Yorker*, "against a bullet-pocked wall in an empty moat surrounding La Cabana, an eighteenth-century stone fortress, on a cliff overlooking Havana Harbor, that had been converted into a prison."

When Díaz sees my map showing our route past all this history, his eyes brighten. He notes that Cruces, where I had talked with Martín Dihigo Jr., is the hometown of Chicago White Sox slugger José Abreu, only forty-five kilometers—twenty-eight miles—from Santa Clara.

I describe to Díaz the two- and four-legged parade on the Autopista near Santa Clara that I had happened upon at dusk six months earlier. He nods. "Chaos," he says. "I have seen this chaos of many bicycles and donkeys—and only one car—quite often. Still, I'd rather have the car. My family is lucky to have a car." We both smile.

"I notice you Cubans aren't going to be denied a Saturday night out, even if you've got to hitch up the donkey to do it," I say to Díaz with a wink.

"Yes," he says, grinning. "It is the Cuban mentality to want to move forward and progress—no matter the hardships or the obstacles. We are a positive, happy people. Move, move, move. Go, go, go. Get out there in it; enjoy life, the best you can. That is our philosophy."

Much is made, and rightly so, of Cuba's identification with not only baseball players, but also world-class ballet dancers and boxers. "The Gift" appears to be a national trait, judging by the girlfriends and wives who ride side-saddle on the rear fenders of bicycles on the shoulder of the Autopista without so much as a wobble.

"Balance," says Díaz, nodding again.

As I converse with the twenty-five-year-old Díaz, I have the eerie sensation that I am interviewing the twenty-five-year-old Tony Pérez during his breakout season in 1967 (twenty-six home runs, 102 RBIs). But had I been around in those formative days of the Big Red Machine, I would have had some trouble conducting such an interview, because I speak about as little Spanish as Tony did English back then—back when there weren't any interpreters available. Which is why the young Pérez often received short shrift in the next day's newspaper; his English was limited, so it was difficult to be "a good quote" on deadline. Pete Rose and Johnny Bench were more easily quoted and, thus, a lot more quotable.

I ask Díaz if he knows who Tony Pérez is.

"What I've learned, I've learned since coming over here (to the States)," he answers. "I have heard his name, but I don't know much about him, except that he was a great player. If I were still in Cuba, I wouldn't know him at all. After the Revolution, as far as baseball is concerned, one of the main priorities was to erase major league baseball from the minds of the people. The Cuban authorities don't want the people to know of the players who left Cuba—the 'deserters,' we are called. I know that Tony Pérez was not a deserter. He was just trying to make a better life for himself, the way I am…"

"Ciego de Ávila, is that where Tony Pérez is from?"

"Close," I say, "about sixty kilometers—thirty-seven miles—from Ciego de Ávila." Tony is from the sugar mill town of Central Violeta, now called Primero de Enero, which is why, I explain, that I had been on the *Autopista* driving past Santa Clara, headed for Violeta.

I can tell Díaz understands English; he answers my questions before the interpreter translates them. He likely speaks English decently, too. But the interpreter is present to keep things moving. Díaz still needs to warm up; team-stretch in twenty-five minutes.

Díaz explains that because he was born in the early 1990s, he didn't have any exposure to American baseball until he began following news reports about the Cuba national team in the World Baseball Classic of 2006. The Cubans lost to Japan in the championship game that year. Diaz was fifteen.

"That opened the doors for me," he recalls.

I am tempted, but refrain from asking: *Aledmys, do you realize how much easier you have it as a rookie than Tony Pérez did?*

I am not talking about *getting* to the U.S.—that was harder for Díaz; it has been harder for all the Cuban baseball players since the Iron Curtain lowered, going on what is now six decades after the Cuban Missile Crisis. No, what I'm talking about seems obvious in 2016, but it wasn't obvious in 2015, let alone fifty-four years ago. In 2016, for the first time, all major-league teams have a Spanish interpreter on staff; they even travel with the teams on the road. Pérez, by contrast, once ate chicken every day for a week in Geneva, New York, when he was in his first year in pro ball. "Chicken"—*pollo*—is the only English food-word he knew. He stuck with that after ordering a "mystery" entrée and winding up with apple pie à la mode.

Díaz also had something Tony didn't have: a father who spoke English. "As a child growing up," says Díaz, "I always liked English because I learned from my father. He had the opportunity to work in South Africa as a professor for three years, and when he came back he taught me. So when I came to the United States, I already had the basics of the English language. Then, coming up through the Cardinals organization, they gave us English classes. And as I went along, I always tried to stay active with my American teammates. Plus, TV has been a great way to learn English. My teammate Brayan Peña (a former Red) has been a motivator for me and everybody else here. I'm going through what he already went through. So I can lean on that for support."

Pérez had almost *none* of that, although he did get some help from Leo Cardenas, the Cuba-born Reds shortstop (1960–1968). Cárdenas wasn't a facile English-speaker, but he could advise Tony on the basics.

As a producer of major league talent, Cuba today is every bit as rich as it was when Pérez, Luis Tiant, Tony Oliva, and Zoilo Versalles, among others, were major league stars.

As we travel through central Cuba in December 2015, we are in the heart of baseball country. Behind us is Mal Tiempo, one of the four distinct barrios of Cruces and the home of José Abreu, who braved fifteen-foot-high ocean swells during his escape to America. Just up the road, in Santa Clara, Cuba's sixth largest city, future Miami Marlins star pitcher José Fernández grew up with Díaz. It was Díaz's father who urged Fernández to take the game seriously, and whom Fernández credits with inspiring his major-league dream. "I owe him a lot," Fernández tells me a few months later in Cincinnati.

The baseball things came rapidly for Díaz, much faster than for Pérez. At sixteen, when Pérez had only a year under his belt at shortstop for his sugar mill team in Violeta, Díaz was already beginning play for his home province, Villa Clara, in the highest level of Cuban baseball, the National Series *(Serie Nacional)*. Díaz couldn't have played for the sugar mill team in Santa Clara had he wanted to. Like so many sugar mills in Cuba, the closest one to Díaz's home was shuttered before he was born. He played for Villa Clara for five seasons—2007 through 2011—before defecting in 2012, when the Cuba national team was playing in the Netherlands. For Díaz, the pro money came quickly, too, much faster than it had for Pérez who, two months' shy of his eighteenth birthday, signed with the Reds for $2.50 (the cost of a visa) and a flight to Florida. In February 2014, the unproven Díaz, who hadn't played a day of professional baseball, signed with the Cardinals for two million dollars a year for four years. Thirty-five years earlier, thirty-eight-year-old Tony Pérez—with 1,400 RBIs under his belt in sixteen major league seasons—signed a three-year free agent contract with Boston for

$392,000 per year, his best-ever paycheck, which even at today's dollars is only half of what Díaz signed for.

I tell Díaz more about Pérez, that he is the only Cuban player who played in the American major leagues to make the National Baseball Hall of Fame in Cooperstown, and suggest to Díaz that he check out the statue of Tony in front of Great American Ball Park.

I recalled mentioning to Pérez that I had once heard cable news magnate Ted Turner had wanted to give a satellite dish to Castro in the 1980s so that the Supreme Commander could watch the major-league games and other programming from the States. Pérez didn't so much as crack a smile or say a word.

Yes, it is hard to believe it was fifty years previous when Tony Pérez first topped the 100-RBI mark (his first of eleven straight seasons of ninety-plus RBIs), and smashed his way to .290/.328/.490.

That same year, 1967—the year Che was wounded in battle and then executed—Pérez hit a 15th-inning bomb off Catfish Hunter to win the All-Star Game in Anaheim, and was hugged in the dugout by his heroes, Roberto Clemente and Orlando Cepeda. The memory *still* brings a smile to Tony's face. He cites that greeting as the moment he "arrived."

I ask Díaz if there is group pride among the present Cuban players in the major leagues.

"Yes," he says. "Most of the Cuban players now in the major leagues played together in Cuba. But it's not just a Cuban thing. It's more of a Latino thing. We help one another. I think that's only natural, because of the language barrier, the culture, the pride. It's like a fraternity. Cubans, Dominicans, Venezuelans, Puerto Ricans…"

In other words, "arriving" now is the same as it was fifty years ago.

I ask Díaz what he thinks of Cuba-native major leaguers Yasiel Puig, Alexei Ramírez, Brayan Peña, and Abreu being welcomed back to Cuba and feted in December 2015—a public celebration of Cuba's American stars that hadn't happened since the Revolution.

"I didn't believe it at first," he says. "But I knew that somebody had to take the first step if relations were going to be normalized. It was a great step for Cuba, for the Players Association, and for the kids in Cuba who want to do exactly what I am doing now—fulfilling my dream to play baseball at the very highest level."

"Would you like to play for Cuba in the World Baseball Classic?" I ask.

"Yes," he says. "I would always like to play for Cuba. But before that, the Cuban government would have to change many things. First of all, by not calling people like me deserters, which they are still doing. Second, I could not in my heart play for Cuba if they would not let me into my homeland to visit my family."

His boyhood pal, Fernández, had said the same thing: First, the Cuban government has to allow some form of freedom of expression for the people of Cuba, and improve the people's economic situation.

Fifty-five years later, Tony Pérez is still waiting for that same embrace. ◆

Tony's boyhood home in 2015, the same few blocks that it was from the Violeta's grade school and sugar mill.

CHAPTER 5
"Vitola"

CENTRAL VIOLETA—Martín Dihigo Jr. doesn't remember exactly why he began calling Tani Pérez by the nickname "Vitola," just that it has something to do with a character in a kids' cartoon he recalls seeing years ago. Oh, and that it's a riff on Pérez's hometown of "Violeta"—Central Violeta, in the rich-soil flatland of what back then was Camagüey province. (In 1976, when the original six provinces were subdivided into fifteen, Central Violeta became part of Ciego de Ávila province. When Pérez refers to himself as being from "Camagüey," as he so often does, he means the province *he* grew up in, not the city seventy-five miles away that is the capital city of modern-day Camagüey province.)

I personally believe "Vitola" has its genesis in the stage name of reed-thin (think cartoon Popeye's girlfriend, Olive Oyl) comedienne and actress Fannie "Vitola" Kauffman, who got her show-biz start in Havana. "Vitola" performed in Havana on stage and on radio until she was twenty-two, then moved to Mexico and became a movie star in the 1950s and 1960s. Her stage name came from the "Vitola" cigar, the thickest ring-gauge of the Cuban stogies—a nickname akin to "Fats" for the skinniest kid on the block. When Dihigo Jr. first met Pérez in 1959, Tani was six-foot-two and one hundred and thirty-eight pounds—the wildly popular "Vitola" in a baseball uniform. Latino coaches, scouts, and players at the Cincinnati Reds camp in Tampa in 1960, however, didn't call him "Vitola." They called him what he was: *Flaco*, Spanish for "Skinny."

Central Violeta was the center of Tani's life for his first sixteen years. The three things you need to know above all else if you love Tani Pérez are found there: the history and importance of the sugar mill, the nature of the way base-ball is played, and the legend and memory of Tani's late father, José Manuel, who by all accounts was as even-tempered, mild-mannered, and well-humored a man as ever walked the royal road from Morón to Magarabomba.

Violeta's formal name since the Revolution is "Primero de Enero"—the First of January, which marks the day in 1959 that Fulgencio Batista flew out and the rebels rolled in. But everybody here calls it Violeta. As we drive up the main street of Violeta in our government-issue, dark-blue, four-door, Volkswagen Passat—it stands out like a full-sized Lincoln Continental in vintage-car Cuba— we come upon the open-air market that is all but finished by the time we arrive. But just beginning is a baseball game at the stadium. The stadium in Violeta is not a big place but has a regulation-sized field: 325 feet down the left- and right-field lines, and 345 feet to center. Two dark-colored horses graze beyond the left-field wall. A soccer game plays out beyond the barrier in center.

A *fanatico*, seeing that I am holding a commemorative newspaper sports section about Tony from thirty years ago, motions toward the field. *El arbitro del meta es sobrino de Tani*, he says—"The home-plate umpire is Tani's nephew." Unlike his famous uncle, the ump apparently can't hit the curveball, but he can call it a ball or strike.

The concrete grandstand, ten seat-levels high, was built in the 1970s, well after Pérez left town in March 1960 and sometime during his lengthy prime with the Big Red Machine, the locals say. Except for that concrete grandstand, Central Violeta hasn't changed all that much since Tani grew up here in the 1950s. The houses are colored sea-blues, corals, and lime-greens, the latter the color of Tani's family home where one of his sisters still resides. Same colors as the houses in Havana but with none of the decay of the capital city evident here. Maybe it's just better-hidden in Violeta. My sense, though, is that Violetans are a particularly proud people and that work at the sugar mill, one of the few things still thriving here, provides Violetans the means to take care of one another and their properties, which clearly they do.

And that is why you need to know about baseball in Violeta, the town that time (but not Tani Pérez) forgot.

As we walk into the stadium, the players are being introduced; the managers then gather at home plate with the four umpires, who are dressed in dark blue slacks and light blue shirts. It is a game between the Violetans and a group of players from a visiting province. No two players are dressed in the same color clothes—no uniforms per se—and the players range in age from what appears to be late high school- to middle-age. Somewhere out there, I imagine, is a sixteen-year-old Tani Pérez. There are about one hundred and twenty people in the stands, two-thirds of them male, of all ages. The Violeta pitcher reminds me of Davey Concepción in his last year with the Reds when he still moved with grace and confidence but without the firm body of youth. Still, this Cuban "Concepción" has a good breaking ball and mows down the opposition.

A foul ball clears the backstop and lands with a thud into a backyard abutting the stadium. A shirtless man picks it up, checking the lettering on it. *Lanzaro de vuelta!*—"Throw it back!"—shouts a thirty-something *fanatico* wearing a basketball jersey in the white, blue, and orange colors of the New York Knicks and adorned with "Sprewell—8" on the back. *No es para mi; para mi bebe.*—"It's not for me; it's for my baby."

"Sprewell" keeps up a non-stop patter of commentary in Spanish directed at the players. It is loud enough for them to hear; everybody around him laughs. I laugh, too, even though I don't understand a word he says. Sprewell is a funny guy, a natural comedian. Among the men chortling are two of his friends who discretely share a bottle of rum, each of them with a paper cup.

It is *beisbol* Cubano style, and although I don't see any gymnastics performed by "Concepción" after he punches out back-to-back batters to end an inning, the game is played with a contagious enthusiasm and camaraderie on both sides. I immediately understand how the former Cincinnati Reds fireball reliever Aroldis Chapman came to do a double forward-roll one night coming off the Great American Ball Park mound after another dramatic save. It is, as they say, how the Cubans roll, in an environment of gaiety, frivolity, and all-around "just-glad-to-be-here."

In watching this game in Violeta I also understand—for the first time—what it truly was like to grow up in America in the 1930s, the way my father did, and play these games between neighborhood teams. And also to play in, or watch, pickup games in the 1950s across America. I ask our guide and he tells us yes, most Violetans have television sets, but most are not turned on, at least not on an early December Sunday afternoon that is sunny and perfect for playing or watching baseball, or going to market to eyeball the fruit and the girls. If I didn't know better, I'd swear I had just walked into a Sunday afternoon in July 1952 on a ball field edged by corn stalks in Whitewater Township outside Cincinnati.

I can also tell that the government must have built this stadium (something I later confirm), because of the words painted on the outfield walls, stretching all the way from the left-field line to the right-field line: *Por todos los tiempos, Adelante Deportistas, Orden, Disciplina, Exigencia, Salud*—"For all time;" "Forward, Athletes;" "Order;" "Discipline;" "Urgency;" "Health."

By the third inning, the soccer—*fútbol*—game being played by twelve-to-fifteen-year-olds has broken up and the players sit atop the outfield wall with their legs draped between *Orden* and *Disciplina*. Baseball is still king here, despite what I read in *The New York Times* before coming to Cuba, suggesting that *fútbol* might be about to take over as Cuba's national game. I like that *beisbol* is still number one here. I especially like hearing that Cubans clung to *beisbol* before and during the War for Independence, because *beisbol* was *their* game, as opposed to *fútbol*, which is what the Spanish authorities wanted them to play. And most of all, I love that even though shortly after Fidel came to power he tried to change the national game to soccer, people by their actions told the Maximum Leader, "No, this time you've gone too far—baseball is our game."

Until I visited Cuba, I thought the Cubans had simply borrowed our game and adopted it as their own. But during my baseball pilgrimage through central Cuba I had my epiphany. It came through as loud and clear as those Voice of America broadcasts that originated in Washington, D.C., and were relayed by the giant Crosley towers in Butler County north of Cincinnati to Central Violeta in the 1940s and 1950s: Baseball is as much the Cuban game as it is the American national pastime. In some ways it is better here; in no ways inferior.

Different. More joyous. It's the game you played when you were twelve. Is there a better baseball than *that*?

Even though Tani didn't play in this *estadio*—by then he was playing in front of fifty-thousand fans inside the spaceship known as Riverfront Stadium on the banks of the Ohio River—he played on this *field*, the one laid out in 1922, the very year after the Violeta sugar refinery's first sugar cane harvest. That is how deeply sugar and baseball are ingrained here in this brightly colored company town of mostly small, single-story, two-bedroom homes. (Yes, in Violeta—where everybody Tani had to leave behind in 1960 is friendly, warm, and family-oriented—the dwellings are "homes," not houses.) But they no longer appear to be overflowing with kids, at least not the way they were back in the day when it was commonplace to have families that numbered as many as the three boys and three girls of José Manuel Pérez and Teodora "Tita" Rigal.

Tani's father played baseball, but the evidence suggests he wasn't exceptionally skilled at it. Tani has said his father didn't teach him the game; rather that he learned from getting involved in the neighborhood games. And he obviously learned it well. In answer to a question not long ago during a Miami Marlins radio broadcast, Tony told his son Eduardo that the reason he was such a good RBI man goes back to those street games in Central Violeta, and to that baseball field carved out by the mill workers in 1922: "We always played with something on the line, and the goal was to *win* it." That "something" could be as simple as a fruit drink—especially refreshing and satisfying when the losers had to watch you drink it. That's when guava juice tasted like World Series champagne.

Tani's skills were not honed with an Iron Mike pitching machine; rather, with the hand-eye games of his youth. Once, during a languid morning walk in Puerto Rico, where the Pérez family has long wintered, Eduardo asked his father how he so often managed to find the hole or simply hit a ground ball up the middle that meant an RBI. "Hit pebbles with a stick," Tony told him. "That is what I did in Violeta." Eduardo, who was a major leaguer at the time, didn't believe it.

Tony's grade school.

"Get me a stick and throw me some pebbles," Tani said. *Whap, whap, whap.* Eduardo was incredulous, but there it was.

And while Tani's father didn't have that hand-eye gift, make no mistake, he *loved* the game. He followed it closely on radio and sometimes on television and instilled in Tani a deep-abiding respect for the competition, habits, and history of the game as showcased on radio broadcasts of the Saturday "Game of the Week" from the States and especially winter league games from Havana. Those latter contests featured mostly Cuban players with an infusion of a half-dozen *gringos* per team, most of the *gringos* up-and-comers like Jim Bunning.

Tony told me he grew up as a National League fan. He told me this when he was touring the National Baseball Hall of Fame in May 2000 during his orientation visit. Tony saw a big photo on the wall of the great catch by Cuba's Sandy Amorós against the left-field fence in Yankee Stadium in Game Seven of the 1955 World Series: "I can still see it. I was watching the game on TV with my dad," Tony said. "I was thirteen years old, and I was a Dodgers fan. My father loved the Dodgers."

Unlike José Manuel's fellow baseball fans in the U.S., who had to wait for another half-century to pass before the Dodgers' Jackie Robinson broke the color line in 1947, José Manuel—who was born in 1895—never knew anything but integrated professional baseball in Cuba. Before the Cuban War of Independence (1895–1898), professional baseball here was a game of whites and mulattoes. But during the War, when the whites and mulattoes and black Cubans fought side-by-side against the occupying Spanish army, integration was born.

Of course, the league's integration was neither smooth nor easy, just as it wasn't in the United States. Most Cuban teams didn't want to integrate. Forced to, many club officials changed their team names, as though to signal that the teams were no longer their real teams, certainly not the teams that continued the lineage of their original teams. But the attitude gradually changed, as super-talented black players—*agentes de cambio*, difference-makers—were sprinkled in. Within a few years, the greatest of the American Negro Leaguers were flocking in: Joe Williams, John Henry Lloyd, and Pete Hill played for big-city La Habana. In between, Cuban black pitcher José Méndez shut out the visiting Cincinnati Reds for twenty-five consecutive innings. ("Walter Johnson and Grover Alexander rolled into one," exclaimed New York Giants manager John McGraw.) And all Central Violeta was abuzz in 1920 when slugger Cristóbal Torriente smashed three home runs in one game to out-slug Babe Ruth who was visiting as an add-on with the New York Giants, and again in 1929 when Cool Papa Bell ushered in the New Year with three inside-the-park home runs. Later came Satchel Paige, Oscar Charleston, Josh Gibson, Mule Suttles, and Jud Wilson.

Tani's father was…sixteen years old when Armando Marsans and Rafael Almeida debuted for the Cincinnati Reds, becoming the first big-time Cuban players of the "modern era" to perform in the majors…twenty-seven when sixteen-year-old Martín Dihigo debuted for the Habana Rojos alongside teammates Almeida, Dolf Luque, John Henry Lloyd, and Torriente in the Cuban Winter League (the same year the baseball field was being laid out in Central Violeta) …twenty-eight when Luque won twenty-seven games with the Reds…and fifty-six—with nine-year-old Tani at his side listening to the radio—when rookie Minnie Miñoso led the American League with fourteen triples and thirty-two stolen bases in 1951.

Know that history, and you understand why José Manuel Pérez told his son to "Go!" when the Reds came calling in 1960 and why he told him to "Stay!" in the States after the 1963 minor league season, even though it meant he might never get to see his son again. The old man *knew*.

In many ways, José Manuel knew *beisbol* better and in a different way than the *gringos* across the Gulf. Had he known it would be 1971 before Satchel Paige became the first Negro Leaguer to be enshrined in the National Baseball Hall of Fame, he might not have believed. Nor would he likely have believed that it would take thirty years after Jackie broke the color line for the last of the class of Mendez,

Williams, Lloyd, Hill, Torriente, Cool Papa, Josh, Satchel, Charleston, Suttles, Wilson, and Dihigo to be enshrined. Or maybe José Manuel would have believed it. Those early streets in Violeta were laid out on a black-only and white-only basis. One thing for sure: The fact that Miñoso is *still* not in Cooperstown, and José Manuel's son is, well, that would have rendered the old man speechless.

As we approach the Central Violeta sugar mill in our Passat, the government travel guide-driver is visibly nervous. We want a photo, and he won't get close enough so we can get one. Eventually, we put two-plus-two together: The sugar factory is government-owned, as is most everything across this 780-mile long, 119-mile wide island. (Some mom and pop businesses and more elaborate "proposals"—restaurants, clubs, and hotels that are matters of foreign investment—are exceptions, because Raul Castro has loosened the Communist philosophy to allow it.)

Our guide is afraid of losing his job—or at least being called on the carpet—if he gets too close. Minimally, it could lead to "at least one bad day at the precinct," he later confides. (This is our first indication that he is in on this bad joke.) He is under forty, so he's never known anything but fear of the State. He's also never had his own car—"I can't afford it, and I won't be able to afford it in two lifetimes of work," he says. But he is delighted to be at the wheel of our $200-for-three-days'-government-car rental, which is ten times the monthly salary of the average Cuban.

Not until I visited Cuba did I realize how blessed I'd been in my forty years as a daily journalist in America, getting to go almost anywhere I wanted, at almost any time I wanted, and freely talk with almost anybody I wanted. That is all but impossible in Cuba. Once people learn you are a journalist, you are done because people won't give you their names to go with their quotes. Everybody is afraid to talk with you for fear of reprisals from the government. In the United States, it is known as "a chilling effect," and citizens and our courts rail against it. In Cuba, if you're a visiting journalist—in my case, writing a book—and the State finds out, which of course it does, you're put on ice.

At one point in Violeta, we were conversing with a couple inside their home and a middle-aged "friend," about the age of their son, walked in, sat down, and listened. Eventually, the husband in this couple left for an "errand." We could tell he was ticked off. We got the distinct impression that the friend was no friend at all, but rather was an agent of the State, reporting to his superiors on the nature of our questions. It was all very disconcerting, and later, when I put two-plus-two together, I got angry. It confirmed what we had been forewarned of by some well-intentioned residents of Havana: "They know where you're going before you do."

To understand who Tony Pérez is, one has to understand Violeta, and one cannot understand Violeta without understanding the sugar business, which I was able to do without getting inside the plant. Books and articles came to my rescue.

Two-thirds of the way through the most recent sugar harvest, the Central Violeta sugar refinery was rated number one in Cuba, generating forty thousand tons of sugar *above* its state-determined goal. An article on the state-run website, "granma.cu," attributed at least some of the success to plant manager, Ernesto Blanco, who in turn attributed his success to the workers: "You have to work with the people *and* with their hands—everything that moves in the Central—talking with them, hearing their concerns and suggestions, because the most important thing is the human capital here." Blanco had "more than forty harvests under his belt." *Forty harvests under his belt? That means his first harvest was in 1975. Another Big Red Machine.*

The smell of molasses permeates Central Violeta during the *zafra*—harvest. The mill was built in 1918. It was the custom of U.S.-backed sugar operations of that era to set up shop on an all but uninhabited piece of land, as happened here. The New York-based financial firm of Sullivan Cromwell Rockefeller met with the representatives of the Violeta Sugar Company and asked them where they wanted to move their Santa Clara operation. The stewards of the Violeta Sugar Company pointed to an empty spot on the map, ten miles from Ciego de Ávila and seventeen miles from Morón. When asked what they wanted to name the plant, and thus the town, they said "Violeta," after the owner's daughter. And that is how Central Violeta, Tony Pérez's hometown, came to be.

Tony's paternal grandfather moved to Central Violeta for the work, and brought his family with him, including son José Manuel, who was the prime working age of twenty-six during that first harvest in 1921. The Pérezes moved into a company house located six blocks from the school, four blocks from the processing plant—and only two blocks from the ball field. The population before work began on the sugar mill here was 633 people working on Violeta's 367 "farms." By 2016, the population had reached twenty-eight thousand, about the size of Xenia, Ohio.

Both of Tani's brothers and all three of his sisters worked at the processing plant with their father; José Manuel's wife, Tita, their mother, ran the family home. Tani didn't particularly like working in the mill, though he loved playing shortstop for the factory team, which is how he was "discovered" in 1958—by which time a Cuban company, Falla Gutiérrez, had purchased the business from its American owners.

Our tour guide, who works for the Cuban government, would not allow us to take a close-up of the government-owned and -operated sugar mill where teenager Tani worked side-by-side with his father, José Manuel.

Falla Gutiérrez was a big-time sugar operator, ranking number three in the country by 1953 and still holding that position in 1959 when Castro took over the government. Castro didn't begin nationalizing everything until the following year. The big myth that Castro perpetuated when he took over the sugar industry is that he had to nationalize the plants because the Americans owned most of them. In fact, the Americans owned only a quarter of them—forty-one of the 161. Cuban companies owned 113 (seven by Falla Gutiérrez), six were owned by Spaniards, and one by a Frenchman.

José Manuel wouldn't have known that breakdown, but he would have known that Falla Gutiérrez lost its profit-making aspect when Castro took over its processing plants, including the one at Central Violeta; Jose Manuel would have found that curious.

I later learned that the powerful Falla Gutiérrez family, fearing revolution, had moved $40 million of its fortune abroad. But there is no way José Manuel could have known that.

Agrarian land reform—taking everybody's land and sharing it (in the case of the Cuba Land Reform of 1959, nobody was allowed to own more than 3,333 acres)—was initially popular among the Cuban rank-and-file, but obviously not among the big landowners, whose property was confiscated and redistributed. All in all, the Castro government confiscated 480,000 acres owned by U.S. corporations—750 square miles (almost the total land area of Rhode Island). On the way from the Sierra Maestre Mountains to Havana in 1958, Che Guevara lobbied hard around the campfire to anybody who would listen about the benefits of land redistribution.

As well as Che might have understood economics—and he certainly read enough books on it back home in Argentina and while in Mexico preparing for the Revolution—the one thing he apparently didn't understand is human nature, particularly that aspect known as "incentive" that led men to work harder and produce more when they knew there was something in it for them.

José Manuel understood incentive better than Che.

José Manuel told Tani to sign with the Cincinnati Reds for the price of a month's worth of fruit drinks to play baseball in America. ◆

Bobby Maduro, founder and owner of the Havana Sugar Kings, grew up in Cuba, eleven miles from Pérez.

CHAPTER 6
Maduro's Dream

In the spring of 1954, just as twelve-year-old Tani Pérez was beginning to feel his oats as a young hitter—his muscles lengthening out, his mind sharpening from watching games played by the Central Violeta sugar mill team—a new professional franchise was beginning play in Havana, three hundred miles away.

The Sugar Kings.

They were a full-fledged, highest-level, minor-league franchise in the aptly named International League (three teams in Canada, three in upstate New York, and one each in Virginia and Cuba). All of the franchises outside the United States harbored dreams of getting major league teams someday, especially Montreal, Toronto, and, most overtly, Havana. Within a generation, two of them—Montreal (1969) and Toronto (1977)—would realize those dreams. Havana's dream was interrupted, if not scotched forever, by Fidel Castro.

Little did Tani Pérez know that the Sugar Kings' bloodlines began less than eleven miles from his hometown, on the road to the beach at Playa Guaney, in another sugar-mill "Central"—this one called Cunagua. It is where in the early 1930s young Bobby Maduro, son of a wealthy sugar planter, took up the game and watched it played on a very high level by the mill's team. Twenty years later, Maduro—by then, a "baseball man" through and through—co-founded the Havana Sugar Kings. In 1954 they opened play at Maduro's thirty-thousand-seat Gran Stadium, which he had built a year earlier for two million dollars—the very same stadium where in 1957 Jim Bunning played winter ball for Marianao, and where in 2015 the Tampa Bay Rays played the

Cuban national team in front of Cuban president Raul Castro and president Barack Obama.

Beyond the center field scoreboard at Gran Stadium there was a small restaurant ("Triple A") owned by Joe "Papa Joe" Cambria, the Washington Senators/Minnesota Twins superscout who scoured Cuba for talent, signing well over four hundred Cuban prospects between the early 1930s and early 1960s, all the way from Bobby Estalella in 1934 to Tony Oliva in 1961. In-between were the likes of Camilo Pascual, Pedro Ramos, Mike Fornieles, Sandy Valdespino, and Willie Miranda. Cambria founded the Habana Cubans, a franchise that played in the low- to mid-level Florida International League from 1946–1953, a forerunner to the Sugar Kings. Cambria later sold the Cubans to Maduro, who had bigger dreams—a major-league team in Havana.

Late in that first season of the Sugar Kings' operation—August of 1954—Maduro reached out to his friend in Cincinnati, Reds general manager Gabe Paul. The representatives of the two clubs signed an affiliation agreement that in essence gave the Reds at least an equal grip, if not the upper hand, on Cambria and the Senators/Twins. Maduro and Paul had known one another since the late 1930s when Paul began his career in the majors as the Reds traveling secretary; by 1951, they were fast friends and posed for a photo in Maduro's private box at Gran Stadium, where Maduro's Cienfuegos' team played winter ball. The Reds would provide the Sugar Kings with some players and much of their field expenses and in turn would have the rights to call their players to the major leagues.

Less than two years later, in March of 1956, Maduro's scouting network, which covered the island from Pinar del Rio in the west to Santiago in the east, had such a hold on Cuba that it plucked outfielder Tony González from Cunagua, Leo Cardenas from Matanzas, Cookie Rojas from Havana, and Mike Cuellar from Santa Clara, sending them all to the Reds complex at Douglas, Georgia, for a tryout in front of the Reds brass. On the spot, the Reds signed Cardenas and Rojas, each eighteen, and González, nineteen. The Reds would later sign Cuellar, nineteen. These four teenagers would go on to play between them an astounding fifty-nine major league seasons. Within three years of that day in Georgia, they were with the Triple-A Sugar Kings, and in that final full season in Havana would win the Little World Series, beating the Minneapolis Millers, managed by Gene Mauch and starring Carl Yastrzemski. Cardenas, a shortstop, and Rojas, a second baseman, were Sugar King double-play mates for that season and the one after.

"When I was growing up, that was my dream—to play for the Sugar Kings," Cardenas told me back in 2002. "All of the young players felt that way."

Miguel "Mike" Cuellar in 1959, who pitched for the Sugar Kings.

There was this lilting phrase when Cardenas was growing up: *querido Cinci.* Beloved Cinci. It went back to Armando Marsans and Rafael Almeida, the first Cuban players in the major leagues (with the Reds, in 1911), and then came the great Dolf Luque in the 1920s.

"We grew up with an appreciation for Cincinnati," Cardenas said. "We couldn't have told you where Cincinnati was on a map, just that it was in the *Grandes Ligas.* For me as a boy, it was all about playing for the Sugar Kings, and (by extension) the Cincinnati Reds. Because of the Sugar Kings and their scouting network, the Reds were getting the best players in Cuba."

Fifty-five years later, Cardenas' friend, Luis Zayas, a second baseman with the 1958 Sugar Kings, sits in front of a plate of calamari salad at El Litoral Restaurant in Havana and asks a visitor to say hello to Cardenas when the visitor gets back to Cincinnati.

"Tell Leo I can still turn the double play," says Zayas, seventy-eight.

Zayas speaks hardly any English; I speak hardly any Spanish. And, yet, we "speak" our pidgin tongue of mostly baseball terms, with lots of hand gestures, and we both laugh after ten minutes because my translator, not a baseball fan, sits by mesmerized—and lost—with our "conversation." That's Cuba for you: The universal language still works fifty-five years after Castro nationalized the sugar mills and the Americans headed for home.

Zayas explains to me that from the beginning the Sugar Kings had an instructional team—called the "Juveniles"—who were housed in Havana and played all over the island. On that team in late 1959 and early 1960 was Tani Pérez, who was first seen as a teenager by Sugar Kings scouts in a tryout near Central Violeta. The primary evaluator at the tryout—the *only* evaluator, really—was Tony Pacheco, the Sugar Kings scouting director. He had taken the job in 1956 at twenty-eight, his playing career cut short by a second beaning. Two months after seeing Pérez, Pacheco was named the Sugar Kings manager, taking over for Napoleon Reyes, who was Jim Bunning's manager in winter ball one season earlier.

Pacheco, like most other Cubans, kept up with the news, but he had his own *pescados que freir*. And among those fish to fry were the small-fry, who could become big-fry, the goal of any good talent scout. And that's where Tani Pérez came in.

"I had hundreds and hundreds of bird dogs (scouts), one in every town," Pacheco told me in the fall of 1986. "The bird dog who was around Tony's town wrote me a letter every week with fifteen prospects listed in it. Pretty soon, he had a hundred prospects listed with me. I said, 'Wait a minute, I'll hold a tryout.' I told the bird dog what I wanted to see in age, size, and main tools. 'One tool is enough,' I told him. I wanted to see anybody who could run fast, had a good arm, or could hit the ball."

The bird dog assembled his fifteen best prospects in late-May 1959. One of them was a 140-pound string bean with brown eyes, a swan's neck, and fluorescent smile.

Even though Pacheco recalled liking Pérez—"his strength was his bat, (but) he was a very poor defensive player, very erratic—I didn't sign anybody out of that tryout, not even Tony," Pacheco said.

Yes, Pacheco, a seventeen-year veteran of managing, coaching, and scouting the American minor leagues, called the Reds star "Tony," not Tani, likely in part because Pacheco's own first name (Antonio) had been Americanized to "Tony" ever since he arrived in the States to play ball in 1949.

"I told Tony we were running a baseball school in Havana, and that we invited the kids there who we liked best," Pacheco said. "We worked with the kids like Tony for some time. It all depended on their progress."

The Sugar Kings kept fifteen juniors in a boarding house just outside Havana, paying all their expenses. (If Pacheco and his scouts decided that a youngster didn't have enough ability, they sent him home without signing him. That way, the boy could maintain his amateur status.)

This is where Pérez was when Cuba president Fulgencio Batista fled Havana with $300 million in the middle of the night just after the gong sounded on New Year's Eve, only hours before the *rebeldes* arrived, eight days before Castro rolled in, literally.

Pacheco, who was six years old when Batista had first taken over in 1933, remembered that in 1958/1959, even early 1960, the Sugar Kings went about their business, thinking there was no reason to doubt their continued existence. Baseball in Cuba, as always, had been immune to the political unrest.

"Tony progressed very steadily," Pacheco recalled. "But he had trouble pulling the ball. He'd hit the ball from right-center to the right-field line. But he'd hit it hard. His hands were rolled in too much on the bat. That brought his elbow into his body. It stopped his hands."

The Sugar King instructors worked with Pérez on his grip so that he could release his elbow from his body. That way he could follow through on every swing.

"At first it was awkward, but he stuck with it," Pacheco said. "Every Saturday, we'd send him (and his teammates) into the interior of the country, where one of our scouts was the manager of the team. Games were played on Sunday. On Monday morning, I'd found out how he did."

"How did you do in yesterday's game?" Pacheco asked Tani.

"Two hits," Tani answered.

"What kind of hits?"

"Two home runs."

"Where?"

"Left field."

Bingo! This was when Pacheco knew: He likely had himself a hugely promising prospect, maybe even a future major leaguer, who knows, perhaps even a star. Soon after that, Pacheco signed Tani for the Reds.

The year 1959 seemed like such a high point for baseball—and perceived freedom—on the island; the promise was so bright. "The top," to use Cole Porter's phrase. The year began with Batista being ousted, and people cheering Castro, who promised free elections within two years. But, as noted in *The Pride of Havana* by Roberto González Echevarría, the tumultuous nature of things led baseball commissioner Ford Frick ("urged by Washington Senators owner Calvin Griffith") to order the American players out of Cuba. However, Alemendares pitcher Art Fowler "replied in the name of the players that they were staying, having been offered guarantees by the new regime." After a five-day hiatus, the Cuban Winter League resumed with a nighttime doubleheader beginning at 7 p.m. on January 6 at Gran Stadium, at which "the *rebeldes*, now being called *barbudos* because of their beards (the length of which indicated time of service in the hills) were invited to attend for free."

"This would be a *Dia de Reyes*—the Epiphany—like no other," continued Echevarría. "The crowd stood to sing the July 26 Movement's anthem and gave a long standing ovation to the soldiers, many of them white *guajiros* from the deepest backwoods who were in Havana for the first time …When Carlos Paula hit a homer, a *barbudos* jumped onto the field and embraced him. It was a time of celebration, as if all of Cuba (and quite a few Americans) had joined in a ritual of celebration…Baseball was, again, the crucible of Cuba's nationalism, even though the new leader had yet to reach Havana. He was slowly approaching in a caravan from Oriente, a new magic king from the East."

That February, Alemandares won the Caribbean World Series in Caracas; that March, the Reds and Los Angeles Dodgers, featuring future Hall of Fame pitchers Sandy Koufax and Don Drysdale, played a tight, exciting series in Gran Stadium; the Sugar Kings played well all season long and went on to win the Little World Series in September against the Minneapolis Millers in Havana. In the middle of it all was Tani Pérez, slugger, baby Sugar King. *La Bomba.*

Yes, 1959 was a great year to be young and a (future) Red.

About the time Pérez's tryout was taking place, the average townsfolk not fighting in the revolution—which was everybody in Tani's hometown of Central Violeta—felt free to move about.

But the reality was something else.

The reality was that three hundred miles away in Havana, Fidel and Raul Castro and Che Guevara had their hands full culling out the Batista supporters and dispatching several hundred of them "to the wall" in 1959 and 1960, according to an unpublished history of Leo Cherne, a wealthy businessman and power broker who had advised several presidents and met in late 1960 with William Morgan, the "Yankee Comandante" from Toledo. All of this was related in that stirring narrative in *New Yorker* magazine in 2012.

Despite the popular perception, the *Revolución* took a long time to be consummated: Castro and his band had come ashore from Mexico in December 1956—while Jim Bunning was six weeks into his winter ball season with Marianao—and a year and a half later was still in the mountains in southeast Cuba near Santiago, 550 miles from Havana, when Pérez turned sixteen on May 14, 1958. May of 1958 is also when Che led a summit in the Sierra Maestre about agrarian land reform, designed to break up giant land holdings, especially those of the rich American corporations, and allot them to the peasants and cooperatives.

A lot of important things happened in the month of May during the two years of armed revolution. On May 19, 1957—five days after Pérez's fifteenth birthday when he was already the shortstop and hitting star of the Central Violeta sugar mill team—a cache of weapons from the failed assault on Batista's palace in

March by the group, *Directorio Revolucionario Estudiantil*, arrived in the Sierra Maestre: three machine-gun tripods, three Madsen machine guns, nine M-1 carbines, ten Johnson repeaters and six thousand bullets. One of the machine guns went to the *jefe estado mayor*, the chief of staff. Guevara was put in charge of it. The American public wasn't aware of this little detail: an in-person visit to Fidel's camp a few weeks earlier by CBS-TV newsman Robert Taber and a cameraman yielded a documentary that aired in the States on that same May 19 night, "The Story of Cuba's Jungle Fighters."

"In this way," Che would later write, "I made my debut as a full-time combatant, for until then I had been a part-time combatant and my main responsibility had been as the troop's doctor. I had entered a new stage."

A year later, in late May 1958, *Ejercito Rebelde*, Castro's revolutionary army, was still operating in the Sierra Maestre, where a major offensive by Batista's army was underway to try to eradicate the two Castros, Cienfuegos, and Guevara, once and for all.

Late that August, as Pérez's training with the Sugar King "Juveniles" was progressing, the Pan Am Games got underway in Chicago. The baseball part of the program was played at Comiskey Park, home of the White Sox, and at the Cubs' Wrigley Field. Cuba hadn't fielded a team in the Pan-Am Games since 1955 in Mexico City. Fidel Castro, a baseball fan who knew what the game meant to his country and its pride, wanted to field a team in Chicago, in part to show that life was "normal" on the island—baseball at center stage, as it were—and also in hopes that the gold medal the team had won in the Pan-Am Games in Buenos Aires in 1951 could be captured again. The problem was that even though the Cubans fielded a good team, they didn't field a great one.

"They were good—but no better than the Duke-Syracuse-Princeton-Harvard teams we had seen at Navy," recalls Chuck Davis, the U.S. Naval Academy pitcher who was the starter against Cuba in that medal game and two years later would be USNA's first baseball All-American. "Most of them were clearly older than our guys—many had bushy mustaches. I had never played with or against a guy with a mustache. The Wrigley Field stands had many Puerto Rico and Cuba fans. There was much 'Puerto Rico, rah-rah-rah!' and 'Cooba, Sí; Jankees, No!' and 'Feedel Cahstro, rah-rah-rah!' There were a lot of guys wearing green military dungarees, and some Sam Browne belts. A few of these guys were walking around on top of the Cuba dugout. We did not see any guns. No doubt many of the Cuban players were pros in Cuba. Looking back on it, the 'uniforms' may well have been there to prevent defections. We were not especially intimidated, mainly because it became a tense, tight game."

The score was 2–2 with two outs and a man on third base when future Hall of Famer Lou Brock (Southern University)—who, along with fellow outfielder Ty Cline (Clemson University) were the only future major leaguers on the U.S. squad—stepped to the plate.

"Just hit it on the ground, Lou!" his teammates shouted. He did, beating out an infield hit, as the go-ahead run scored for the 3–2 lead that held up. The gringos went home with the bronze. Nobody outside Castro's inner circle knew it at the time, but he was already an avowed Communist. The result of this game, especially against the team representing Castro's archenemy, could not have pleased the Maximum Leader.

But what if the then-twenty-one-year-olds Leo Cardenas and Cookie Rojas had been the double-play combination on that Cuba team, and twenty-one-year-old Tony Oliva and twenty-two-year-olds Mike Cuellar and Tony González had worn the Cuba "C," and seventeen-year-old Bert Campaneris was a late-inning defensive replacement, and eighteen-year-old Tani Pérez as a pinch-hitter and nineteen-year-old Luis Tiant Jr. was in the bullpen?

What *then*? Weren't these the type of players the Cuba national team had in the Pan-Am Games when it recaptured the gold at São Paulo in 1963, the silver in Winnipeg in 1967, and then ten straight Pan-Am gold medals every four years from 1971 through 2007?

"It might well have been different had those big guns been in that game," contemplates Davis, looking back. "Two ways to look at it, though. They may have won it, but we could look back with pride on competing with them. As it

Chuck Davis, one of the stars of the 1959 Pan-Am Games who held the Cuban team at bay in the medal game until teammate Lou Brock could infield-single home the go-ahead run.

was, we got the win against a good team, and a medal. Most of us would take the win."

From a Cuban standpoint, it all comes down to what a narrow window the youngsters Campaneris, Oliva, and Pérez were lucky enough to climb through. They were among the last of the future stars to get out; Campy and Oliva were even later than Pérez: Pérez, March of 1960, Oliva, a year later, just before the CIA-backed Bay of Pigs invasion in mid-April 1961, Campy a week after.

In *Tony Oliva: The Life and Times of a Minnesota Twins Legend* by Thom Henninger, former Reds farmhand Minnie Mendoza recalled a telling moment. The Reds had signed Mendoza in Cuba in 1954. After four years, they released him, only to see him hook up with the Senators organization and play another eleven years in the minors. (He would get a sixteen-game call-up by the Twins in 1970, and then play two more seasons in the minors.)

Mendoza's telling anecdote is this: In February 1961 in Havana, Castro told a group of Cuban professionals who had been playing ball in the States that soon they wouldn't be free to come and go. Mendoza remembered Castro appearing out of nowhere at a Havana ball field where the players had gathered for an informal softball game just after the conclusion of the Cuban Winter League. This is what Castro told them:

"If you want to go and continue your career in the United States, you are free to go. But if you stay here, you're going to stay for good."

Castro was not as concerned about the younger players, but someday he would be. ◆

Tony thinks he may've been issued one of Ted Kluszewski's old uniforms to wear in his first spring training in 1960. Perhaps it is this one from four years earlier ("Klu" is No. 18.) The sleeve-holes came down to his waist. "I looked ridiculous," Pérez recalls.

CHAPTER 7
The Geneva Accords 1

Geneva, New York—I knew as soon as the Cuban Missile, Aroldis Chapman, told me in Cincinnati in January 2010 that he didn't know who Tony Pérez is, that hardly anybody in Cuba knows who Pérez is. After two days in Geneva, New York, it dawned on me how close Tony Pérez came to nobody in the United States knowing him, either.

Havana Sugar Kings scouting director Tony Pacheco had to fight for Pérez from the very first day the young Cuban took the field in Tampa, Florida. "Tani" had been issued an old Reds uniform that would have required the girth of at least a 180-pounder to avoid looking foolish. Pérez was two bowling balls shy.

"I looked ridiculous in it," Pérez told me years later. "I think it was Ted Kluszewski's uniform. But what was I going to say, 'It doesn't fit me?'"

Pacheco: "It was one of those sleeveless ones. The hole (where the sleeve would have been) went all the way to his waist."

During the first intrasquad game in Tampa, second baseman Pérez made some errors and struck out a couple of times. Dave Bristol, a Reds coach who had managed the first-year Geneva franchise to the New York-Penn League Championship in 1958, remembers.

"He was so tall and gangly that when somebody hit him on a double play, and it took him five minutes to fall down—he came down in sections," Bristol told me at his home in Andrews, North Carolina, in the summer of 2016.

After that intrasquad game, Reds farm director Phil Seghi asked the other Reds scouts if any of these greenhorns looked overmatched and should be sent home. Pacheco suggested that a seventeen-year-old catcher, last name of Miller, be shown the door. Pacheco didn't know that Seghi had signed Miller.

"The other scouts, they signaled to me to shut up," Pacheco recalled. "But I had already started, so I figured I'd finish…Seghi was getting angrier by the minute. He said, 'Well, your guy (Pérez) looked so bad I felt like going out there and taking the uniform off him and sending him back to Havana on the next plane!'"

By then, Pacheco knew he had gone too far.

"I just said, 'Phil, maybe he's better than you think.'"

There is no record of a "Miller" at any of the Reds' "D" level affiliates in 1960—Geneva or Tampa or Palatka—or at "C"-level Missoula or "B"-level Topeka, so Pacheco must have had a pretty good eye.

As for Pérez, he was headed for Geneva, New York, for a memorable first season of rookie ball. Geneva is on the northern end of Seneca Lake, halfway between Syracuse and Rochester in the heart of Finger Lakes Country. Watkins Glen at the southern end is thirty-four miles away.

And Cincinnati?

Cincinnati was a million miles away for an eighteen-old Cuban kid who didn't speak a word of English and had no idea what the future might hold.

Geneva Redlegs manager Reno DeBenedetti, thirty-two years of age, had put in seven minor-league seasons by the time the Reds hired him in 1959 to begin grooming as a manager. He knew his team could hit. But he also knew they would have to hit like the '27 Yankees to make up for all the runs they were going to give up.

"The infield will (eventually) settle down," DeBenedetti told the *Geneva Times* the day before the season opened. "But right now they are weak from a fundamental standpoint."

Translated: The Redlegs were such rock-handers around the horn they made Fred Flintstone and Barney Rubble look like surgeons.

The rock-handers cost DeBenedetti his job.

And Tony Pérez, who didn't know Fred and Barney from Fannie and Tin-Tan, cost himself his position.

Pete Rose is second from left, top row in this 1960 Geneva (N.Y.) Redlegs team photo. Tony is in the row beneath him, second from right. It is extremely rare that two future Hall of Fame-quality players would be on the same rookie team; even rarer is that both played the same position (second base). Pete pushed Tony to third base.

Opening Day, New York-Pennsylvania League, Falcon Park, Auburn, New York, Sunday afternoon, May 8, 1960. Overcast, forty-three degrees.

"Cold," Pérez told me in 1986, shaking his shoulders in a shiver. "I will never forget the (early spring) cold of Central New York."

Tani was accustomed to the warmth of the May sun in central Cuba, where the mean temperature runs seventy-nine degrees, twice what it is in CNY. Auburn is twenty-eight miles west of Syracuse, which is in the center of the state and hosts the annual New York State Fair. (I don't want to say it snows a lot in Syracuse, but I'm from there and I can relate to what Pérez said. In 2013, Syracuse received its latest snowfall on record—*Memorial Day weekend*. And it wasn't as though the locals were shocked; it broke the previous record by only nine days.)

There was a decent crowd at Falcon Park on Opening Day 1960: 1,694. They drank twelve hundred cups of coffee that day at the park. Assuming that at least half the crowd was kids of pre-coffee-drinking age, that's a lot of java, a cup-and-half per adult.

"Not many were around for the thrilling finish four hours later," observed the *Auburn Citizen Advertiser,* and the Geneva Redlegs lost 6–5 in thirteen innings.

"Tanney" Pérez (note the newspaper taking a wild stab at the correct spelling of the young Cuban's first name) displayed the whole package in his first professional game: booting the very first ground ball hit to him (Auburn took a 2–0 first-inning lead on that error), blasting a triple, and scoring a run.

Seven weeks later, he was "Tani" in print and in the clubhouse (phonetically: TAH-nee), and he was starting to hit the ball a ton. But, oh, the fielding. Nobody had a better view of it than the guy backing him up whenever a groundball came right at Pérez, or to his glove-side, than Geneva right fielder Ron Flender.

"He was a *terrible* fielder," Flender recalled. "He couldn't pick up a ground ball. It was a far-out thing for him."

Marty Dihigo Jr., who played center field, would say the same. But he was more mesmerized by Tani's power than he was horrified by his friend's fielding. The Reds brass was trying to find a position for Pérez. The brass even ran him out to the outfield seventeen times in 1960.

"Man, you could see it in his wrists," Dihigo said. "He could generate a lot of power. When he hit 'em, they went a long way."

Early evening, Friday, June 24, 1960, Shuron Park, Geneva, New York.

Norm Jollow, the late legendary sportswriter for the *Geneva Times* was talking with manager DeBenedetti in his ballpark cubicle when a crew-cut kid walked in, two bats slung over his left shoulder.

"Who are you?" skipper DeBenedetti asked.

"Pete Rose, your new second baseman," the crew-cut kid answered.

The season was already seven weeks old. Back then, school in Cincinnati always went into the third week of June. Rose had graduated West High—shorthand for Western Hills High School—only a day or two before. West High had produced a bevy of future major leaguers going back to the 1940s, Rose being the brashest, but as a high-schooler, far from the best. Among the others: Don Zimmer, Jim Frey and—before the 1961 season—bonus baby Eddie Brinkman.

And now, here was Rose telling his first pro skipper where to play him.

Two veteran journalists of the *Finger Lakes Times* (née the *Geneva Times*)— Mike Cutillo and Alan Brignall—heard it right from Jollow himself.

"Absolutely true story," Cutillo told me in the summer of 2015. "Pete's first day on the job, he's telling the manager where he should start, the sooner the better."

Here's what Rose saw his first night in Geneva:

A relatively well-fielded game by the Redlegs (Rose couldn't have known how rare that was), a well-pitched game by Dan Paul (who was accustomed to doing that in 1960, but not coming into this game) and a near game-costing ninth-inning error by a crazily skinny Cuban second baseman who could barely speak a word of English. Rose didn't know it, but only a week earlier the Redlegs had had their collective psyches shattered by a rash of errors so voluminous that the number stood out even on a rookie-league team.

And that was the back story of the Pérez error and the tension it caused in the Geneva dugout where Rose had been riding the hardwood the entire game. A week ago, Dan Paul had also been on the mound and couldn't get out of the first inning because of four Geneva errors that led to six unearned runs. All *ten* of the opponent's runs that day were unearned. That defeat had capped a five-game Geneva losing streak in which the Redlegs made, count 'em, *twenty-eight* errors, an average of almost six a game. In a three-game stretch over the previous weekend (two of the games coming in a Sunday doubleheader), the Redlegs had made 16 errors—and Pérez made an error in each of them.

In the first of those games, which was on the road, the Redlegs blew three-run leads in the ninth and 14th innings, those errors opening the door for game-winning rallies. The next night, the Geneva home fans—having personally borne witness to the continuation of the faux pas—"were cheering easy popouts louder than they normally would a good play," Jollow observed. It was the Geneva fan's equivalent of the expansion New York Mets manager Casey Stengel saying of his team, "Can't anybody here play this game?"

And now here Pérez had almost caused another cave-in with an ill-timed error. Soon as it happened, DeBenedetti vowed to himself that he didn't care how brash the crew-cut kid was from Cincinnati, *I'm going to make him a prophet. He's starting tomorrow. And Pérez? I'm putting him on the disabled list because I've got no place else to put him.*

Rose had arrived too late at the ballpark to get a start. But not, as would turn out for his entire career, too late to make an impression.

Fortunately for the Redlegs' shattered psyches and the manager's mental health, the next Elmira batter after Pérez's error, Dick Allen—yes, *that* Dick Allen—popped out to Geneva's sure-handed catcher, Greg Nash, to end the game.

I had always heard that Rose knocked Pérez off second base in 1960. But the DL wrinkle to the story is an eye-opener. As an historical note, it is no small thing, because Pérez would go on to play twenty-three big-league seasons without so much as a day on the DL. Rose doesn't remember the Friday night error, either, but suffice to say it was an easy play.

And it's worth detailing a bit more because it's rare enough that two future all-time greats would be on the same rookie-league team, but even rarer, *maybe even all-time rare*, that one's exit from the lineup would be the other's entrance to it.

Here's how Jollow described it in the next day's *Geneva Times*:

"With runners on first and third base and two out and his team down 2–0, Elmira batter Paul Price promptly hit a popup in back of first base that (second baseman) Pérez called for and moved under."

Jollow, in the style of the day in low-level minor league towns, not only never openly criticized Geneva's players for errors—they were eighteen-, nineteen- and twenty-year-old kids usually in their first year of pro ball, fer cryin' out loud—but often didn't even give the name of the young men who made the errors. Fans and followers could find that information if they wanted. Jollow tagged the stone-fingered culprits with an "E," the scarlet letter for the crimson-faced. He was the official scorer of the Geneva Redlegs.

Jollow had his fun and took his shots in print (June 18: "Unless the Redlegs stop treating the baseball like it was a live hand grenade…") but rarely named the perpetrator, although in Pérez's case he just had to. That's because button-holing the player could be critical to describing the game action, and that was Jollow's hallowed forte. He didn't use any adjectives to describe this final error on that fateful night, but one can tell he absolutely believed Pérez should have made the play.

"Then the ball popped into and out of Pérez's glove. Elmira had a run, the tying tally was on third and the lead run was on second."

As in, "If you've been following this team for the past two weeks, you know what I'm talking about. That was an error with a bold-faced capital 'E.' "

It says something about Pérez—and the pitcher—that fifty-five years later Paul remembered neither the error nor the fielding reputation. Paul did remember the way Pérez swung the bat and the ease of his demeanor.

"I've never seen a guy swing the bat that hard, but that under control," Paul recalled. "And I remember what a pleasant disposition he had. He was a great teammate, and that's saying a lot because he could hardly speak any English."

The other thing that stands out about Pérez's first season in Geneva is that he was one of six Cubans on the team. Six on one team could be matched only by some of the Washington Senators farm clubs.

Pérez's double-play mate—until Rose knocked Pérez off second base—was shortstop Ignacio Nelson "Nellie" Morera. How was Morera as a shortstop? Let's put it this way: Only a shortstop from Havana—who made eighteen errors in his grand total of only twenty-six games—could make a second baseman from Camaguey look major-league-ready by comparison. (As bad as Pérez was at second base—twenty-three errors in sixty games—Rose was even worse, making more than half again as many errors in only twelve more games.)

Although what Pérez said at his introduction to the New York media at the time of his Hall of Fame election in January 2000 was true for most of his time in Geneva— "I couldn't even talk to the players on the field, didn't know what they meant when they said, 'Hit the cutoff man,' or 'Throw home'"—it is also true that for twenty-eight games in 1960, he had a double-play mate in shortstop

Morera with whom he would have communicated in Spanish regarding double plays, pickoffs, and covering second base on attempted steals. (Of course, it is also true that Pérez likely knew more about playing shortstop than Morera did: Pérez grew up in Central Violeta playing shortstop—Morera had been converted that spring to shortstop from his natural position as an outfielder.)

And when right fielder Flender said Tony's fielding a groundball was a "far-out thing," the same could be said about life in general for the six Cuban transplants in Geneva.

In the unpublished questionnaires that the *Geneva Times* collected from some of the Redlegs players the following spring, one can see in their handwriting just how tough it was. Under "Hobbies," the Havana-born pitcher Delio Suarez wrote "Movies" in fairly legible script; he had been with the team in 1960, and had obviously learned something. The next questionnaire in the file is that of teammate Roberto Iglesias, a rookie from Havana, who under "Hobbies" wrote "M... O... V..." in halting, barely decipherable script, as though he was learning English for the very first time.

Besides the culture- and food-shock ("I remember the Cuban guys eating chili at a drugstore downtown—it was the closest thing they could get to their cuisine, with the beans and spices," Paul said), there was the bone-chilling, CNY temperatures of early May of which Pérez spoke.

Besides Pérez, only two of Pérez's five Cuban teammates would advance in professional baseball beyond "Geneva—1960":

Outfielder Martín Dihigo Jr.—Yes, *that* Martín Dihigo Jr., son of *El Inmortal*, Cuba's greatest player ever. Dihigo Jr. hit only .247 at Geneva that season without much power (.332 slugging percentage), but survived to play three more seasons before returning home to be with his family.

Pitcher Arsenio Sotolongo—He also played four minor league seasons, the first two of them with the Reds organization, and he made it to the Cleveland Indians' Single-A Burlington team of the Carolina League, where in 1963 he played with the soon-to-be far more renowned Cuban, Luis Tiant Jr.

By the end of the 1960 season, Sotolongo (presumably injured), and Morera and pitcher Miguel LaRosa (each presumably released) were gone. Only Pérez, outfielder Dihigo and pitcher Delio Suarez (incorrectly identified in some base-ball statistical compendiums, but not the *Geneva Times*, as "Delio Díaz") were with the Geneva Redlegs at season's end.

Speaking of the confusion over Suarez's actual name, there was and is even *more* confusion over Pérez's full name. In the Spanish/Hispanic tradition, the final name of the three-name trilogy—e.g. "Delio Suarez Díaz" —is the mother's maiden name (Díaz). The second name (Suarez) is the person's actual family name. Thus, the *Geneva Times* got it correct from the get-go: The pitcher's true first-and-last-name was "Delio Suarez."

If Tony Pérez's full name were written in the Spanish tradition, it would be Atanasio Pérez Rigal. But it appears in American baseball compendiums as Atanasio Rigal Pérez, because it has been Anglicized, which is fine: His true first-and-last-name is Tani "Tony" Pérez. My favorite-cited mistake involving Pérez's name involves an incorrect identification of his wife, Pituka. Hal McCoy, the re-nowned baseball writer from Dayton who is enshrined in the writer's wing of the National Baseball Hall of Fame, told me of the caption he saw in an Associated Press newspaper photo of the couple: "Tony Pérez and his wife, Atanasio." We both howled at that one.

Now, for the kicker: The *real* first name of Tony Pérez—or "Tani" as he was and is called back in Cuba among those who played there with him—is *Atanacio*, with a "c," not an "s." I first learned of this in July 2016 on Induction Weekend in Cooperstown, New York, from Cincinnati sculptor Tom Tsuchiya, who has crafted all of the statues of famous Reds outside Great American Ball Park, including the Tony Pérez. (In 2016, Tsuchiya debuted as plaques sculptor for the National Baseball Hall of Fame.)

Tsuchiya first learned of the misspelling in a visit to Pérez's winter home in Puerto Rico while doing research for Tony's statue. Tony and Tom visited the Caribbean Baseball Hall of Fame in San Juan. "Hey, Tom, check this out," Tony said when they came to his plaque. "They misspelled my first name. Everybody

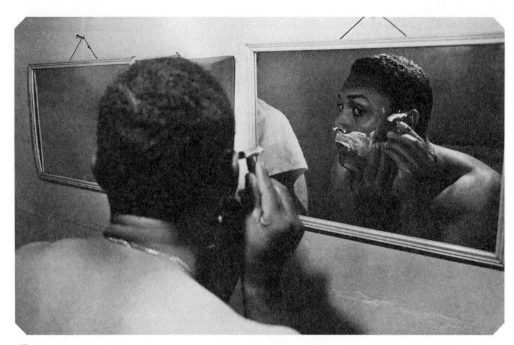

Tony received the figurative "good look in the mirror" when, despite a decent rookie year in pro ball (.279, six HR, 43 RBI), he learned he would be sent back to Geneva, N.Y., for a second consecutive season, while fellow rookies Pete Rose and Art Shamsky moved up.

does, including my plaque in Cooperstown." He is totally nonchalant about it, as in "Why bother to fix it?" Only the Topps baseball card series has it correct: "Atanacio." Tsuchiya knows this because he has Pérez's 1975 Topps card: "Atanacio (Rigal) Pérez."

I looked up the full name of Tony's son, Eduardo, the former major leaguer turned instructor, coach, and broadcaster. Sure enough, it was crystal clear in the online baseball bible used by every baseball writer worth his or her salt, Baseball-Reference.com:

"Eduardo *Atanacio* Pérez."

Meanwhile, most Reds fans old enough to remember the Big Red Machine can tell you that Atanacio Rigal Pérez and Peter Edward Rose played together in Geneva in 1960.

What most can't tell you is *where* Pérez played in 1961.

It would change Atanacio's view of everything. ◆

Tony (kneeling third left) made the most of his second year in rookie ball in 1961, smashing 27 HR with 132 RBI in only 121 games. He won the league MVP award. "Not until then did I realize I was a prospect," he said.

CHAPTER 8
The Geneva Accords II

Atanacio Rigal Pérez was sent back to Geneva for a second straight rookie-ball season in 1961. That wasn't normal treatment for any player coming off a decent year, let alone a future major leaguer. But it was, and is, especially unusual for a future Hall of Famer. It's indicative of an organization that wasn't totally sure what to do with Pérez, so they sent him back to Geneva for more seasoning to build his confidence. The Reds wanted him to get his feet underneath him—figuratively and literally.

"Definitely not the typical thing to do with a guy coming off a pretty good year (.279, twenty-one doubles, four triples, six home runs and forty-three RBIs in only 384 at-bats)," proclaims Chuck Agonito, who was an eleven- and twelve-year-old fan when Pérez played his two seasons in Geneva. Agonito pedaled his bike three blocks from his house to Shuron Park almost nightly from the time Geneva got its New York Penn League franchise in 1958. "I didn't see many guys, if any, of Pérez's caliber as a hitter being sent back here."

Agonito, being so young, was able to get up close and personal with the Geneva players without them giving him a second thought, playing backstop in the nightly "pepper" games, sometimes sitting in for an absent batboy, hauling the burlap-on-chains across the infield dirt between the top and bottom of the fifth innings to rake it smooth, occasionally inserting the white tin numbers into the allotted spaces in the scoreboard—runs, hits, errors.

"Looking back on it as I got older," says Agonito, "I think they (the Reds brass) just wanted Pérez to get more comfortable, maybe learn the language better—he never really tried to do that, as I recall; he mainly hung out with the other Hispanic players—and become a better fielder."

As Agonito and I talk, he points to a bench near a light stanchion in right-field foul territory at what is now McDonough Park, though it is the same field Pérez played on. A half-dozen pitchers from the Geneva Red Wings—a team in the Perfect Game Collegiate Baseball League, a wood-bat circuit—are talking and cutting up. In the same spot, Geneva's Hispanic players cut up in 1960–1961. (Geneva lost its New York Penn League franchise to Williamsport, Pennsylvania, after the 1993 season.)

Also still in the same place: the thirty-foot high scoreboard in right field, refurbished, of course, and the ghostly twenty-five-foot-tall metal pole and rib-remnants of the Marlboro Man billboard (the billboard itself long gone). Pérez likely smashed home runs off both these landmarks—or at least came close—given that he hit a league-leading twenty-seven bombs in his second season in Geneva.

"Tony was an easy-going guy," recalls his 1961 teammate, former Geneva Redlegs outfielder Sal Minetta. "As a hitter, he was great. He could hit everything—fastballs, curveballs, change of paces. He was a wonderful guy, but man, oh man, if an opposing pitcher or player got under his skin, he'd make them pay. That's what I remember about him. He'd have a good time in the clubhouse but on the field, if you got under his skin, he was a tiger. He stood out in that way."

By 1961, the group of Hispanic players in Geneva was considerably smaller than it had been in 1960: Dihigo and Sotolongo had moved up a level, LaRosa and Morera had been released, and Díaz—last heard of in the upstate New York newspapers in late April when the Geneva club was breaking from spring training camp in Tampa—apparently didn't make the last cut that spring; he vanishes from American baseball statistic books immediately thereafter.

One thing the Cubans who were let go wouldn't have missed is the car rides. "We had the long rides like everybody else in the minors, but it was the three-game road trips to places like Wellsville, New York—not just three games, but three round *trips*, a separate trip for every game—that tended to do you in," recalls pitcher Dan Paul, fifty-five years later. "A road trip, every day and night, ninety miles each way. And we're not talking expressways, not in those days."

One of the two Latinos on the club was Venezuelan infielder-outfielder César Tovar. "Happy guy, always smiling, could make you laugh even if you didn't speak a word of Spanish," recalls former Geneva pitcher Stanley Proffitt, five-and-a-half decades later. "He and Tony would've been close, because Tony liked to laugh—and nobody could make you laugh like Tovar."

There was also a sawed-off (5-foot-7, 185 pounds) eighteen-year-old outfielder named Roberto "Bobby" Iglesias from Havana, a left-handed hitter and thrower, missing the tip of the index finger of his throwing hand, just above the knuckle. Iglesias had a good year in 1961, albeit a short one (sixty-one games, half of Pérez's total, but with nine home runs and forty-eight RBIs in only 249 plate appearances) and paired nicely with Pérez for power at the corners. Too bad for Iglesias' sake that Geneva's new skipper Karl Kuehl hadn't acted more quickly on something he had heard at spring training—that outfielder Iglesias had played first base in high school. Part of what kept Iglesias off first base early in the season was that the twenty-three-year-old Kuehl was also player-manager and his position was first base.

On Opening Day 1961, Kuehl batted himself in the three-hole ahead of Pérez. But by June, to Kuehl's credit, he had moved Iglesias into first base and got him a lot of at-bats. By early July the Redlegs were in first place by four games. That's when the bad news struck: On Saturday night July 8, Iglesias broke two bones in his hand when he was hit by a pitch. Five days later—at the same time it was announced that Pérez would be out of the lineup for at least four days due to a bad bone bruise of his hand after also being hit by a pitch—the *Geneva Times* beat writer Norm Jollow shared what had to be a heartbreaker for Pérez, now being called "Tony" in the paper: "Bobby Iglesias, the hard-hitting 1B-outfielder seems to have decided to return home to Cuba."

It would have been no consolation for Tony that the cheers from the Latino fans at Shuron Park would now be all for him and the Venezuelan Tovar.

"We had lots of migrant workers and a good-sized Puerto Rican population here in town back then, and quite a few of them came out to the ballpark," explains Agonito, pointing to the upper rows of the grandstand where the Puerto Ricans sat as a group. "They cheered really loud—in Spanish, of course—for the

Hispanic players. They were glad to have Pérez back in '61, that's for sure. He gave them lots to cheer about."

In particular, one two-week stretch stood out. It began only the day after Iglesias returned home to Havana.

After Pérez suffered the bruised hand, he sat out the next night's game at Erie, Pennsylvania, then told skipper Kuehl that he wanted to play Friday's game, which he did. On Saturday night, with Geneva ahead 2–1 in the top of the ninth, Geneva catcher Greg Nash led off with a triple. Then Pérez—he of the sore hand that was supposed to keep him out of the lineup for another two days—stepped to the plate. The count went to 3–2...*Ka-boom!* Pérez's seventeenth homer of the season was a signature two-run, opposite-field shot, with that distinctive *crack* of the bat and surprising power to right-center that had first caught scout Pacheco's eye two years earlier in Camagüey. "Tony's hitting those blue darters," said the late skipper Karl Kuehl, admiringly. "And when he's hitting, you don't need that much more help."

Four nights later came a Pérez grand slam, his eighteenth home run. It keyed a Geneva split of a doubleheader with Jamestown (New York), the birth-place of comedienne and TV star Lucille Ball, whose teaming with Cuban-born husband and actor/musician Desi Arnaz was the only exposure many average Americans in the 1950s had to Cuba. (Well, that and the consumption of lots of Cuban sugar.)

The next night, a Thursday, Pérez and Tovar (he stole eighty-eight bases in a hundred tries that season), were up to their own antics. They dressed as "men in blue," umpiring an old-timers' game at Shuron Park that featured former big-league pitching stars Lefty Gomez and Johnny Gee. Pérez was obviously feeling a lot more at home. He and Tovar "took great delight in calling third strikes on bad pitches to Art Denard and Lou Ventura, two standby umpires in the NYP League," observed beat writer Jollow. "Pérez also called out league president Vince McNamara on an inside pitch..."

Fielding, though, for the occasionally ham-handed third baseman, was still an adventure. Six weeks after going on his hitting tear, Pérez was charged with an error even though it was an especially hard-hit ball. Tani's reputation had preceded him, and perhaps some assumptions were being made that weren't totally fair. The Geneva pitcher had a no-hitter going that he eventually secured, but this was one of those nights when not even the opposition thought Pérez deserved the "E," and the opposition let the entire ballpark know it.

The Geneva that the Latinos experienced in 1960 and 1961 is a lot different from the Geneva that Hispanics, or really, anybody, experiences these days. The first time I dropped into McDonough Park in the summer of 2015 for an early look-see of what would become the familiar ground for this book, I talked with Joe Marone, a young man who owns his own restaurant in downtown Geneva, "Joe's Hots." That night at the ballpark, he was making and selling tacos of pork, shredded pork and beef, with various toppings including honey, diced celery, and blue cheese crumbles. (He also made custom burritos at his restaurant.)

"I bet Tony and his teammates would have loved some of these back in the day," says Marone, who didn't know how right he was. I share a story about Pérez eating chicken every day for a week in Geneva, once he learned the English word for *pollo*. Replies Marone: "I'm guessing the ballplayers ate a whole lot of basic hot dogs at the ballpark after road games, because that's all they had. Hot dogs couldn't have sat too well with those Cuban guys. Do they even *have* hot dogs in Cuba?"

Only at the restaurants catering to Americans, I tell Marone, who laughs when I add, "and no self-respecting gringo in Cuba even *wants* a hot dog unless he's off his rocker."

Yes, life in ways great and small has changed in Geneva in the past six decades.

I go looking for the family home where Pete Rose had lived while playing ball in Geneva in 1960. Turns out the house came down when the Wegmans Supermarket went up on Hamilton Street in 1991. The movie house the Cuban players were so fond of, "The Smith," aka "The Geneva Theatre," is barely recognizable, having been beautifully restored and reverting to its original nineteenth century name—the Smith Opera House.

The tip of Seneca Lake where the players went swimming is now a state park. There's a skateboard course just outside McDonough Park now, and a soccer field beyond the left-field fence.

John Oughterson, the inimitable "John O," longtime fan, booster, and Geneva baseball executive, remembers rifle-armed Stanford University quarterback John Elway "pulling them in here" in 1982 with the Oneonta Yankees when he hit .318 for his 45 games. "John O" remembers big crowds for Geneva Redlegs and Geneva Cubs games. I know from reading game stories in the *Geneva Times* from 1960 and 1961 that often crowds of over a thousand gathered to watch Rose and Pérez leg out doubles and triples and find creative ways to boot groundballs. The night I stopped in to take in a Geneva Red Wings vs. Utica Blue Sox collegiate-level game in the summer of 2016, I counted eighty-six fans.

The Shuron Optical manufacturing plant next door to the ballpark is long gone, the space occupied by a senior citizen facility. Up the road, a $400 million gambling casino is going up.

"We had a lot more industry here in the 1960s than we do now, and more (non-grape-growing) agriculture than we do today, that's for sure," says Agonito, now a musician and writer of music and entertainment news for the *Finger Lakes Times*. He notes that back in 1960 and 1961, there weren't any wineries dotting the shores of Seneca Lake; today there are almost a hundred. "Tourism is big business now."

Tourists aren't always baseball fans, but plenty of longtime residents familiar with the names "Pérez" and "Rose" know that Rose was named the most popular player in Geneva in 1960 and received two Samsonite suitcases from the fans as a parting gift ("even though he wasn't very popular with the team," pitcher Dan Paul remembers), and that Tovar won the same award in 1961, and that Pérez and Tovar finished first and second in the NY-Penn batting race that same year (.348 to .338, respectively), and that the Geneva Redlegs won the pennant that year.

The best of Geneva's two-year flirtation with future big-time and all-time players was basically over, although nobody knew it at the time, of course.

Geneva residents old enough to remember it know as true what 1960 Geneva Redleg Art Shamsky told me in Cooperstown in 2016: "Two Hall of Famers and me—a future eight-year major leaguer—were so bad in 1960 that the owners had to fire the manager late in the season."

Yes, Tani was a starter with the team that ran one manager off the rails, and a star with the next team that catapulted the new skipper to a big-league managerial and coaching career. Karl Kuehl, who had been a modestly successful seven-year Reds minor leaguer, found his traction with the Pérez-Tovar team and by 1976 was the manager of the big-league Montreal Expos, when Pérez won his second of two world championship rings.

Kuehl would never forget how monstrous Pérez's 1961 season was: .348, twenty-seven home runs, and 132 RBIs. *El Monstruo,* "The Monster," is what the Cubans call somebody who puts together a season like that.

"I started to think of myself as a prospect that year because I won (the league) MVP," Pérez said in 2015. "Before that, I didn't know what I was."

Meanwhile, in early May of 1960, a new team arrived in Geneva to get ready for a new season. Six of those players were from a mysterious island country ninety miles from Florida with a bearded president in green military fatigues, and one of those rookies went on to make the National Baseball Hall of Fame.

"We're part of that history, too," says Agonito, proudly. "And now, with things opening up in Cuba after all these years, and us still around to see it, well, that's pretty amazing, too." ◆

This is the team—the 1962 Macon Peaches (Pete Rose, seated third from left; at his left hand is closest friend, Tommy Helms)—that set the standard and created the excitement that bled into 1963 when Tony Perez arrived. Helms out-hit Rose .340 to .330, but Rose already was displaying the eye (60 more walks), power (eight more home runs) and unparalleled aggressiveness on the bases (10 more triples) that earned him the Reds starting second baseman's job in 1963. Upper right corner, Dave Bristol, who managed both the 1962 and 1963 Peaches.

CHAPTER 9
These Arms of Mine

Macon, Georgia—In the three autumns ending each baseball season from 1960 through 1962, Tani Pérez returned home to Central Violeta, Cuba, and then, the following spring, flew to Tampa, Florida, for spring training. He eventually made his way with his team to wherever he was assigned that season: Geneva, New York…Rocky Mount, North Carolina…and, in 1963, Macon, Georgia.

From the very start—from in-season to offseason—the news of rising tensions between the United States and Cuba had been daily and non-ending. No sooner had Tani left Cuba for his first spring training than President Dwight D. Eisenhower announced an embargo on sugar, oil, and guns; Cuba nationalized all U.S. companies and properties; President Eisenhower canceled the seven hundred thousand tons remaining in Cuba's sugar quota for 1960; a mere two days later, the Soviet Union announced it would buy up those seven hundred thousand tons. Practically overnight, the shipping stamps that José Manuel Pérez had been placing on the bags at the Central Violeta sugar mill changed from "U.S." to "U.S.S.R." The Soviets immediately absorbed the shortfall.

During that first offseason—February of 1961—the Supreme Commander, Fidel Castro, held his unannounced meeting with a group of Cuban major and some minor leaguers and told them they soon would be no longer free to come and go from Cuba. They had to make a choice: the States (where the Comandante knew the money was), or Cuba, for home, hearth, and the motherland.

Tani knew his days were numbered. But he figured, correctly as it turned out, that he wouldn't be forced to make a choice until later. He was a long way from the majors. It was the high-profilers Fidel didn't want coming and going. In February of 1961, Tani was far from a quick-rise; he was the lowest of the low. He would take it as it came—the way he took everything—and he had every reason to believe he could operate under the radar for another couple of seasons.

Still, tensions continued to rise...Cuba nationalized all U.S. banks...sixteen days after he was inaugurated as thirty-fifth President of the United States, John F. Kennedy banned all trade with Cuba excepting foods and medicine...CIA-backed counter-revolutionaries invaded Cuba and were crushed at the Bay of Pigs...

Tani was home when, on December 2, 1961, Castro proclaimed to the world: "I am a Marxist-Leninist." And he was in Rocky Mount, North Carolina, when Castro announced the formalization of Cuba's relationship with the Soviet Union.

So much was happening covertly that there was no way any average American citizen—let alone a non-English speaking Cuban visitor—could know what was going on: Castro told visiting Soviet officials that, yes, he would accept deployment of nuclear weapons. The Soviet military buildup in Cuba began in the second half of July, 1962. American surveillance and intelligence reported suspicious movements of Soviet ships laden with arms bound for Cuba. Through August, the buildup continued. From what the *New York Times* could piece together after the fact, thirty ships carrying two thousand Soviet technicians and instructors "and such war matériel as surface-to-air missiles, patrol boats with missiles, and MIG-21 fighters" unloaded in Cuban ports.

The first high-altitude U.S. surveillance from a U-2 flight confirmed that there were eight different surface-to-air missile sites in Cuba. There was no way Tani or his family could have known in August of 1962 the risks of his returning home that offseason. They couldn't have even known it on Labor Day, 1962, the traditional season-ending weekend for minor-league baseball, which is when President Kennedy finally publicly acknowledged the presence of surface-to-air missiles in Cuba, saying there was "no evidence of any offensive ground-to-ground missiles. . .Were it otherwise, the gravest issues would arise."

Six weeks later, by which time Tani was back in Central Violeta, all hell broke loose. On Tuesday night, October 22, 1962, Kennedy went on national TV to announce the "unmistakable evidence" of long-range nuclear missiles in

Cuba and that he was instituting a "strict quarantine of all offensive military equipment" (a naval blockade, in other words). He said that if the missiles were launched in Cuba, the United States would automatically launch its nuclear arsenal. This sent Cuba into lockdown, and put Tani and his family on notice: This time, it wasn't going to be so easy getting out. Castro believed that an American invasion was imminent.

History has only recently revealed—in 2012, the fiftieth anniversary of the Cuban Missile Crisis—that not even the U.S. brass in 1962 knew the full capability of the missiles in Cuba. There were ninety-six nuclear warheads with the ability to reach New York City at sixty times the destructive force of the Hiroshima A-bomb. Not knowing the capability meant that many of the top brass in October 1962 could (and did) urge an invasion. Even President Kennedy didn't know if American air strikes would be sufficient to take out the missiles if force were needed. Had the United States invaded Cuba, everybody agreed: The nuclear arsenal in Cuba would have been unleashed, and then, in an eye-blink, Washington would have responded with its arsenal—mutually assured destruction.

On October 14, 1962, only the American top brass knew that one of its U-2 spy planes, flying over western Cuba from south to north, had provided the first hard evidence of medium range ballistic missile sites—offensive weapons—in Cuba. That was the date that began the *Thirteen Days* of Robert Kennedy's book about the missile crisis. Parts of those thirteen days played out so publicly that even in Cuba, where the press was state-owned and -operated, the citizens were aware of the standoff, given the orations of the Maximum Leader on radio and television. On October 27, the Soviets shot down an American U-2 spy plane over Cuba, killing its pilot, Air Force Major Rudolf Anderson. Castro cabled Soviet premier Nikita Khrushchev and told him that the Cubans expected Khrushchev to launch the Soviet nukes as soon as it was obvious that an American invasion was underway; Castro told Khrushchev that he and the Cuban people were prepared to die fighting.

Eventually, Khrushchev blinked and made a back-channel deal with President Kennedy to dismantle the missiles in exchange for the removal of

U.S. missiles from Turkey (even though Kennedy made it clear to Khrushchev and everybody else that this was not a quid pro quo). Castro and his top man, Che Guevara, were livid. Castro learned of Khrushchev's double-cross the day after the fatal U-2 shootdown. Wrote Jon Lee Anderson thirty-five years later in the book, *Che Guevara: A Revolutionary Life*, "Fidel was incredulous and furious, and reportedly smashed a mirror with his fist when he was told. When (Che) heard the news, he tersely ordered his troops to sever his command post's communications line with the adjacent Soviet missile base, and rushed off to Havana to see Fidel."

What news Tani and his family could glean in Central Violeta was, of course, limited. Tani had to hang out in his sugar mill town a full two months longer than he had in the spring of 1960, 1961, and 1962, while bureaucrats in Havana sat on his visa paperwork. He was anxious to get back to playing ball, but he knew from talking with his dad that he should make the most of his time home; he might not get back for a while. This high anxiety was felt not only by the players trying to get out, but also by the major-league organizations waiting to receive them.

Not until late May, 1963—almost a full seven months after the de-escalation of the missile crisis—did Tani's paperwork come through authorizing him to leave Cuba. (There was a news item in the Geneva paper around that time referring to Pérez having to fly into Canada and then make his way to the States, but it's difficult to tell whether it was a reference to 1962 or 1963. It could have been either, or both. Plenty of Cuban pros stayed in the States after the 1961 season, fearing they wouldn't be allowed to leave if they went back home.)

Tani was cutting it close, but he wasn't the only one pushing it. So was his Macon teammate, the "short and stocky" (5-foot-9, 160 pounds) right-handed relief pitcher Andres Ayon.

By the time Tani got out, he had missed all of spring training and the first five weeks of the Macon season, arriving at the ballpark just in time to hear the fans' transistor radios blasting WIBB-AM disc jockey Hamp "King Bee" Swain's introduction of "These Arms of Mine," the first big hit of Macon's own, Otis Redding. Otis, like Tani, was twenty-one years old that summer.

"Slugging third baseman Tony Pérez has finally gotten out of Cuba and is expected in Macon today," announced the *Macon Telegraph* on May 28, 1963. "Pérez is not in (game) condition and isn't expected to be ready to play for some time.

"He was preceded to the city by pitcher Ayon, who got out of Cuba a few days earlier," wrote Harley Bowers, the *Telegraph* sports editor and Peaches' beat writer, who then quoted some of Pérez's numbers the past two seasons (27 HR in 1961 at Geneva, and 18 in two-thirds of a season at Rocky Mount). "Best of all, Pérez is a right-handed batter which would give the Peaches a much better balance since most of the Macon power is from the left side."

Tani had already missed five weeks' worth of games, and now he was going to miss another month's worth getting ready. Macon skipper Dave Bristol didn't want to have to take his slugger out of the lineup once he put him in. It was only a four-and-one-half-month-long season. Tani was going to miss half the games.

Where would that leave him?

Peaches' fans couldn't wait to get a look at Pérez, given his power—but Bristol knew he had to be patient. ("Pérez has been on the Geneva roster for the past two springs and has been coveted by Bristol on the basis of what he saw of him in spring training in 1961," wrote Bowers.)

For twenty-eight days, Tani took batting practice, smacking *pelota* after *pelota* all around Luther Williams Field. The baseballs were whitewashed, rubbed down scrupulously with PET evaporated milk and a towel by the early-arriving Bristol and Macon Peaches groundskeeper Willie "Smokey" Glover. ("That stuff smelled so bad they had to sit outside the clubhouse and do it," recalls former batboy Cam Bonifay, later the Pittsburgh Pirates general manager and longtime scout.) Finally, on June 28, Bristol declared Tani ready, and placed him on the active list.

The primary beneficiary of the big Cuban's long absence was Tom Dotterer, the last of a storied Central New York baseball family, i.e., the son of the esteemed major league scout Henry "Dutch" Dotterer, a thirty-six-year veteran, thirteen of them with the Cincinnati Reds, 1949–1961. Tom was a much better fielding third baseman than Pérez, having ten fewer errors in only twelve fewer games, and turning six more double plays. ("But, man, could Tony ever hit that ball," Tom remembers.) Tom's brother, Dutch Jr., had been a backup catcher for the Reds from 1957 through 1960 and played two years for the Triple-A Havana Sugar Kings. Dutch Jr. spoke several languages, including various dialects of Spanish, all fluently. Dutch Jr. had told Tom about all the great Cuban players. In Macon, Tom Dotterer was replaced by one of them, then he went on to become, at Christian Brothers Academy in Syracuse, one of the country's great high school coaches.

Bristol remembers the first time Tani reached base as a Peach after getting out of Cuba. It included, among other things, a happy gallop through Bristol's hands-up "stop sign" in the third-base coach's box.

"Tony had reached on a single or walk," Bristol recalls. "The next guy up hits a deep fly ball to right-center, but I could see it was going to be caught. Tony just kept on running, like a horse kicking up his heels. He was so happy to have gotten out of there (Cuba)—so happy to be playing ball again—that he couldn't contain himself. He kept right on running all the way home, and, of course, they doubled him up at first base. I brought it up to Tony (many years later), and he said, 'No, no, it was a gapper, the guy made a great play.' I told him, 'No way. Everybody in the ballpark knew that ball was going to be caught!'"

Undoubtedly such a sequence happened, but not that first night. The box score shows an 0-for-3 debut for Tani, batting sixth in the lineup in a 3–0 defeat; the Peaches could muster only three singles and a walk. Tani went 0-for-10 in the next two-and-one-half games before finding some success: On July 2, his fourth game back, he won it with an RBI single in the ninth inning to beat the Knoxville Smokies 4–3. Two days later—on the Fourth of July—he hit his first home run as a Peach to help beat Knoxville by one run. The Smokies outfielders—Willie

Horton, Jim Northrup, and Mickey Stanley, all future major league stars—had to be wondering, "Who is this guy?"

Macon was a rough tough town for persons of color. On one hand, it was producing great black entertainers. Richard Wayne Penniman, aka "Little Richard," was born in Macon and made frequent appearances in all the Macon clubs and the Douglass Theater, and was an inspiration to the great Redding. But none of that, recalls longtime Macon resident Leon Simmons, could mask what a difficult town Macon could be for any minority, be they African-American or a dark-skinned Latino, like Pérez.

"It would have been tough for him, very tough," says Simmons, born and raised in Macon, and only two years younger than Pérez. "He wouldn't have been allowed to live at the YMCA, unlike his white teammates and manager. He would have had to live at either the Brooks Motel or with a black family in town, and that of course would have been in the black section. And he couldn't have taken his meals in the restaurants with his white teammates when they all went out together on the road. They would've had to bring him his food in the car, and that's where he would have eaten it."

The only dark-skinned players on the Macon Peaches were Pérez, short-stop Francisco Obregon, and second baseman Gus Gil, both Venezuelans. And Simmons was right: None of the three could live at the YMCA where Pete Rose, Tommy Helms, Art Shamsky, and manager Bristol had hung their hats as Macon Peaches in 1962 and where most of the single white Peaches also lived in 1963. Dan Neville, a Covington, Kentucky, native and 1963 Peach, confirmed that Pérez, Obregon, and Gil had to eat their road meals in the car.

"I felt terrible for them, because that's the way it was throughout the South, including the southern cities where the Reds had farm teams that I played with—in Macon, and Tampa and Palatka, Florida, and Rocky Mount, North Carolina, and Columbia, South Carolina," Neville remembers. "We all rode together in three large white station wagons, red interior, three rows of bench seats in each

Macon packed them in in 1962 (Pete Rose, Tommy Helms), 1963 (Tony Pérez) and 1964 (Lee May). But Macon was a rough town for persons of color. It is not visible here, but a rope ran up the middle of the grandstand at Luther Williams Field, home of the Macon Peaches—whites on one side, blacks on the other. The white power structure applied segregation everywhere in public places in the south. The clubhouses—the teams' private enclaves—were not segregated. Those and the field were Pérez's sanctuary.

car, the last bench-seat facing backward. The last two benches could lay down flat, which we'd do when guys wanted to get some sleep. One of the wagons pulled a U-Haul with our equipment in it. Sometimes one of the wagons would be in the shop, and we'd have to ride three players to a bench. All the Reds farm teams, with the exception of Triple-A San Diego, had those two or three white or red station wagons. And the players, black and white, rode side-by-side, and we all got along. But it's true, the black guys couldn't go in restaurants with us and they couldn't stay in our hotels. It was terrible."

Luther Williams Field is the second-oldest (1929) minor league ballpark in America. The only older one is in Birmingham, Alabama, where the famed Birmingham Barons of the Negro Leagues played. The demographics of baseball have passed Macon by—the last organized team played here in 2002 and it was an Atlanta Braves affiliate; the last pro team here was the Macon Music, an independent team. Only occasionally does even a high school game grace Luther Williams Field anymore. But Luther Williams Field is still attractive to filmmakers. In 2012, the Jackie Robinson movie, *42*, and Clint Eastwood's *Trouble with the Curve*, were shot there. Three decades before that, Luther Williams had been the setting for *The Bingo Long Traveling All-Stars and Motor Kings*.

In late August, 2016, I stood in the third-base coach's box at Luther Williams Field, looking out at the diamond and the right-field warning track beyond and tried to imagine a certain baseball game here from fifty-three years ago. Very few twenty-one-year-olds who weren't in the armed forces experienced anything like Tani Pérez and his fellow Cuban ballplayers did. They had one foot in a Communist country and the other in a "free" country. Suffice it to say, for an apolitical black Cuban in the Deep South who knew only a few words of English, Tani Pérez had almost no idea of what was going on.

He shared his story with *Sports Illustrated* in June 1986, in his final major league season. "Things were different in the South then," Pérez recalled. "The black players and I could not stay with the rest of the team. We were put in a hotel in the black section of town. I had never had that problem in Cuba or New York. We also couldn't eat with the white players, and sometimes we would wait in the (cars) outside a restaurant until the white players finished their meals and brought us hamburgers. After Rocky Mount, I played in Macon, Georgia, and everywhere I found the same situation until, in 1964, they outlawed segregation. It was hard for me to understand why people of different colors couldn't live and eat together, but it was explained to me that it had been that way for a long time, and that this was part of the history of the (United States). I was sent to San Diego in the Pacific Coast League in (1964), and I never had discrimination problems again."

As a player, the better the year you were having, the better the sanctuary of the ballpark. Everybody on the Macon Peaches knew that Tani Pérez loved the ballpark—it's where he felt most at home. The routine at Luther Williams Field was all baseball all the time—7:30 a.m. to midnight "shifts," certainly for groundskeeper Willie "Smokey" Glover, who not only maintained the field but laundered the wool uniforms daily, hanging them on the chain-link fence outside the clubhouse to dry by the sun. At mid-day, ol' Smoke would take a break. He'd walk with his occasional helpers, Nape and Johnny, to lunch at the nearby little soul food joint, Maybell's. He'd then take a short snooze on a couch in his "office" under the stands before resuming work on the field at two o'clock every day, because batting practice was at five. Glover, an African-American,

Tony took his lumps in the minors (and even, as shown here, in his early years in the majors). Former teammates on every level recall "patience and persistence" as being among his greatest traits.

always had to make sure the rope was up in the grandstand separating the blacks (third-base side) from the whites (first-base side). The blacks had separate bathrooms. It was true in 1949 when Jackie Robinson broke the color line at Luther Williams Field—he was the first black to play among whites there—and it was true when Tani Pérez played there in 1963.

"There were a lot of days where if (manager) Bristol wasn't happy, he'd hold workouts for players after the games—you know, to get it right," Cam Bonifay remembers. "We wouldn't leave 'til midnight. My dad and I would lock up. Smokey still'd be in there, working. He had his own way out."

On July 6, 1963, with a pair of 1-for-3s in the first and second game of a doubleheader, Pérez began a month-long hitting barrage that didn't end until he had hit safely in twenty-eight straight games. On August 10 at front-running Lynchburg, Virginia, he doubled home shortstop Obregon in the tenth inning to give the Peaches a 5–4 lead, and after Lynchburg tied it up again in the bottom of the inning, Pérez led off the 13th inning. He ran the count to 3–2, before blasting a long home run to put the Peaches up to stay and move them to within a half-game of first place.

Northern Kentucky native Neville, who pitched ten innings that night and was 13–9 with a 2.70 ERA that season, rode to the games with sixteen of his Peaches teammates, including Pérez. Manageable for sure, if you were in your early or mid-20s, as were most of the Peaches. But the very sight of this sardine treatment of her beloved Peaches caused one female fan, considerably older than those she adored, to take it hard. Wrote the *Telegraph*'s Bowers: "There is a lady in town who sheds honest tears every time the Peaches take off on a road trip. 'I just feel sorry,' she says, 'for anybody that has to ride as far as those fellows do jammed up in a station wagon. It's just inhuman.'"

"Oh, it wasn't so bad," Neville tells me. "You can do anything when you're twenty-one or twenty-two."

The week of Tani's 13th-inning home run landed him in *The Sporting News'* Sally League leaders for the first time that season. Despite missing sixty-five games, his fevered stretch of twenty-eight games had elevated him to .294 with eight home runs and thirty-three RBIs, and had earned him the sixteenth-best batting average in the league, sandwiched between his Venezuelan teammates Teolindo Acosta at .299 and Gil at .289, with three weeks to go.

"Good group of hitters," Bristol recalls fifty-three years later, "but Tony was the guy who did the most damage—he was the one with the power."

Even when Pérez's twenty-eight-game hitting streak ended, it didn't end quietly: He backed up left fielder Jim Hicks to the wall in the third inning and "rammed a savage one-hopper to short in the sixth inning," before striking out to end the streak in the eighth.

At season's end, the "short and stocky" (not to mention small-handed and generous) Cuban relief pitcher Andres Ayon gave his Rawlings "Trap-eze" model pitching glove to the ten-year-old batboy Bonifay, who the very next spring introduced it into Little League play in Macon.

And "Tony Pérez" was back in *The Sporting News,* making first-team All-Sally League at third base, even though he had played only half a season.

There'd be no going home to talk about it.

Not this time. ◆

1964 Triple-A San Diego Padres' Murderers' Row. Tony, far left; fellow power hitter, Art Shamsky (with bat, far right). Manager Dave Bristol, upper right.

CHAPTER 10
The Other Minnie

As hard as it had been to get out of Cuba in the spring of 1963, Tani Pérez agreed with his father that he should not return that winter. Of course, it would mean staying away from home for the first time in the three years of his yet-to-blossom big league career, but Tani understood. He always understood that his father knew best.

"I already knew I wasn't going home to Cuba that winter," Pérez explained to me many years ago. "I stayed (elsewhere) that year and every offseason after that. My father made the decision. He told me: *Si la pelota va a ser su vida, usted debe hacer esto*—'If baseball is going to be your life, you should do this.'" It was a life-altering decision, but, looking back, the right one.

That fall, Tani participated in the Florida Instructional League in Tampa and met his friend for life, Lee May. "I guess I helped Tony some with his English; I never thought much about that," the late May recalled during a long interview in 2003. "I was just trying to learn enough Spanish to communicate with him, and he was trying to learn enough English to communicate with me. We didn't have a problem.

"I remember well that he fell in love with barbecued chicken that fall. On weekends, I'd have to go find a place that sold barbecued chicken. It reminded him of *pollo asado*—roasted chicken—and he couldn't get enough of it."

May told me something else then, and it gave me pause: "Tony could've gone back to Cuba after the 1963 season, but he wouldn't have been able to get back out. That would have been it."

That would have been a helluva decision, wouldn't it? To go home for good, as teammate Martín Dihigo Jr. had done after the 1962 season in Macon? From what I could tell when I visited Dihigo Jr., he appeared mostly at peace with his decision to go home, even though it meant a loss of freedom and opportunity. He appeared filled up by the warm memories of having chosen to be with his family.

The big difference was this: Martín Dihigo Sr. wasn't telling his son to stay in the States. José Manuel Pérez was. But what if José Manuel had told Tani to come home because the Pérez family's roots were too intertwined in Cuba for any of the family members to ever even consider joining their loved one across the Straits of Florida, that his mother needed him in Cuba, that *la familia* needed him in Cuba, what then? Tani would have gone home. Tani always listened to his father.

Cristóbal Rigoberto Mendoza Carreras—another "Minnie" from Cuba, but far less famous—had notched ten minor-league seasons as a slick-fielding third baseman, but he was more valuable as Latin-ballplayer-*whisperer* than as a ballplayer. By the time Tani Pérez came along with the Macon Peaches in late May 1963—in the same South Atlantic League as Mendoza's Charlotte Hornets—"Minnie" had settled into the role of "organization man" for the Minnesota Twins. (The Twins had been the Washington Senators until 1961.)

"Minnie" was from a little town thirty miles southwest of Havana called Ceiba del Agua. Minnie mentored Pérez in that 1963–1964 offseason when Tani's dad told him not to come home. The Cincinnati Reds had signed Mendoza in 1954, the year before the Havana Sugar Kings became its Triple-A affiliate. After a couple of seasons in the low minors, including two short stints in the Mexican League, "Minnie" had *una taza de café* —a cup of coffee—with the Sugar Kings (four games, twelve at-bats, one hit). He was just never quite good enough with the bat to impress. But in 1956, the Washington Senators traded for him, anyway, believing he could help. They immediately moved him to Missoula, Montana, for two seasons; then came two seasons at Charlotte on his way up to Triple-A Vancouver in 1962. The Senators-turned-Minnesota Twins were hoping against hope that the twenty-six-year-old Mendoza might be a late-bloomer.

By 1963, Minnie was back in Charlotte where the Twins—and, apparently, the Reds' Tani Pérez—needed him. Minnie was a vivacious, hail-fellow-well-met-type with good command of every Cuban ballplayer's hoped-for second language: English. They talked mostly in Spanish, of course, but some of Mendoza's English rubbed off on the young Central Violetan.

Minnie had his own personal, compelling life story, as did every promising Cuban player of that era. Their stories always had "1961" or "1962" in them, usually both. Those were pivotal years for every Cuban player. For Minnie, "1963," "1964" and "1965" were also pivotal years. (Author Thom Henninger tells Minnie's story well in *Tony Oliva: The Life and Times of a Minnesota Twins Legend*.)

Mendoza was playing in Charlotte when news of the Bay of Pigs debacle hit the air in mid-April 1961. His wife, Julia, was in Havana, pregnant with their second child. The Cuban government wouldn't let Mendoza's wife and two children leave the country until Mendoza returned to Cuba to sign their passport papers. Minnie was finally able do that in the 1962–1963 offseason, but when he returned to Charlotte in May 1963, circumstances required that it be by himself. In 1964, the Mendozas reunited in Nicaragua, where Mendoza was playing winter ball. Not until 1965 were they able to settle together in the United States.

Consider: When Tani was wintering with Mendoza in Charlotte during the offseason of 1963–1964, he was living with a father of two young children who was separated from them and their mother by geography and a dictator's edicts. To Mendoza's credit, he didn't let his personal difficulties dampen the enthusiasm he poured into his cooking. He was an excellent cook—especially of Cuban food, and took great pride in it.

Macon Peaches skipper Dave Bristol had given Tani specific instructions to "put on some weight" during that offseason. Bristol knew that Tani would be living with Mendoza. That pairing would ensure that Tani would be eating well. Somebody inside the Reds, not Bristol, had arranged for Tani to receive a stipend of $300 a month to winter with Mendoza, who they knew would be a good influence. Mendoza knew what he needed to do; he took in his countryman Pérez and added him to his growing stable of Cuban protégés.

"Great guy," remembers Reds Hall of Famer Tommy Helms. "I knew Mendoza because I was from Charlotte and that's where I spent my winters. I'd check up on Tony a little bit, you know, go over to Mendoza's to see him or go out somewhere. One night, Tony even stayed at my place. Mendoza was always taking care of the Latin players and would cook them just what they wanted. He was the perfect guy to put weight on Tony: Unlimited black beans, rice and those fried green bananas—plantains. No wonder Tony put on about thirty pounds that winter!"

When Bristol saw his protégé that following March in Tampa, his eyes bugged out of his head: "Tony, you need to lose some weight!" To which Tani, in greatly improved English, replied: "Dave, make up your mind!"

Bristol had special reason for counseling Pérez: They were moving up to the Triple-A San Diego Padres together.

Buoyed by his friendships with May and Mendoza—and strengthened by their *pollo asado* and black beans and rice—Tani blasted the ball all over Tampa in the spring of 1964. By the time he arrived in San Diego, he was ready. Judging from the photos taken of the Padres in that 1964 season, Bristol's spring-training advice of "lose-some-weight" had taken hold. Pérez was a far cry from the "Flaco" that Bristol had witnessed that first spring in Tampa in 1960, but he was also a hoot and a holler from the two-ton-Tani that greeted Bristol in Tampa in 1964. The Cuban filled out his uniform at a crisp one hundred and eighty pounds.

"You could just see his eyes light up and what lay ahead," Helms recalls. "Everything in San Diego was major league: The ballpark (Westgate Park) was new, as good as any of the parks in the major leagues; just didn't seat as many as them, ten to twelve thousand, I would say. The owner and general manager were great. We stayed at the Stardust Hotel, six bucks a night if you stayed two to a room, which we did; pool, fashion shows, golf course nearby, with driving range. Six bucks a day meal money...flew everywhere—in our division,

Tony Perez (left) and Lee May became close friends in the Florida Instructional League in October, 1963, when Tony couldn't return home to Cuba for the first time in three years. They helped teach the other their native tongue. May was a natural comedian, which helped lighten Perez's load as well.

CHAPTER 10

Tony, not long after he had won the International League's Most Valuable Player Award in 1964 as a Padre. He hit 34 HRs and had 107 RBIs. No less amazing were his eight triples, only one off the team lead of nine (Tommy Helms).

it was Seattle, Spokane, Tacoma, Portland and, oh yes, Hawaii." In the other division of the Pacific Coast League were Denver, Dallas, Salt Lake City, Oklahoma City, Indianapolis, and Little Rock.

"It's hard to imagine how good Tony was that season," Helms recalls. "The best way I can put it for Reds fans is, 'Do you remember 1970 when Tony had ninety RBIs for the Reds at the All-Star break?' Well, that's the way he was in San Diego. Man, he was getting the game-winning hit every other night! It was unbelievable. San Diego agreed with him—it agreed with all of us—and he was coming into his own. He was named the league's Most Valuable Player (thirty-four HR, 107 RBIs and eight—*count 'em, eight*—triples, only one fewer than Helms' team-leading nine), and we won the pennant."

Tani had always been, by his example, a leader. He was becoming a man.

"There's no bigger fan of Tony Pérez than me," related Bristol in the summer of 2016. "The players will tell you that I was big on small fines as a way of getting their attention and keeping them engaged in the game. But I can't ever remember having to fine Tony Pérez. His head was always in the game."

Yes, Tony's head was in the game, but he also saw the business side of baseball. The Reds had been trading away, one after another, his Spanish-speaking idols and friends from Cuba and Venezuela. Tony realized then that baseball was a lot more than a finishing school. It was cold, hard, and downright Darwinian. Tony González (outfielder) and Cookie Rojas (second baseman mostly) were the first to be traded—both as twenty-three-olds (mid-1960 for González; after the

1962 season for Rojas) after only brief major league looks. The same for Cuban Mike Cuellar (age twenty-five, before the 1963 season) and Venezuelan César Tovar (twenty-four, after the 1964 season, following five straight minor league seasons of absolutely crushing the ball). Three of Tovar's five seasons were with Pérez, including the last of them in San Diego.

Tani was supposed to play ball that winter in Venezuela, but had trouble securing a passport.

"Never mind," Reds assistant general manager Phil Seghi told him. "Go to Puerto Rico. (Cuban native) Preston Gomez is there. He will take care of you."

Pedro Gomez "Preston" Martinez—like Pérez, born and raised in a sugar mill town (Central Preston, from which he drew his name in professional baseball, in eastern Cuba's Oriente Province)—had been signed by famed Washington scout Joe Cambria. After Gomez's playing career ended, he began managing—most notably, in Cuba lore, as the skipper of the 1959 Havana Sugar Kings, the year they won the Little World Series over Gene Mauch's Minneapolis Millers. Tani's reunion with Gomez in Puerto Rico was almost like returning to his roots as a Sugar Kings junior player.

Seghi was absolutely right: Gomez would definitely take care of Tani.

And so would somebody else. ◆

The Day Love Came to Town—Tony and Pituka met in October 1964, married four months later, and honeymooned in Tampa at spring training in 1965. "It felt like my career really began when I met her," Tony said.

CHAPTER 11

Pituka

Tani Pérez, one-hundred and eighty pounds of tightly wound sinew and eager to show it off in the Puerto Rican League, quickly connected in San Juan with another displaced Cuban, José Martínez, a Pittsburgh Pirates' minor-leaguer who also had signed on to play winter ball on the island.

Martínez, like Pérez, was twenty-two. The difference was that Martínez was from Cárdenas, Cuba—*Calle Calzada, Cárdenas*—and was notably well-acquainted with the de la Cantera family of the same city, they of the three beautiful daughters—Pituka, Matty, and Mercedes—who had all by then relocated to San Juan.

Martínez was eager to call upon the de la Canteras so he could introduce his roommate to Pituka, twenty, the eldest of the sisters. But she was working that day when the young men arrived. Tani—by now having gotten two eyefuls of Pituka from her picture in Pablo de la Cantera's home—kept making excuses why he really didn't have anywhere to go. Pablo, who had been a building contractor in Cuba, was more than glad to have the young men hang around. He was a huge baseball fan. While Fidel Castro and Guevara were still in the Sierra Maestre Mountains in October 1957, Pablo was of sufficient means and time to travel to New York to watch Games One and Two of the World Series between Mickey Mantle's New York Yankees and Henry Aaron's Milwaukee Braves.

Yes, it had been a good life in Cuba in the 1950s for the de la Canteras. But in 1960, things began to change—*dramatically*—as Fidel Castro started to nationalize everything. And those who had a goodly share of that "everything" had no choice but to leave it behind. In Castro's world, that "everything" was no longer theirs; it was the State's. The bulk of this nationalization was of property owned by Americans, but not only the Americans lost their property.

Socialism was taking over. In 1961, the de la Canteras family fled to Puerto Rico. Pituka was seventeen. The de la Canteras were far from alone. According to the Heritage Foundation, a conservative think tank based in Washington, D.C., close to a quarter million Cubans were forced by circumstances to emigrate between January 1, 1959, and late October 1962 (the Cuban Missile Crisis). In early 1959, it was mostly members of the political and military elite, followed by members of the propertied and professional sectors (this would have included Pablo de la Cantera), then clerical and sales workers and skilled workers.

This same period also saw the arrival of some fourteen thousand unaccompanied Cuban children in the United States, most of them between the ages of six and sixteen, sent to America by parents fearful of Castro's control of their lives (*Operación Pedro Pan*). The thinking was that the families would soon be reunited. But when the Cuban Missile Crisis occurred in late October 1962, air travel between the two countries was officially halted—some, if not many, of the families could not be reunited. Even those that were reunited often had heart-wrenching stories of young children cut off from their parents for several years.

And therein resides the pathos of Pérez: He knew that as tough as it was for him to be separated from his mother, father, and sisters and brothers from May of 1963 forward, there were—and are—those who had it worse. For Tani, knowing that it was even worse for others made his own separation anxiety harder, not easier. Tani never was—and never will be—one who cares only about himself. From the very beginning, empathy and understanding are what made him a great teammate.

On that October 1964 day in San Juan—the day love came to town—Pablo de la Cantera had plenty of opportunity to ask Tani about his rapidly rising baseball career.

Earlier that season, Tani had gotten a six-week taste of the big leagues, a month of it in the dead of summer before Reds Triple-A manager Dave Bristol successfully lobbied Reds owner/general manager Bill DeWitt for Pérez's return to San Diego. ("Tony wasn't playing in Cincinnati, and we were trying to win a pennant in San Diego," Bristol explained a half-century later. With Pérez's help, San Diego won the West division—by a game—and beat the East's Arkansas in seven games for Pacific Coast League Championship.)

What about your major-league debut, Tani? What had that been like?

It had come on July 26, in a Sunday doubleheader at Crosley Field against two Pittsburgh Pirates lefthanders, Joe Gibbon and Bob Veale. Tani's minor-league team—the Triple-A San Diego Padres—had been in Denver the night before when Tani got the call. He had to catch a red-eye flight to Cincinnati.

Manager Fred Hutchinson greeted Tani warmly, but not with the bear-like shake of the hand that was Hutch's signature. (A career-long smoker, Hutch was suffering from lung cancer, and three-and-a-half months later would be dead.)

Tani went 0-for-2 in the first game, a 7–2 Reds victory over Pittsburgh. Most memorably, he had gotten to watch Puerto Rico's own Roberto Clemente and the impressive slugger Willie Stargell. Pablo de la Cantera knew all about "The Great One," Clemente. What baseball fan didn't? Here on the island—where Pérez and Martínez were playing for the Santurce Crabbers—Clemente was king, player-manager of the San Juan Senators.

Tani explained that in his debut he had gotten up-close-and-personal with the Pirates' second baseman Bill Mazeroski's flashing hands in the very first inning. After Pete Rose led off with a home run, Tommy Harper struck out, and Frank Robinson reached first base on an error and Deron Johnson singled, Tani walked on a 3–1 pitch from Joe Gibbon to load the bases. But Don Pavletich bounced one to shortstop Dick Schofield who flipped it to Maz who *whoosh-whoosh* got rid of it before he seemed to really ever have it—the fastest double-play Tani Pérez had ever seen—and *asi como asi*—just like that— the first inning was over.

In the fourth, Pérez flew out against Gibbon, and in the fifth struck out against reliever Don Schwall. Before the eighth inning began, Tani was replaced by Deron Johnson at first base; Marty Keough would bat for Tani, in the fifth spot. As the Reds nursed a 3–2 lead in the eighth inning, Reds starter Joey Jay— yes, that same Joey Jay who had pitched a little for the Braves in their World

Series season in 1957 and a lot in their World Series season of 1958—gave up singles to Clemente and Smoky Burgess and had to be relieved by Sammy Ellis.

The young Ellis got Maz to line out to end the inning. Deron Johnson led off the bottom of the eighth with a walk, and Keough followed with a single, and then young Don Pavletich smacked another single to load the bases. This is where Cuban-born shortstop Leo "Chico" Cárdenas—with none out and three men on—blasted a grand slam off Elroy Face to win it going away. Now that made Señor de la Cantera smile. How exciting of a debut that had been, despite Tani's 0-fer!

In the second game of the doubleheader, Tony went 0-for-4 against 6-foot-6 left-hander Bob Veale in a 5–1 loss, but he wasn't the only one who didn't hit. The Reds mustered only four singles.

After Tani's 0-for-6 in the doubleheader, he flew with the team to Milwaukee. That Monday night, he redeemed himself by going 2-for-4 against the Braves' seventeen-game winner that season, Denny LeMaster. Tani's first major-league hit was a rifle-double to left-center following a home by Deron Johnson in the Reds' two-run second inning, and his second hit was an RBI single scoring Frank Robinson in the Reds' five-run seventh.

Those were Tani's only two hits in twenty-five at-bats for the Reds during the 1964 season, but Tani was excited about the Reds' future. His teammates really could hit the ball—*oh mi,* that Frankie Robinson!—and the pitching was underrated. Tani had seen some fine examples of winning baseball down the stretch, including all six games of a six-game winning streak in mid-August that had started in the final game of the series at the Houston Colt .45s and included three straight victories at the San Francisco Giants and two straight at the Los Angeles Dodgers.

Tani glanced at his watch and at his *amigo,* José Martínez Azcuis. Tani loved talking baseball—and the de la Cantera family had put out some good snacks to eat—but…*is Juana "Pituka" Pérez ever going to get home?*

Seemingly oblivious, Señor de la Cantera was interested in hearing more. He wanted to hear about Tani's first big league manager, Fred Hutchinson.

Tell me about "Hutch," Tani.

Tani explained that he had been there to witness the end of an era in Cincinnati, the Hutch era. On August 12, 1964, at Crosley Field, the Reds held a pre-game forty-fifth birthday party for their beloved manager that left everybody in tears; they all knew—including Hutch himself—that he was gravely ill. Hutch was hospitalized two days later and never managed again. In the bottom of the fifth inning that day, Tani pinch-hit for pitcher Jim O'Toole. It gave Tani the heady experience of facing the Dodgers' Sandy Koufax, who whiffed him on a 2–2 pitch, and went on to win the game 4–1.

Tani took another look at his watch, glanced again at Martínez.

Pituka?

No Pituka.

So Tani talked some more, about his return to Cincinnati that September, and the collapse of the Phillies, who blew a six-and-a-half-game lead with twelve games to play.

What had that been like, to witness that?

Tani explained that he and fellow Padres Tommy Helms and pitcher Dan Neville had joined the Reds on September 22 in Philly, just in time to watch the Reds take the last two of three in a row at Shibe Park. The day before they arrived, Cubano Chico Ruiz had stolen home with Frank Robinson at the plate to win the game 1–0—what would later become known as the Phillies' Day One from Hell. It was the Reds' second victory in a nine-game winning streak that by September 27 had rocketed them into first place by a game. The Reds then lost four of their last five games to finish a game behind the Cardinals.

Yes, seeing seven of the nine games of that winning streak in the fire of a September pennant race, all but one game of it on the road, had been *asombroso*—amazing. Until losing four of the last five games of the season, all at home, the Reds were 28–12 including 18–7 on the road. The Reds were a very ho-hum 11–9 at home down the stretch. Tani wasn't sure what to make of the home attendance, though. Only 860,000, about ten thousand *fanaticos* per home game. *We did almost as good as that in Triple-A San Diego!* But yes, all in all, the pennant race had been a blast. Unfortunately, Hutch couldn't be there down the stretch. Dick Sisler had taken over the reins. The club was trying like hell to win for Hutch. Tani remembered the tears in the players' eyes when they couldn't quite do it.

Which is when love walked in the room.

This time, it didn't go quite so *así como así* (just like that) for Tani. The strapping Violetan respectfully stood up from his chair, and Pituka—a tall, brown-haired, brown-eyed beauty, full of confidence and strength—smiled. But, in this moment, she also felt herself dissolving.

Ay, Dios Mio! she said to herself. ("Oh my Lord!") She went weak in the knees at the sight of the quiet and smiling young man.

"He was looking straight into my eyes," recalled Pituka, telling me the story many years later. "I went into the kitchen and said to my cousin, *Ven aca. Te doy una peseta si averiguas si esta casado o es soltero.*—"Come here. I will give you a quarter if you find out if he is married or single."

"After two minutes, I was still in the kitchen when I felt a tapping on my shoulder. I turned around and it was Tani. He said, *¿Eres tú el que quien saber acerca de mi estado?*'—"Are you the one who wants to know about my status?"

Four months later they married.

The entire courtship was liberating for Pituka and Tani. They rediscovered their homeland in one another. And Puerto Rico felt so much like Cuba to Tani. Close in climate, culture, and chord. Tani couldn't go back to Cuba, and Pituka didn't have anything nearly as much to go back to—her mother, father, and two sisters were already together in Puerto Rico.

"Tani's family is so big and so close," Pituka told me. "How could they all leave? So many of them were married and had babies."

Pituka and Tony soon added babies of their own—Victor and Eduardo—and later, after forty-some years of marriage, two granddaughters, Andreanna and Juliana, Eduardo's children.

"We miss Cuba," Pituka told me many years later. "Your mother is your mother. Your country is your country. It is in your heart."

She also told me, "Tani's life was very different than mine." The de la Canteras sisters had grown up in an upper-middle class home. "Tani had to start working very hard, very young," she said. "But our families had the same heart, the same tradition of love and respect to the parents."

Tani, of course, told Pituka everything, especially in those early days together, when one learns so much about one's soulmate. Finally, Tani had somebody outside Cuba in whom he could confide. He had especially missed Cuba that first year away (the winter of 1963–1964), but finding Pituka that second winter reconfirmed for him that he had done the right thing.

Truth be told, Tani had always stretched the bounds going home to Cuba in the offseason, not so much after the 1960 season—that was a no-brainer—but definitely after the 1961 season, and especially after the 1962 season. The Reds brass, through Geneva (New York) Redlegs manager Karl Kuehl, had tried to convince Tani to stay in the States after the 1961 season in Geneva. The Reds brass had its connections from its Sugar Kings days, and the Reds had its Cuban players, past and present. Nothing would have slipped by them. February of 1961 had brought Castro's famously spoken orders to the gathered ballplayers in Havana: Stay or go, nothing in between. Those players would have quickly passed the word to their brethren.

Tani ignored the orders of the Supreme Comandante. Pituka, of course, knew about the Bay of Pigs invasion in April 1961. She didn't know, until Tani told her, that he had returned to Cuba after the 1961 season. She knew what a calculated risk that was. The de la Canteras had already fled Cardenas by that time. A year later—April 12, 1962—with Pérez still stuck in Cuba and the 1962 season about to begin in Rocky Mount, North Carolina, here was the headline and brief story in the April 12, 1962, *Geneva Times*:

> Where's Tony Pérez?
>
> In a continuing report, there is still no word on the whereabouts of Tony Pérez, who led the NY-P League in batting average and set a record for Geneva home-run hitters with 27.
>
> "They (the Reds brass) haven't been able to get hold of Tony," manager Kuehl reported. "They tried to place a call yesterday but the last I heard they hadn't been able to get the call through to Cuba."

Pérez, one of the best prospects to play for the Redlegs, is somewhere in Castroland, but where is still anyone's guess.

It was jokingly suggested that perhaps the four-man negotiating group seeing Castro about release of the ill-fated (Bay of Pigs) invasion survivors also include Pérez in a package deal.

Bruce Montgomery, a teammate of Pérez's in 1961 at Geneva and briefly at Rocky Mount in 1962, remembers how much Pérez missed home and distinctly recalls him as having trouble getting out of Cuba in 1962. The Reds brass had always let Monty attend Montclair State College (New Jersey) for the full spring and fall semesters, then report to his farm-team assignment in June.

"I paid attention to what was going on with Tony," Monty remembered, "because I was close to him and other Cubans, all the way back to the Geneva days. Don't ask me why; I just had an affinity for them, and they had the same affinity for me."

Being so aware of Tani and the other Latinos gave Monty empathy for the Cubans' separation from their homeland that he otherwise wouldn't have had. And when it came to the dark-skinned Latinos, well, Monty was affected in such a deeply negative way that one could hear the catch in his voice more than a half-century after the fact.

"To have to give up your family and your homeland, that is one thing," Monty says. "But what made that deprivation even worse in the South (for the dark-skinned Latinos) is that we'd drive to a city to play and stay the night and we'd have to leave the black guys in a different hotel, not as nice, in the black section of town. Meaning that now they were in a situation where not only were they deprived of 'home,' their new country was treating them like they weren't even human beings. I was taken aback by that. It rattled me.

"I cannot believe what we (as Americans) made those guys endure. The fact that no 'whites-only' hotel was going to let those guys in doesn't make it any easier to live with. I think about it to this day. At the same time Castro had taken their homeland away from them, we took away their humanity. When I see all that Tony has accomplished and overcome, I can only say to people, 'If you only knew...'"

Tani told Pituka that he eventually made it to Rocky Mount for the 1962 season, but that he was late. And yet, he went home to Cuba again *after* the 1962 season. The Cuban Missile Crisis erupted less

Frank Robinson (last in the line here at the far right of the "Meet the Reds" luncheon early in the 1965 season) was a role model and mentor for Tony that year. It was Robby's last year with Reds, Tony's first full year. "I learned a lot from him," Tony said. "I would have learned even more had he stayed."

than month after he was home. Tani told Pituka that he had to fly to the States through Mexico or Canada in order to join his team, because no flights from Cuba were granted access into the United States. (Even the *Geneva Times* had picked up on that creative and exceptional way of routing a Reds' Cuban minor leaguer to his destination in those incredibly tense days.)

Why had Tani gone home after the 1962 season? Undoubtedly, he wanted to see his family again. He would have understood that the days of seeing them again might very well be numbered. Maybe he felt he had some sort of special protection because he knew Martin Dihigo Jr., whose famous father ran the national sports ministry in Cuba. Maybe Tani felt he was under the radar, being a relatively obscure, mid-level minor leaguer. But, either way, clearly he was stretching it.

All that changed after he met Pituka. Tani would always love his family, of course, but Pituka's family helped fill a void. Tani had Pituka, and soon, God-willing, they would have a family of their own. It was a very special belonging that Tani felt in the arms of Pituka de la Cantera. ◆

CHAPTER 11

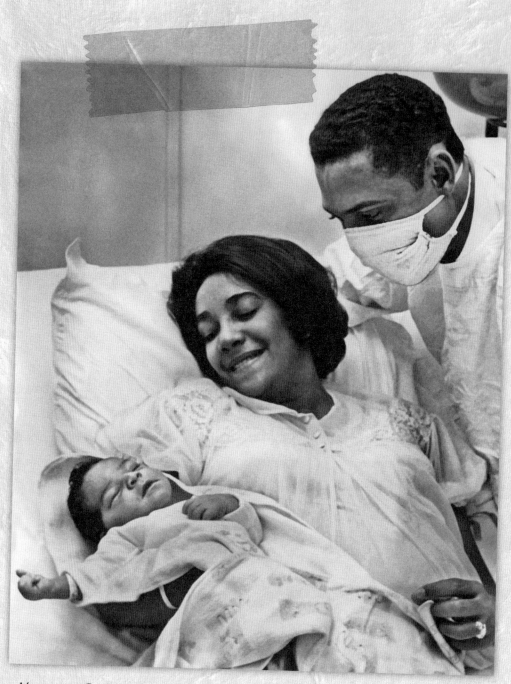

New mom Pituka cradles first-born Victor, two days old and ten-and-a-half pounds strong, at Good Samaritan Hospital, May 13, 1966, as proud papa Tony looks on.

TONY PÉREZ

CHAPTER 12
Out of the Shadows

When Tani arrived at the Grand Hotel in Anaheim, California, at eleven o'clock the evening of Monday, July 10, 1967—the night before the thirty-eighth Major League Baseball All-Star Game—he had every reason to expect a room. Anaheim was Tani's first All-Star Game, and rooms had been reserved for all of the players. Standing at the front desk, though, with his wife, Pituka, and fourteen-month-old son, Victor, Atanacio Rigal Pérez was told there was no room at the inn.

Remembering his treatment as a person of color in Tampa, Rocky Mount, and Macon—where he stayed with African-American families or in segregated hotels in the black section of town as he made his way through the minors—what he had just heard was absolutely unacceptable. He had to have a room, and he had to have it now. And so, at 11 o'clock the night before his first major league all-star game, Tani Pérez stood his ground. He knew it's what Pituka would have done.

By the All-Star Break of 1967, Pituka de la Cantera was not only Tani's wife of two-and-a-half years but also his friend and counselor. Pituka had the strong, stand-up-for-yourself conviction of so many eldest daughters, and imparted it to her Tani. For example, when Reds manager Dick Sisler had said to Tony at the end of spring training 1965 that he had made the club—as though Sisler was doing him a favor—it got back to Pituka who, as always, let her husband know what she thought of such disrespect.

"I wasn't going to take any guff," is the way Tony explained the scene at the hotel in Anaheim the next day (although he might have used a different word than "guff," the choice of *Long Beach Independent* executive sports editor Hank

125

Tony's son, Victor, is too young to go to bat on August 14, 1966, at Reds' Family Day, so watched over by Papa Tony, he sleeps through the festivities.

Top left: Tony and Pituka walk Victor, spring training, 1967.

Top right: Tony works on fundamentals with Victor, spring training, 1967 (Pituka in background).

Bottom: A month after his father won the Major League Baseball All-Star game with a fifteenth inning home run, this time it's fifteen-month-old Victor Perez's turn at the Reds' Father-Son Game at Crosley Field. Victor was at the All-Star game in Anaheim, but didn't see the historic homer. He was sleeping in the arms of his mother, Pituka, who couldn't stand up and cheer.

Hollingsworth who wrote the story). Tony wasn't aware when he arrived at the hotel's front desk that night before the game that Hammerin' Henry Aaron—the thirteen-year-straight All-Star—sat cooling his heels on a big sofa in Grand Hotel's lobby for quite awhile because he, too, couldn't get a room. (Eventually, the Hammer departed for neighboring Los Angeles, where a hotel room had been secured.)

Eventually, Tony got his room. The presidential suite, no less. The Pérezes couldn't fall asleep until two o'clock in the morning (five a.m., Cincinnati time), and therefore had to dispense with plans to take Victor to Disneyland the next day. Instead, the royal couple slept in and was well-rested by the time Tony had to go to the ballpark.

"I felt like a queen, er, I mean a king," Tony would later say.

Truth be told, Tony Pérez had more than made a "reservation" for himself at that All-Star Game in Anaheim. The Reds' twenty-five-year-old third baseman had finished second in the National League fan balloting and named to the NL team by Dodgers manager Walt Alston, who recognized a young star about to blossom. Pérez was not in the same league as frontrunner Richie Allen at that point in their careers. Despite breaking into pro ball at the same time as Pérez, Allen already had two All-Star appearances going into the 1967 season. As the Phillies' first black superstar, he burst onto the scene as a twenty-two-year-old in 1964, winning the NL Rookie of the Year Award and finishing seventh in the MVP balloting. In 1966, he hit forty home runs and finished fourth in the MVP.

Nor was Pérez the equal of Ron Santo, the Cubs great who was the third-place finisher in NL All-Star balloting in 1967. But Tani was slightly outpacing both Allen and Santo in the first half of 1967. Respectively:

Player	HR	RBI	Batting Avg.*
Pérez	17	56	.291
Allen	11	40	.314
Santo	17	53	.283

Pérez, a freer swinger who didn't walk a lot, didn't outpace his two rivals in one statistic: On-base percentage (OBP). Pérez was .323 to Allen's .423 and Santo's .371. OBP hadn't yet come into the mainstream, not even in major league board rooms. But Reds general manager Bob Howsam knew and used it.

How is it that Tony finished second in the NL balloting in what at that point was his first and only "good half" of a season? Both Allen and Santo were established stars in 1967; for fans to give Pérez an edge over Santo because of three extra RBIs and eight points of batting average (basically three or four hits) is a stretch. The Reds, Cubs, Phillies, and Pirates were at the bottom of NL attendance, drawing an average of four thousand fewer fans per game than the next-best Giants at fifteen thousand.

So it wasn't home-voters. It very likely had to do with the way Pérez carried himself on the field: gentlemanly, genteel, and gracious. Fans around the league noticed. Pérez was popular not only at Crosley Field; he was appreciated *everywhere*. When fans saw him having a good year, they noticed it and marked his name on the All-Star ballot. Clearly, 1967 marked the popularization of Tony Pérez, a phenomenon that would follow him his entire career, no matter the stadium or city in which he played.

Within the Reds organization in 1965 and 1966, Lee May and Tommy Helms were the more highly regarded players, and even going into 1967, Pérez was no more than in a dead heat with them. This fact jumps off the pages of *The Sporting News* and the Reds season programs.

Within the organization, the attitude about Pérez was typified by something that then-Reds scout Jimmy Bragan told the *Cincinnati Post/Sporting News* writer Earl Lawson in 1965: "Lee May will make you forget about Pérez." Even Colt 45s second baseman Joe Morgan noticed from way down in Houston, Texas, that the Reds field staff was moving mountains to find a place for Helms. "Tommy Helms was seen…as the second coming of Pete Rose," wrote Morgan in his autobiography, *A Life in Baseball*.

It was understandable: Long-time shortstop Helms had hit .340 in Double-A equivalent Macon, Georgia, and .309 and .319 in back-to-back Triple-A seasons in San Diego. But he was blocked at shortstop in Cincinnati by Leo Cárdenas. The Reds found Helms a spot at third base in 1966, and he responded with a Rookie-of-the-Year season: .284 with 23 doubles and nine homers.

During this time, Tony's big-league learning curve was beginning as a rookie at the hotel bedpost of future Hall of Famer Frank Robinson. Tony and other young players would go to Robinson's room on the road and talk hitting. It was Robinson's last season as a Red. "I would have learned a lot more had he stayed," Pérez told me. "I'd watch his actions, and I'd do what he did. He was very good talking hitting." In that season of 1965, Tony platooned productively with left-handed-hitting first baseman Gordy Coleman. (They combined for twenty-six home runs and 104 RBIs.)

Despite that successful sharing, gaining a foothold wasn't easy for the lithe Cuban. He endured a difficult time as a second-year platoon player in 1966, coming close to the same batting average as the year before, but hitting eight fewer home runs. His friend Lee May, a year younger, came up from Triple-A in mid-August of 1966 and batted .345 the last six weeks of the season, effectively burying Pérez on the bench.

One might expect an athlete's wife to not particularly like her husband's competitor, or at least look askance at him. But Pituka de la Cantera wasn't like that. She found May's ebullient good nature to be a perfect blend with her own. She was also great friends with Lee's wife, Terrye Perdue, who had been Lee's high school sweetheart. And Pituka knew that Tani loved the "Big Bopper from Birmingham."

It was Helms who gave May that nickname, later shortening to it to Big Bopper, a takeoff on one of that era's most famous rock stars, J.P. "Big Bopper" Richardson, who died in a plane crash in an Iowa cornfield with Buddy Holly and Richie Valens in February 1959. And it was Helms who at Triple-A San Diego in 1964 insisted on calling Tani by the Americanized "Tony." That's what Pituka told me.

"Tommy liked keeping things simple," she said. Simple as that, "Tani" became "Tony" in the clubhouse and on the field. Pituka was fine with it, because

Pituka serves up a Cuban dish, chicken and yellow rice, to Tony and Victor.

131

she liked Tommy. Who didn't? Even the Macon Peaches' batboy, future major league executive Cam Bonifay, remembered Helms fondly from those days: "He kept things light in the clubhouse," Bonifay recalled.

Back in 1964 at spring training in Tampa—Pituka and Tani honeymooned there, having neither money nor time for any place extravagant—she laughed when she heard May call her husband, "Doggie," and "Big Dog."

The nickname was over a year old, but Pituka hadn't heard it yet. It dated back to Tani and Lee's first instructional league together in Tampa in October 1963, when Tony couldn't return home to Cuba. May explained the nickname to me this way: "He's the big dog, the top dog, the king of the hill. You could always depend on Doggie to drive in the big run or keep you loose in the clubhouse."

At baseball's winter meetings in Columbus, Ohio, in late November 1966, the name "Tony Pérez" was bandied about at the Beasley-Deschler Hotel and the Sheraton-Columbus Hotel and Tommy Henrich's Steak House, like pretzels at happy hour. Tony's name kept coming up. Everyone knew the Reds had a luxury: two studs at first base, both right-handed hitters—and room for only one. "Everyone wanted Tony," Reds manager Dave Bristol recalls, "but nobody wanted to give us anything...It wasn't like we were shopping him, but we kept hearing his name."

While all this was going on, Tani was tearing it up in Santurce, Puerto Rico. He had adopted a country and a family. They, in turn, had adopted him, including his Cuban first name. Obviously comfortable in his new home, he won the 1966–1967 Winter League's batting title, RBI crown, and Most Valuable Player award. Early that winter-league season, Tani moved from first base to third base to make room for first baseman Orlando Cepeda, who was also the team's manager. This move benefited Pérez tremendously, sharpening his skills at third. Even though he had been pegged to battle it out with May at first base in Cincinnati in 1967, Pérez had a feeling this winter work at third base just might pay off.

From the very beginning, Puerto Rico was an incubator for Tony becoming a major leaguer. He picked the brain of Orlando Cepeda and every Latinos' idol, "The Great One," Roberto Clemente, who managed and played for the San Juan *Senadores* (Senators), who shared the same ballpark with Santurce's *Cangrejeros* (Crabbers).

Clemente had a prideful demeanor that demanded he speak up about perceived slights even when not spoken to. Although Pérez's nature was not Clemente's nature, the big Cuban recognized there was merit to standing for himself, in part because he saw that same spirit in Pituka. Tony's way took longer than Clemente's and Pituka's, but in the end, his way worked for him—mainly because he had the exceptional and godly patience to see it through.

In the winter going into 1967, Dave Bristol told Earl Lawson that he had no idea how he'd find room for both May and Pérez in the daily lineup: "Helms is my third baseman, and if he doesn't play there, Deron Johnson will," May didn't have the arm to play the outfield, and neither he nor Pérez had the speed. Speaking up as Clemente would have done, Pérez told Lawson in spring training: "I don't want to be traded. I know I can hit in the major leagues if I'm given the opportunity."

Bristol called Pérez and May into his office that first day of spring in 1967 and told them, "You'll each play first base every other day here, and at the end, the guy

Three of Tony's closest buddies, the young men with whom he had come of age in the Reds minor and instructional leagues, (left to right): Lee May, Tommy Helms, and Pete Rose. It was May who gave Tony his nicknames, "Doggie" and "The Big Dog."

CHAPTER 12

with the highest batting average is my first baseman." Bristol also asked Pete Rose to switch to left field, so Helms could move to second and make room for Deron Johnson at third. Rose did...and wound up loving it. "A stroke of genius," said Phillies' Phi Beta Kappa manager Gene Mauch. Pérez won the first base job on the last day of the exhibition season, needing multiple hits to out-bat May.

But in early May, Deron Johnson pulled a hamstring and was out of the lineup for three weeks. Pérez took over at third (that made room for May at first base)—and never looked back. Pérez would play 139 games at the hot corner that year, and between 148 and 160 each of the next four seasons. Before the 1972 season, May was traded to Houston in the deal that brought Joe Morgan, among others, to Cincinnati. That opened up first base, and Tony became a fixture there on the Big Red Machine.

Legendary Chicago Cubs manager Leo Durocher marveled at the way Bristol had maneuvered Pérez to third base, May to first, Helms to second, and Rose to the outfield: "The Reds are the most versatile team in the league," he said.

On May 15, 1967, the day after his twenty-fifth birthday, Pérez muscled the Pittsburgh Pirates at Crosley Field in what *Pittsburgh Press* sports editor Lester Biederman described as "an unbelievable finish to an unforgettable game." The unforgettable was courtesy of Clemente. He smacked three home runs, driving in all seven of his team's runs. In the bottom of the ninth inning, right fielder Clemente went high above the fence and slickly slapped back what would have been a home run, thus sending the game into extra innings. The unbelievable was courtesy of May (two-run homer in the ninth to tie it up, driving home Pérez, who had singled), and courtesy of Pérez again in the 10th inning (his fourth hit of the evening, the game-winner, a double off his Puerto Rico winter ball teammate and Santurce neighbor, Juan Pizarro, to drive in Rose). "One of the most thrilling comebacks ever staged by the Reds at Crosley," wrote Lawson.

Two days later "the likable Cuban," as Lawson referred to Pérez, "rapped out" two hits and drove home two runs to complete a three-game sweep of the

Pirates in a 3–1 victory. Also during the series, third baseman Pérez ranged "far to his left to grab a smash off Clemente's bat, whirled and fired" a strike to May for the putout. Lawson: "An awed Clemente was still gawking in amazement at Pérez when he returned to the dugout." Forty-nine years later, one could feel Pérez's heart swelling. Take one away from *Arriba*? First time for everything. Bragging rights!

It was right about this time of the season that Helms recalls manager Bristol telling his pitchers, "Just keep it close; if the game goes long enough, the Big Dog will win it."

On May 30, the Reds went into the eighth inning down 1–0 to the St. Louis Cardinals at Crosley Field when Pérez led off with a triple to center field. Chico Ruiz pinch-ran for him, Vada Pinson doubled, and Leo Cardenas singled. The Reds headed for the ninth up 2–1. When Orlando Cepeda and Tim McCarver singled off Reds starter Jim Maloney, Bristol called on reliever Don Nottebart. He induced Phil Gagliano to bounce to Cardenas at short, who flipped to Helms and on to Deron Johnson at first base: double play.

But wait! Cepeda was running from second base and charging around third, hell-bent to score the tying run. From the dugout, Pérez, watching Cepeda all the way—having seen the Baby Bull pull this one in Puerto Rico—bellowed from the dugout: "Watch home, HOME!" First baseman Johnson threw a strike to catcher Johnny Edwards to complete a *6-4-3-2* triple play to end the game. It is the only time in their history the Reds had pulled a triple play to end the game with the tying run being the final out. It made for a jubilant Reds clubhouse, and an exasperated one on the Cardinals' side.

The Cards didn't like the Reds to begin with; they saw themselves in the Reds. Rose personified it: hard-charging, step on your throat, and keep your foot there. The next day, May 31, the Reds purchased 6-foot-3 right-handed reliever Bob "Moose" Lee from the Dodgers. The Reds were two games and two-hundred and twenty-five pounds up on the second-place Cardinals. Bob Howsam, the first-year

Reds general manager who had come over from the Cardinals after the 1966 season, was girding for a run at the pennant. Everybody knew the road ran through St. Louis. That was fine with Bristol and the players; they didn't particularly like the Cardinals, either. And it started with intimidating ace Bob Gibson, who thought nothing of backing hitters off the plate and daring them to do something about it.

But by the second week of June, the Reds were considerably banged up (shortstop Leo Cardenas, broken hand; left fielder Rose, badly jammed right shoulder). On Sunday, June 18, in Los Angeles, Bristol had to pencil in Pérez for a start at second base. It was the only time in twenty-three years that he would play second base in the majors. (He hadn't played there professionally since his rookie year of pro ball, back in Geneva, New York, when Rose arrived and pushed Pérez to the disabled list.) At Pérez's shortstop side on June 18 was Cuba-born utility man Chico Ruiz. Pérez and Ruiz each got three hits that day (one of Pérez's was a home run), but the rest of the Reds team got only six between them and lost 5–3. Pérez and Ruiz even turned a double play that day.

A few days later, Ruiz drew a huge laugh in the Reds clubhouse when he unveiled a pair of thirty-one-dollar, custom-made, alligator hide baseball shoes that he'd bought the previous winter while playing winter ball in Venezuela—and then proceeded to wear them in the game. Ruiz was a favorite of Pérez's. The big Cuban from Central Violeta cracked up when he recalled what the wife of the smaller Cuban from Santo Domingo had said upon watching Chico crutch-hop into the family home late in the 1965 season after breaking his ankle sliding into third base that day:

"Chico, what happen? You fall off the bench?"

But it was the Reds who were falling: By mid-June 1967, they were out of first place after fifty-seven days' occupancy. It had been a smoke-and-mirrors run: Not only were Cárdenas, Rose, and Johnson out, so was outfielder Tommy Harper. And infielder Helms was on weekend duty with the Marine Corps reserves.

The powder exploded in St. Louis the day before the Fourth of July, and one week before the 1967 All-Star Game in Anaheim.

Something that Pérez's rookie-ball teammate Sal Minetta noticed back in 1961 at Geneva proved true: Tony Pérez was a really nice guy off the field—and a hail-fellow-well-met most of the time on it. But he was also somebody who gave no quarter when anybody was trying to take food off his table.

The Cardinals had gotten off to a 7–0 first inning lead on that July 3, 1967. Nevertheless, after leadoff hitter Lou Brock reached base on a fielder's choice in his *second* at-bat of the inning, he tried to steal second base. Although Brock was tagged out, the attempt led Helms to say after the game: "He must be nuts." It wasn't a 5–0 lead as Gibson later remembered in his 1994 autobiography, *Stranger to the Game*. There's a heck of a difference between a 5–0 and a 7–0 lead. Even though Brock was thrown out trying to steal second base, the Reds filed it away.

All was otherwise quiet through the next three innings. Gibson was dealing: He struck out Helms and Rose in the first inning, punched out Deron Johnson, Pérez, and May in the second, baffled Art Shamsky and reliever Don Nottebart in the third, and dazzled Vada Pinson and Rose in the fourth—nine strikeouts in only four innings.

Then Brock came to bat again, leading off the Cards' bottom of the fourth. It was his first at-bat since the first inning, and Nottebart drilled him. When Pérez led off the top of the fifth, Gibson retaliated, throwing a fastball at Pérez's head, leaving him sprawled in the dirt in front of 34,241 fans. (Gibson's reasoning was accurate, and offered an explanation borne of experience. When a pitcher is hell-bent to drill a right-handed batter, he throws the ball just behind the victim's left front shoulder; batters *always* back into that pitch.)

Nonetheless, a fastball at a batter's head gets his attention. Pérez brushed himself off and got back in the box, intent on driving a pitch up the middle or over the wall like Frank Robinson so often did. But Tony flied out to right field. He trotted around first base as he watched the ball get caught. He then trotted across the infield on the way to the Reds dugout. Lou Smith, the *Cincinnati Enquirer* sports editor/Reds beat man, watched from the press box. In the next day's paper, Smith described Pérez as "leaning in" when he snarled his epithet; Smith said that he, the observer, sensed that Pérez was about to throw a punch. ("He said something nasty," Gibson later recalled. Presumably, that "something nasty" was in English—one another's cuss words are among the first-learned by English- and Spanish-speaking players, and in that sense, every baseball player is bilingual.)

No matter what was said, that lean-in was all anybody needed to see. ("The only time I ever saw Tony Pérez get mad—at anybody," Rose recalled, many years later. "You're going to have a teammate's back in any situation—but particularly that one, when it's Doggie.")

As the benches emptied, Cardinals first baseman Cepeda sprinted in from his position to restrain his friend, Tani, and keep tempers from escalating. It appeared that Cepeda's action had tamped the uprising, but that's when the Reds' Deuce-and-a-Quarter roared in from the bullpen. "Where's Cepeda?" Bob Lee exhorted. "I'm going to punch his lights out!"

"All hell broke loose then," recalled Bristol a half century later in his living room in Andrews, North Carolina. "As a team, we were in a foul mood. We'd gone from first place to fourth in the past two-and-half weeks, dropped fourteen of our past eighteen games. Nobody likes seeing an opponent steal a base with a 7–0 lead. It's like Tommy Helms later said: 'It's like having your face rubbed in it.' The brawl got so bad they called in the police, who responded with billy clubs. As I was coming out of the dugout, I didn't see the cop about to smack me over the head with his club. But Ray Shore, one of my coaches saw it. He unloaded on the guy and broke his jaw."

Nowhere had I ever heard—nor found anywhere in my research—that Shore is the one who broke (actually, dislocated) the cop's jaw in St. Louis. But that's just the way it was back in the days before a game was televised or at least video-taped. Some of the written accounts after the fact expressed the possibility that Bristol, a noted scrapper, had thrown the punch. But Bristol and Shore (who died thirty years after the incident in Saint Louis), managed to keep it quiet all these years. It's a testament to the times that the Saint Louis County prosecutor didn't get involved. It was more of a boys-will-be-boys atmosphere back then. But in baseball lore, that Reds-Cards brawl on July 3, 1967, is still the gold standard for baseball-brawl comparisons. If your donnybrook didn't have nineteen cops, most of them with billy clubs drawn, well, it wasn't much of a donnybrook.

The brawl said as much about Pérez as it did about Gibson. Pérez wasn't going to sit back and take it, not even from one of the game's legendary intimidators.

Anaheim Stadium was only fifteen months old. It was already known as the "Big A" because of the twenty-one-story high, red-metal "A" that served as the scoreboard with the giant halo atop it. A full house—forty-six thousand—would be on hand for the All-Star Game of July 11, 1967. More important, a projected forty-five million would be watching on NBC-TV. Curt Gowdy, Pee Wee Reese, and Sandy Koufax were in the booth for the first MLB All-Star Game in prime time. Most of the viewers were in the Eastern Time zone, and that's why the game had to start on or slightly before 5 p.m. on the west coast.

The concern, well-founded, was that the dreaded shadows would envelop home plate. The pitchers would be throwing out of the sunlight. The batter's box, for almost the entire game—certainly from five o'clock to half-past seven, which is 8 p.m. to 10:30 p.m. on the east coast—would be in shadow. This was one of the first times "The Shadows" had happened in modern major-league history for a national event; the first prime time World Series game was still four years away. The hitters also were concerned about the liberal strike zone of home-plate umpire Ed Runge. The shadows and Runge's wide zone were almost certain to conspire to make for a ton of strikeouts, neither the batters' nor the fans' favorite outcome.

Tony didn't start the game, and that didn't surprise him. He knew the start would go to Richie Allen, as the leading vote-getter. On the bench with Tony were his Reds teammates, Rose and Helms. (How could one possibly be upset at riding the Anaheim pine, knowing that Willie Mays—after fourteen straight years as the NL All-Star center fielder—was on the bench, too?) In Willie's place in center was Lou Brock; he was flanked by Hank Aaron in left and Clemente in right. At second, shortstop, and catcher for the National League were, respectively, the Pirates' Bill Mazeroski and Gene Alley, and the Atlanta Braves' Joe Torre. On the mound for the NL was the Dominican Dandy, Juan Marichal of the San Francisco Giants. Slotted to follow him were the Cubs' Ferguson Jenkins and the Cards' Gibson.

Pérez wasn't slotted for anything. Political correctness hadn't yet arrived—not on the baseball diamond, anyway. Managers played the players they thought gave them the best chance to win—for as long as necessary. Clemente, Aaron, Cepeda, and Alley played all fifteen innings for the NL; for the American League, Brooks Robinson, Harmon Killebrew, Tony Oliva, Carl Yastrzemski, Tony Conigliaro, and Bill Freehan (the catcher!) played all fifteen innings. The headline atop the box score in the *Los Angeles Times* the next morning read: "The Longest Day."

Of the twenty-one All-Star Games between 1950 and 1966 (there were *two* each in 1960–1962), the NL had won fifteen and tied one; it had won the last four in a row. A major reason for this was believed to be that the NL was much faster to integrate, and therefore gained the advantage brought by the African-American players, beginning with Jackie Robinson, followed by Roy Campanella and Don Newcombe, Mays, Aaron, Banks, and Frank Robinson, and the dark-skinned Latinos, Clemente and Cepeda.

As Brooks Robinson put it, "I'm not saying the National League is superior as a whole, but their best eight are probably better than our best eight." True, an AL team, the New York Yankees, had dominated the World Series for decades, right through 1962. Not even a young Central Violetan could escape the Yankees dominance of the Fall Classic.

But in 1967, coming-of-age Tani was most impressed by the Minnesota Twins who had won the AL in 1965, and in 1967 were looking as though they were about to make another run at the World Series. Tani was well-versed in the story of the Washington Senators, who had moved to Minneapolis in 1961. He knew about the Senators super-scout Joe Cambria who had been based in Cuba, signing scores of islanders to play *beisbol* in the States. Tani was well aware of the joke about "TC" on the Twins caps as standing not for "Twin Cities" but "Twenty Cubans." People could joke about it all they wanted—Tony knew it was good-natured—but it was also a source of pride.

The Twins had Tony Oliva, Sandy Valdespino, Zoilo Versalles, and Camilo Pascual on their World Series team. Versalles had won the 1965 Most Valuable

Player Award, and Oliva had won his second of two straight AL batting championships as a second-year player that season.

"Yes, I know all about Tani Pérez," Oliva told me fifty-one years later in spring training. I had driven up to Fort Myers to meet with one of the idols of my youth. "I remember when I first saw him—*whew*, those wrists," Oliva continued. "Very distinctive rocking motion at the plate, then *pow*, great power to right-center—that stood out. But he could pull the ball when he wanted—like that night in Anaheim."

Pérez was equally impressed by Oliva, who had grown up on the tobacco-rich west side of the island, Pinar del Río. Oliva's story is even more compelling than Pérez's. Oliva had flown out of Havana in early April 1961 with twenty other Cuban signees bound for the Twins spring training facility in Florida. Oliva's group of Cubans had only four or five days to prove themselves, and Oliva got cut.

At the same time as those tryouts, the CIA-backed Bay of Pigs invasion was unfolding on the southern coast of Cooba; Oliva and the others who wanted to return home couldn't. "I wouldn't be sitting here talking to you if I had returned home, because I never would have gotten back out," Oliva told me. "I hooked up with a minor-league team thanks to Dick Howser, the general manager of the Charlotte franchise in the Southern League. The rest is history. The Bay of Pigs saved my career. Nobody would ever have heard of Tony Oliva if not for the Bay of Pigs.

"That's not true for Tony Pérez. Tony Pérez wasn't going to be (deterred), no matter what."

In the second inning of the 1967 All-Star Game, Richie Allen homered off the Twins' Dean Chance, and in the sixth Brooks Robinson homered off the Cubs' Jenkins. It remained tied at one run apiece through fourteen innings. Pérez entered the game at third base in the tenth inning, and Catfish Hunter entered it in the eleventh. ('Catfish' had gotten the nickname not because he came home with a string of catfish as a boy in Perquimans County, North Carolina, but because in 1965 Kansas City Athletics owner Charlie Finley believed his nineteen-year-old pitcher needed a colorful handle.) Hunter struck out four batters in his four innings of work (including Tony in the top of the 12th) and then retired, in order, Mays, Clemente, and Aaron in the 14th. Not bad for a twenty-one-year-old pitching in his first All-Star Game.

When the NL's Don Drysdale struck out the Twins' Harmon Killebrew in the bottom of the 14th on a called third strike, it was the twenty-ninth strikeout of the game. (The previous high for an All-Star Game was twenty in 1955, in twelve innings.) At that point it seemed the game might never end. Cepeda almost broke the tie in the top of the 15th, sending Red Sox right fielder Tony Conigliaro to the wall.

Up stepped Pérez.

Pérez: "I was thinking, *Okay, now I know what kind of pitcher he is.* I thought maybe I could hit him because I was more relaxed. I was looking (for a) fastball. He started me off with a curve, but I knew a fastball was coming because he struck me out by throwing two fastballs the first time."

It was Hunter's fifth inning of work, tying an All-Star record. Sure enough, here came the fastball down the middle to the Big Dog…7:45 p.m. Cali time, 10:45 p.m. on the East Coast…And there it went! *Pow! Bang-zoom!* in the vernacular of Jackie Gleason/Ralph Kramden of *The Honeymooners*.

Hunter had wanted to scrape the outside corner. As soon as Pérez hit it, Catfish knew it was gone. Doggie had pulled it, got it "right on the screws," in the baseball parlance. A "rising line drive" as the papers later described it, way out of the "Big A" to deep left field. The Big Dog floated around the bases. When he reached the dugout he drew big hugs from Clemente and Cepeda.

Years later, when his playing days were over, Tony told me that it was the greatest individual moment of his career. "It doesn't get any better than that for a Latin player," Pérez said. "That home run…Clemente and Cepeda congratulating me…That's the moment I felt I arrived." When Tony was at the plate, Helms was "in the hole"—the next batter due up after the on-deck hitter (Tim McCarver). Recalled Helms: "I'll never forget the look on Tony's face as he came around third."

Twenty-two-year-old New York Mets pitcher Tom Seaver, the last man standing in the National League bullpen—Claude Osteen had pitched ten innings two days earlier—received a nice ovation from the southern California crowd when he came in to pitch the bottom of the inning. Seaver, only two years out of the University of Southern California, received a firm reminder from first baseman Cepeda on his way to the mound: "Keep the ball down." Seaver got Conigliaro to fly out, walked Yaz, flew-out Freehan, and punched out Ken Berry to end it.

"Oh man!" is all Seaver could say as he entered the NL clubhouse for the celebration. "I'll never forget this—what a thrill!"

The post-game activities were just getting started, though. The Big Dog won the Most Valuable Player Award. He also let his true self come out just a little bit with the Long Beach scribe Hollingsworth, who himself acknowledged that he didn't know Pérez's full story and then proved it: "Anthony…is one of the least publicized, great hitters in the game today," wrote Hollingsworth, who also called him "the Puerto Rican."

But, by any name, Tani, Tony, Atanasio, Atanacio, or the newly bestowed Anthony, the Big Dog knew how far he had come. He channeled Pituka, Clemente, Cepeda, and, yes, even his father, José Manuel, when he said this:

"It did my heart good to get that hit. I hit good all year and nobody talks about it. Then, today, I just hit one ball out of one park and I'm famous. I'm glad to get this hit, but shouldn't people think about all the other hits I got all year?" ◆

Davey Concepción and his first Reds' road roommate, fellow Venezuelan Angel Bravo, in 1970. Davey moved in with Tony Pérez the following season. They became road roomies for the next six years, and friends forever.

CHAPTER 13
Davey and the Men of The Machine

As Tony Pérez jogged off the field in Cocoa Beach, Florida, in late March 1970 following a game against the Astros, Houston manager Harry "The Hat" Walker cranked it up a couple of decibels from the top step of the home dugout: "If you get any stronger, they will have to put you in another league!" The only answer from Pérez—who had three hits in the game (including a double off the center-field fence, 410 feet from home plate, and a long home run over the left field fence)—was "a smile bright enough to blind," recalled a writer there that day.

Tony—nobody called him "Tani" anymore—was twenty-nine years old and in his hitting prime. He filled out his 6-foot-2 frame at right about two hundred pounds. Walker, a former National League batting champion, spoke with Cincinnati writer Earl Lawson after the game about his high regard for the Big Dog.

"He's a lot quicker with the bat now than when he first came up," Walker said. "And he handles that inside pitch much better. He's liable to hit a ball to any field and over any fence—right, left and center. Those are the toughest hitters to pitch to. It's the hitters who do nothing but pull the ball who are the easiest to get out."

Doggie had had a great winter-ball season. He had been reunited in Santurce with his idol and mentor from 1965, Frank Robinson, who managed the local Crabbers for a second straight season. Tony hadn't played winter ball in Robby's first year there. But under Robby's watchful eye in year two, Pérez led the league in doubles, was second in home runs, fourth in batting average, and fifth in RBIs—the latter three the Triple Crown that Robby had won with the Orioles in 1966. Pérez prided himself on being more than just a power hitter; a true RBI man was never just about power.

Two days later in spring training, Pérez smashed a three-run homer way over the left-field fence in Clearwater against the Phillies. A reporter asked him what were his goals for the season. After all, Pérez was coming off a really good season—thirty-seven home runs and 122 RBIs in 1969. Could he do more in the coming season? Pérez said his goal was simple: "Put a World Series check in my pocket. If we win the pennant, I wouldn't care if I hit .250."

Tony Pérez took Davey Concepción under his wing right from the start, but as his mentor, not as his friend. As Davey and I looked back at those early Reds' days a half-century later, the still graceful Number 13 could not believe how raw and naïve he was as a twenty-one-year-old in his first major league camp, and how great an impact Pérez had on him.

"I needed some direction," admitted Concepción between bites of a vegetable omelette at a downtown Cincinnati hotel on the weekend of Pete Rose's induction into the Reds Hall of Fame. The waitress, in her thirties, kept calling him, "Mister Pérez." Davey didn't bother telling her otherwise; he didn't want to make her feel badly.

Davey went on to tell me about spring training 1970, how he'd been invited to camp as a non-roster player, but knew the Reds liked their No. 1 draft choice in the secondary phase of the 1967 June free agent draft, Stanford University shortstop Frank Duffy. And why did Concepción get that invite?

"Because in 1969, the San Diego Padres pitching coach (Roger Craig) was a good friend of their third-base coach, Sparky Anderson, and the following winter, he (Craig) was my manager in Venezuela," recalled Concepción, smiling. "I played good for him. He told Sparky: 'This guy's ready for the big leagues right now, even if he does weigh only one hundred and fifty-five pounds.'"

Tony provided what Davey needed most. In the spring of 1970, Concepción didn't realize that only seven years earlier, then-Reds manager Fred Hutchinson had a twenty-one-year-old kid in camp named Pete Rose, who hadn't even experienced Triple-A ball. Rose wasn't a lock to make the club, let alone win a starting job. But Hutch was open to anything.

In spring training 1970, newly hired Reds manager George "Sparky" Anderson had a twenty-one-year-old kid in camp named David Concepción who had experienced only forty-two games in Triple-A ball. Concepción wasn't a lock to make the club let alone win a starting job, either. But Sparky, too, was open to anything.

"We had four shortstops going for what we thought were, at most, two spots on the big club," remembered Concepción, who had been a pitcher and second baseman until turning pro. He had never played shortstop, except for occasionally filling in there.

Which is when Pérez's mentoring of Concepción began—the day Pérez recognized that Davey was in the hunt for a major-league job. Davey roomed on the road that first season with Venezuelan extra outfielder Angel Bravo but talked to Tony all the time.

The timing and the camaraderie were good for Tony. He had roomed for six years with fellow Cuban Chico Ruiz, but Chico had been traded to California the previous Thanksgiving with Alex Johnson for relief pitcher Pedro Borbon and starter Jim McGlothlin. Chico's final, premeditated public act for laughs—"I knew I was going to be traded, anyway, so I might as well go ahead and do what I'd been thinking about for three years," Chico said—was to "ambush" the Braves' mascot, Chief Noc-a-Homa as the Chief ran to his tepee in left field on the last day of the regular season in Atlanta, October 2, 1969. Chico himself was humiliated when the Chief flipped him on his back with a slick wrestling move.

Pérez had never been one of the organization's fair-haired boys, but in Concepción he sized up a fellow Latino who *could* be that favored son; he counseled Concepción to work for it, not rely on it. He saw in Concepción a young man who could be like the recently traded Leo Cárdenas: in the Show at twenty-one, in Cincinnati to stay at twenty-two, and the Reds' full-time shortstop at twenty-three. Maybe Concepción could rise even faster.

Pérez saw and felt that Concepción had a good sense of humor and wasn't overly sensitive in the baseball sense; he could take the needle, something the senior members of the fledgling Big Red Machine were already famous for dishing out. Pérez always had been good at sizing up people, knowing what they could and couldn't take. Players will tease, they will tempt, just to see if a teammate can take it—be one of them, in other words. Cardenas was a good guy, a give-you-the-shirt-off-his-back kind of guy, but he could be a little sensitive. His pouting led to an ignored popup that helped cost the Reds a key game against the Phillies in the waning days of the infamous 1964 pennant race, something that Pérez saw firsthand as a September call-up from San Diego.

"Look at this not as a reward, but as an opportunity," Pérez told Concepción. "Every day, do something to impress them. Make it impossible for them to send you down. In your head, know this is where you belong. But don't *act* like you belong. *Believe* you belong. For the most part, just keep your mouth shut and play."

This is what great players do: They pass it along. *Pásalo*. And the successful-players-to-be, this is what they do: They *listen*. So it was with Concepción, who reminded Pérez of himself during his earliest minor-league days.

"Davey was skinny, like I had been when I first signed," Pérez told the writers in Tampa. "He's what? About 6-foot-2, one hundred and fifty-five? *Flaco*. Skinny."

Tony was much quieter than Concepción at Doggie's first major-league camp. Tony wasn't one to easily converse with veterans unless he was spoken to. Davey, on the other hand, was outgoing, an *insoucianti*, a natural comedian. "Tani" had to grow into his skin; Davey was already in his. "I had a good spring," Davey remembers. "But I figured they'd send me back to Triple-A when the big club broke camp. Instead, on the last day, Sparky told Tani, 'Tell Davey he's made the team.'"

"And then, on Opening Day at Crosley Field, I was the starting shortstop—in front of Duffy, Woody Woodward, and Darrel Chaney and thirty thousand people! I said to myself, 'You gotta be shitting me!' And even though I was the starting shortstop on Opening Day, Tony wouldn't let me go out for a drink with him. He was that way until 1974 or 1975," recalled Concepción on the day we had breakfast. "He'd say to me, 'I'm going to have a drink. You're not allowed to be with me. You want a drink? Call room service. But not in the bar.'

"By the time I came along, Tony had been in the league for six or seven years. He didn't want me big-timing it. He kept me in my place. One step at a time. It was his way of saying, 'You're good, but you're not a star. You've got to earn it.' I'd go to some dinners at opposing players' homes with him—you know, when we were on the road. We'd go to his friends' homes, guys like (Roberto) Clemente and (Orlando) Cepeda. They'd say, 'Bring that Concepción kid with you. He's a fun guy to have around.' Those big guys, they liked me. But go out to the bar and have a drink with Tony? No way."

Wait a minute. Did you say 1975? Tony made you wait until 1975—the year the Big Red Machine won its first World Championship—before he let you go out for a drink with him?

"Yes," says Concepción, eyes twinkling. "It was 1974 or 1975. Right in there. I'd already had four years in the big leagues, played in two World Series, and Tony finally lets me go out for a drink with him!" (Concepción laughed at the telling, and so did I.) "He wanted to get my feet on the ground. He made me work for it. It's not a case of, 'You're in the big leagues; you've arrived.' Nothing like that. You have to work for it; you have to earn it. That's Tony's way."

Concepción, too, was having a great spring in 1970, especially with the glove. And the bat wasn't being knocked from his hands by opposing pitchers as some had predicted. Sparky had called his batting coach aside, the beloved former Reds slugger Ted Kluszewski, and said, "Make a hitter out of him, Klu."

Just as Davey was beginning to tell me his Klu story, Davey's close friend and mentor of forty-six years came over the table to say hello. I told Tony that the waitress had mistaken Davey for him.

"You don't look *that* bad," Tony told Davey.

"I don't look that *old*, either," Davey replied.

They both laughed.

"Tell her you're not Tony Pérez," the Big Dog suggested.

"That's okay," Davey said. "She's treating me like a Hall of Famer."

We all laughed at that one. But all three of us believed Davey belonged in Cooperstown. I voted for Concepción every year for the fifteen years he was on the ballot of the Baseball Writers Association of America. The highest percentage of votes he received in any one year was 17 percent; 75 percent is required for election. His highest percentage with the veterans committee was 50 percent; the same 75 percent is required.

From the beginning, Reds general manager Bob Howsam loved working rookies into the mix. (One can't help but think Pérez might have been brought along a little sooner had Howsam been the Reds GM in 1965. At the very least, Tony might not have spent September 1966 on the bench while his buddy, Lee May, got all the at-bats at first base.) Giving young guys a shot was something Howsam had learned from Branch Rickey.

Howsam had a formula: Bring three rookies north every season. He didn't always reach that goal, but he tried. It was a reap-what-you-sow approach to scouting and development, a "keep 'em coming" incentive for the developers and the players in the talent pipeline. In 1970, especially, Howsam saw a great opportunity to apply his formula because the new manager would be open to it and because there were plenty of immensely gifted Reds youngsters on the cusp: twenty-two-year-old outfielder Bernie Carbo and twenty-four-year-old Hal McRae, twenty-one-year-old starting pitcher Wayne Simpson and nineteen-year-old Don Gullett, who if he made the club, would start the season in the bullpen.

The Reds, it turned out, opened the season with five rookies in key positions, which is why none of the experts picked Cincinnati to reach the World Series in 1970—they were too young, had a rookie manager, and had been wearing the "not enough pitching" label for so long that it was practically branded in.

Also, amazingly, the Reds opened the season with four shortstops, an unprecedented display of their new manager's conviction about the importance of the "6" position…and utter lack of faith in the ability of any one of the four to fill it.

Ed Liberatore, a former Reds scout who by this time worked for the Dodgers, had the line of the spring: "The Reds are crazy if they think they have anyone who can play shortstop better than that Venezuelan kid."

When Davey got the start at shortstop on Opening Day, 1970—the last Opening Day at Crosley Field—third baseman Pérez felt like a proud papa, even though Davey went 0-for-4. Pérez took an 0-fer as well. First baseman May hit a two-run bomb in the fourth inning, followed by solo shots from Bernie Carbo and Bobby Tolan, and the Reds never looked back.

Going into the Friday night game of April 17, the Reds were 9–3 and hosting the San Francisco Giants. Anybody who was hoping for 1970 to be the Reds' year—which in Cincinnati was everybody—didn't have to wait long. With the Reds down 5–4 going into the ninth inning, McRae tied it with a home run, and then, with two men on base, Pérez stepped to the plate. *Pow!* Three-run walk-off home run.

"I felt good last year when the season opened," he told Lawson, the *Cincinnati Post* Reds' beat man, "and now I feel even better. I was a little overweight at the start of last season. Now I'm not because I play winter ball…That's why I like to play winter ball. It's not the money. It's that I never lose my stroke."

On Sunday, April 19, the Reds beat the Giants 6–0 at Crosley Field on a one-hitter by Wayne Simpson, whom Sparky was already touting as "a young Bob Gibson." Pérez was 3-for-3 with a two-run homer, two RBI singles, and a walk. Seven of the Reds' first fifteen games had been against the Giants. Although the Reds won only four of them, Pérez was 15-for-25 (.600) against the Giants, with thirteen RBI and four home runs.

"I go up there thinking, 'Nobody can get me out,'" Pérez said. "Every time I go up, there's a man on second and third. I like it that way. I think I hit better with men on base. When there are men on base, I just try to meet the ball. With no one on, I swing too hard sometimes."

St. Louis catcher Joe Torre couldn't believe it when he looked at the paper. Ten days into the season, "T. Pérez" was hitting, what, .500? *Wow!*

On April 23, Pérez and pitcher Simpson were the subject of a national story by the Associated Press. By then, Pérez was "down" to .462, with six homers and eighteen RBI. "Everything I swing at seems to go for a hit," Pérez said.

On April 25, *The Cincinnati Enquirer*'s young baseball writer Bob Hertzel, who had started on the beat in 1969 and greatly energized the morning newspaper's baseball coverage, went head-to-head with the *Post*'s vaunted beat writer Lawson for scoops. Hertzel gathered plenty of quotes and clubhouse color, just like Earl. "Hertzie" sat down with Pérez in the coffee shop of the Chase-Park Plaza Hotel in Saint Louis three and a half hours before the Saturday night game. The writer got the ballplayer to open up a little bit. The story appeared in the next day's *Enquirer* under the headline "From Sugar Cane to Fame." Pérez had already hit nine home runs, setting a National League record for April.

There is more to Tony Pérez than just his ability to hit a baseball; there's a certain glow about the man, a gentlemanly attitude that exudes from him with every word he speaks, began Hertzel, putting the lie to the contention by some baseball writers decades later that Pérez was pretty much ignored by writers because of the language barrier. *Unlike some players who get off to a fantastic start as Pérez has, he has managed to keep his head through it all. There's none of this chatter about a changed stance or getting stronger or learning what it's all about.*

"I don't know what happened," Pérez said. "I never hit like this before."

It is things like this modesty that make Pérez one of baseball's most admired men. No popping off, no predictions of greatness. Only a sincere confidence that he displays on the field, not off.

And then, amazingly, Hertzie got Pérez to open up about his homeland.

He traces his confidence in himself back to Cuba. He knows what his baseball abilities got him away from.

"I just a country boy," he says. "I live out where they have sugar cane, and when I was young I start to work in the sugar cane factory with my father. I no like that. My mom, she want me to go to college, but I no like that either. I tell them I want to play ball. 'Oh no,' my mother says, 'you can't do that. You too skinny.' I was built like Dave Concepción."

Tony went on to say he played only baseball and basketball in Cuba.

"*Basketball was really something,*" he said. "*We had this team and every night someone would break an arm or a leg. We took the game very serious. It got so bad that I quit.*"

Pérez named Minnie Miñoso as his idol.

"*Minnie was the best player to ever come out of Cuba,*" Pérez said. "*He's still playing in Mexico, and I think he led the league in hitting with about a .380 batting average (last year). He's fifty something years old!*"

No, Miñoso wasn't quite *that* old in the spring of 1970. He was player-manager of the Mexican League's Union Laquno Aldodoneros, where the shortstop was Zoilo Versalles, who only five years earlier had been the American League Most

A lot of spring trainings from 1965 through 1972 preceded the Big Dog's settling into the position for which he would be forever remembered: "TPérez, 1B, Big Red Machine." Former Reds slugging first sacker Ted Kluszewski, the BRM's hitting instructor, was a key mentor.

Valuable Player for the AL champion Minnesota Twins. Miñoso was forty-four years old—the same age Pérez would be when he hung it up as a player.

On the night of April 28, Tony hit his tenth home run for the month, a blast off the Crosley Field flagpole in center field, tying the major-league record set the previous year by his mentor, Frank Robinson. "He deserves everything he gets," Reds starting pitcher Gary Nolan (4–0) said of Pérez. "You pull for guys who pull for you." Said Rose: "Pérez is hitting everything and everybody."

Pérez's homer and 2-for-3 performance with three RBI gave the Reds a 4–2 victory. Once again, nobody ignored Tony. (Lawson's lead: "A happy smile wreathed the moon-shaped face of Tony Pérez as he peered out from behind a phalanx around his locker which had been formed by the writers.") "I'm just trying to follow Little Victor's orders," Tony told the writers, noting that his son, Victor, was four years old. "Every day when I head for the park, he say, 'Hit a home run, Daddy!'"

When Tony came to the plate in the first inning of the Monday night May 4 game at Crosley, catcher Torre couldn't resist. The Crosley Field scoreboard flashed that the Reds third baseman was hitting .424. From behind his mask, and with a straight face, Torre said to the big Cuban: "I don't want to hurt your feelings, Tony, but I didn't think you'd hit .500 all season." Pérez grinned. And Torre, ever the good guy, a ballplayer's ballplayer, grinned back.

Pérez went 1-for-4 that night with a double and RBI. The double was a pop fly that fell between two Cardinals outfielders. When Tony hustled into second base on the heels of that gift, umpire Chris Pelekoudas asked, "They scored that a hit—you gonna take it?" That drew a belly laugh from Pérez, who knew everything was dropping. Tony's protégé, Concepción, was heating up, too: 2-for-3, raising his batting average to .260.

In a 10–7 loss at Wrigley Field on May 8 that ended the Reds' eight-game winning streak, the Reds hit five home runs (two by Pérez—his league-leading eleventh and twelfth home runs). Pérez was so hot he hit one of his long balls off a greaseball—illegal pitch—from Phil "The Vulture" Regan that didn't break sharply, leading off the ninth inning. Home plate umpire John Kibler continually stopped play in the ninth and went out to the mound to check Regan, but couldn't find the source of the grease. (Two years earlier in a Cubs-Reds game, home plate umpire Pelekoudas had called fourteen illegal pitches against Regan but couldn't find his source. That day, Pelekoudas even told Pete Rose to stay put after he struck out against a spitball, and Rose singled.)

After Bench popped out in the May 8 game, Lee May doubled, but was stranded when McRae grounded out and Concepción struck out to end the game. "It's pitiful that a man is allowed to make a farce out of the game," Sparky said of Regan. "He's got the grease hidden in about four good spots. I don't know where they are, but it's on him somewhere."

Concepción wondered where that somewhere was, too. He'd had a good day at plate (3-for-5), but didn't like the idea of a pitcher gaining an advantage through illegitimate means. Davey was hoping to keep his strikeout total lower than his walk total: Now, he had 12 whiffs (two this day) and only ten walks. His 2-for-3 performance on May 4 had triggered a 9-for-14 stretch that raised his average to .310. "I been telling you all along the kid's going to be a pretty good hitter," Klu told the writers.

On a long day at Crosley Field on May 17, the Reds swept a doubleheader from the Braves, including a wonderful second game in which Henry Aaron logged his 3,000th career hit, and Pérez was 5-for-7 with a double, as the Reds won in fifteen innings, 7–6. Relief pitcher Don Gullett singled home Rose to earn the win and struck out four in his two innings of work. The Reds were already six games in front, and the season was only six weeks old.

It was a loose clubhouse, and twenty-two-year-old Johnny Bench loved it. He loved the role that Pérez and Lee "The Big Bopper" May played in it. In Bench's 1979 autobiography, *Catch You Later*, he laid it down in such a way that it would stay down.

"Nobody had more of an influence on me than Pérez," Bench wrote. "Much of what the Reds became in the 1970s, beginning in that first big year of 1970, was due to Pérez. Don't let anybody tell you different."

For Davey, it was the same: Tony, plus Sparky, plus Klu.

"I learned a lot talking to Tony," Davey remembers. "And every day that season I had to go to Sparky's office before I went in the clubhouse. It was obligatory. Sparky talked to me every day. He said, 'Hey, you're going to be my shortstop. Don't worry about your hitting.' So, I worked on my fielding, but I worked on my hitting, too. Sparky was saying not to worry about my hitting, but Pete Rose was getting on my ass. Johnny Bench used to get on me, too. We had a bunch of good hitters, and I was the Punch-and-Judy guy. I knew I had to work on my hitting, which is why I was always went to see Klu."

After Pérez's 2-for-3 night and a three-run homer off the Mets' twenty-three-old Nolan Ryan in a 5–4 Reds victory, Sparky said "Here it is June 5 and Pérez has twenty home runs, fifty-seven RBI, and is hitting .375. And this is against major-league pitching. It's incredible."

Sparky was plenty encouraging to his veterans but could be prone to anxiety with his younger players when they were doing what young players do—making mistakes. Concepción was hitting .274 and showing tons of range in the field but had made fourteen errors, some at inopportune moments.

The day after extolling Pérez, Sparky benched Pérez's protégé Concepción, calling on the veteran Woody Woodward to take over at short. But Woodward's days were numbered, because he didn't have anywhere near Concepción's defensive range, and at bat was prone to only the occasional warm streak. For a born utilityman, the Ice Man always cometh. Watching Woodward's extended turn at short was the genesis of one of Sparky's more famous bromides: "Play a substitute long enough and you'll find out why he's a substitute." By September, Concepción was getting some starts again.

Even in losses, there was one constant: Pérez kept hitting. He had two hits including a homer and single in an 8–4 loss to Montreal June 11, although that single should have been a double. It was a shot that bounced off the fingertips of the glove of right fielder Rusty Staub. Concepción's roomie, Angel Bravo, who was on second, failed to run, thinking the ball might be caught, which caused Rose, who was on first, to run up on Bravo. In turn, that caused Pérez to pull up on his way to second and then get thrown out trying to return to first. Said Rose: "I felt like a guy waiting to grab the baton in a relay race. There was Bravo a few steps in front of me, and Tony a few strides behind me."

By June 17, the Reds were coming home triumphant, winners of thirteen of their past seventeen games. That included the last game of the road trip when the last of Woodward's three hits was a surprise bunt single in the ninth inning of a tie game in New York that touched off a winning three-run rally. "Woody" was hitting .296. *Paciencia*, Pérez counseled his protégé. *Patience*.

On June 20 in Los Angeles, the Reds' Big Three—Pérez, Bench, and May (and that's the order they hit in, 3-4-5)—all launched early homers. Pérez's was of the killer three-run variety. The Reds ran their record to 46–19 (.708) to send the second-place Dodgers to ten games back—even though Da Bums were playing .611 ball, fourth best in all of baseball.

On Crosley Field's closing night—June 24—Pérez took the collar against Juan Marichal, grounding out to end the seventh. But Bench and Lee May picked him up immediately in the eighth, with back-to-back homers to give the Reds a 5–4 lead. The Reds hung on to win and closed out their fifty-eight-year-old home in style. Four days later, Pérez was at it again, with a ninth-inning go-ahead bomb (number twenty-seven) in Houston. Two days after that—June 30—the Reds opened their new home, Riverfront Stadium. Again, Pérez didn't do much (1-for-3) in an 8–2 defeat by the Braves, but he liked the looks of the banner in the outfield seats that read, "Pérez's Pounders."

The Reds went into the second game of a doubleheader in Atlanta having lost three in a row, the first time it had happened that season. In the nightcap, Davey's all-out hustle on a two-out groundball in the top of the ninth inning of a scoreless game allowed him to reach first base safely and the Reds went to win 3–1. Even though Woodward pinch-hit for the Reds pitcher and took over defensively in the ninth, Concepción showed himself not to be a pouter, and everybody knew he had the speed. It felt good when Pérez gave him a big grin and thumbs-up in the Reds dugout.

"Tony kept me balanced," remembers Davey, "and Klu kept my habits good." Thinking back forty-six years, Number 13 could still see and hear Big Klu as though it were yesterday: "'Pitchers don't put you in a slump; bad habits put you in a slump. Come with me, we will watch the film.' He'd show you the movie of your hands, your stance, how close to the plate you were when you were going good. 'You see the length of your stride? It's shorter. And you hit that ball good. So let's go outside on the field and we'll work on it.' And with me, he'd wrap those massive hands around my head—his hands held my head in place like a vice grip—and he'd say, 'You know what I'm gonna do with your neck if you don't listen to me, right, Davey?'" says Concepción, mimicking his own trembling voice from back then, "'Y-y-y-yes, Klu. Y-y-you are going to snap it like a chicken.' He'd do that to me all the time, from the first day to the last." And Klu would nod, and silently laugh to himself, not a mean bone in his body. "Fun guy, nice guy," recalls Concepción. "He taught me how to hit."

On July 13, 1970, the day before the 41st All-Star Game at the still-not-quite-done Riverfront Stadium, *Sports Illustrated* captured the men, the myth, and the early legend of the Big Red Machine. In a cover story titled "The Cincy Cannonball," William Leggett wrote: "Not since 1955 and the old Brooklyn Dodgers has a club in traditionally baseball's tightest league entered the month of July playing over .700 ball. Yet last week, as the Reds transferred from Crosley Field to their new home in Riverfront Stadium, the Reds were 52–21." (Pérez had gotten them there with a ninth-inning home run in Houston to win the game 3–2.) "Most of baseball was in awe of the machine, and well it should be. At a time when expansion has obviously thinned out the talent in the majors the Reds had arrived with a busload of stars.

"By last weekend they had hit 110 homers. Tony Pérez, with twenty-seven, and Johnny Bench, with twenty-five, are close to the pace that Roger Maris and Mickey Mantle set back in 1961 when they collected 115 between them. Pérez is known as a big RBI man, having driven in 122 runners in 1969 (he has eighty-four so far this year), but Bench…is now in the same class. Not only can he hit, but he is a superb fielding catcher…'When John Bench throws,' says Harry Dalton, the director of player personnel of the Baltimore Orioles, 'everybody in baseball drools.'"

At the All-Star break, Pérez was the toast of baseball, a modern-day Martín Dihigo who was finally getting his due—except in Cuba where only Martín Dihigo Jr. knew his name. Pérez was the odds-on favorite to win the Most Valuable Player award, although Bench—being at the more valuable position of catcher—was close behind. Pérez had added two home runs since *SI* went to press, to make twenty-nine, with ninety RBIs, and a .356 batting average—a great *full* season for most players.

That's when people began to think really special of Pérez. Only three times before 1970 had a player ever accumulated ninety RBIs at the All-Star break. Part of this exclusivity, of course, stemmed from the fact that before 1933 there *was* no All-Star Game. And only the passage of four decades had served to show how rare and how fast a start it took to get ninety RBIs by the break. Lou Gehrig had done it in 1934 (ninety RBIs in seventy-three games) and Hank Greenberg in 1935 (103 in seventy-six games). The only player to have done it since 1935 was strongman Harmon Killebrew in 1969. The six-time American League home run champion and two-time RBI champion had ninety-one RBIs in ninety-six games—eight more games than it took Pérez to reach ninety.

It was rarefied air. To have what Pérez had at the 1970 All-Star break—*more RBI than games played*—was trafficking in the sublime. Bench has a phrase for it in his autobiography, *Catch You Later*: "Pérez was so hot you couldn't get near him." And, yet, everybody wanted to get near Pérez. He was the glue to the clubhouse because he moved easily between the white and black players, and of course was the leader of the Latino contingent.

"He calmed me down," Concepción recalls. "I'd get mad easy when a pitcher would knock me down, pitch me tight. Tony would say, 'Don't let them know you're mad; if you do, they're going to throw it in there all the time. When somebody knocks you down, get up, dust yourself off, and try to get a hit. Try to hit the ball good up the middle. Same way off the field. Don't get mad. When the ball club asks us to dress a certain way, do it. Respect the game. Be a gentleman. Save your energy for what you do on the field.'"

There was an anecdote from Earl Lawson in the *Cincinnati Post* in mid-May, 1970, that illustrated Pérez's role in the clubhouse. During the homestand that included the Braves and Cubs, Lee May had driven up to Kettering, Ohio—only a fifty-minute ride up I-75 from Cincinnati—to check out some new cars at Rose and Bench's Lincoln-Mercury dealership. The Big Bopper had no intention of buying a car. But buy a Lincoln Mark III he did. Here is how Lawson's description began of the clubhouse scene in the aftermath of that purchase:

> Tony Pérez, doubled up with laughter, was on his knees, pounding the Reds' clubhouse floor with his fist. Rookie outfielder Hal McRae, doing a pantomime skit that would have made Red Skelton envious, was performing.
>
> "Have you seen Lee's new car?" exclaimed McRae. "Why, it's got so many gadgets on it that Lee stayed awake until three o'clock in the morning studying the instructions. And he still doesn't know how they all work." Pérez: "It's even got a vacuum cleaner built into it." Rose: "Johnny and I are gonna sell one to every guy on the club. Then we'll have to win the pennant so they can pay for them."(All of this sent McRae only deeper into pantomime): "Here's Lee," said McRae, sitting straight-backed on a clubhouse stool, his hands grasping an imaginary steering wheel and his head swiveling left to right as he flashed a blinding smile at imaginary pedestrians. Pérez, still laughing, pounded the clubhouse floor a little harder....

If Pérez wasn't starting something in the clubhouse, he was keeping it alive and bringing everybody in on the joke. Bench, far more a student of the clubhouse dynamic than anybody gave him credit for, said it best in his autobiography, written with William Brashler.

"Tony cast a net over the entire team with his attitude. He was always up, always had a sense of humor. He could rag you like nobody else. And always with that accent of his. You never got offended when he got on you, and you never felt insulted or injured to where you couldn't laugh yourself. It was an art with him—one I don't have.

"What helped us that year was a little thing we had going between us that just seemed to make a lot of difference," continued Bench. "It started with Pérez and May, another guy with a steady, solid personality. When somebody screwed up, the other guy would say, 'Stay with 'em'…I remember a lot of times when I struck out with men on base and I'd be so pissed that I would try to crush the bat in my hands and Tony or Lee would run by and say, 'Stay with 'em.' And I'd know that it wasn't the (end of the) world, that there would be another chance.

"To survive, and to thrive like we did that season," Bench continued, "that sense of equilibrium was beautiful. Tony always had it. He usually took the most ribbing himself. He could cut you up, just nail you like a kid with his fingers in the frosting. And you'd know you'd been caught. But he'd never turn the knife, never cut you to the bone and hurt you or belittle you to where it wasn't fun anymore. A team goes through a lot in a season—fatigue and wear-and-tear set in no matter how well it's going—and a personality like Pérez is just so valuable."

Although Bench was much more celebrated nationally than Pérez, in Reds Country the fans knew what they had in the Big Dog. Of course, they celebrated the hometown kid, Rose, the most. Occasionally, a ray of light would shine through. *"I like Johnny Bench,"* began the letter on the sports page from Gary Smith, 8960 Plainfield Road in Cincinnati. *"But why does he continue to dominate the publicity while it's basically Pérez, not Bench, who holds a big responsibility for the Reds' 11 ½ game lead?"*

On July 14, the starting All-Star third baseman was "T. Pérez." Hitting in front of him were W. Mays, D. Allen and H. Aaron, and hitting after him were R. Carty and J. Bench. Tony went 0-for-3 in that All-Star Game before 51,838 fans at Riverfront Stadium. The game belonged to Rose who ran over American League catcher Ray Fosse in the 12th inning to win it for the NL'ers, 5–4.

CHAPTER 13

Two weeks later, July 26, the slumping Pérez wasn't in the lineup—"Probably time to give him a rest," Sparky said—when Bench hit three homers off Steve Carlton in consecutive at-bats to beat St. Louis 12–5 before 40,202 fans at Riverfront Stadium. Three years earlier, Lee May had nicknamed Bench "The Little General" because of the way he took charge; now, five months shy of his twenty-third birthday, "Jay Bee" was a four-star.

Sparky hadn't wanted to rest the Big Dog until he showed some real signs of tiring. "He has a chance to make a bundle of money this year," Sparky explained. "I'll just let him go and try to get all the individual accomplishments he can." But the Reds skipper missed the early signs: Pérez was already in the midst of a 15-for-76 slump (.197) that began right after the All-Star Break. Still, all seemed well in Redsland. The Reds' 70–30 start was the best since Stan Musial's 1944 Cardinals went 73–27.

The winning pitcher on July 26 was the rookie Simpson who ran his record to 14–2. But five days later, Simpson blew out his shoulder—he had pitched five hundred innings in the previous year-and-a-half—and six weeks after that, fourteen-game winner McGlothlin left in the first inning with a sore elbow and was done for the year. The Reds had been greatly compromised, something that would reveal itself in the postseason.

The night after the Reds went to 70–30, the Cardinals' Dick Allen smoked a ball off the concrete facing of the upper deck red seats. It set press box tongues to wagging. Everybody knew Richie "Call Me Dick" Allen's reputation as one of the longest of the long-ball hitters. *Would anybody ever reach "the reds?"*

On July 30, Bench hit his thirty-fifth homer and Pérez his thirty-first. "I don't worry about catching Johnny," said Pérez, although it came out "Yonny" in Pérez's Spanish basso profundo. "Every time he hits a homer, it's more glue (money) in my pocket."

On August 8 in Los Angeles, Pérez hit two 400-foot-plus bombs, but both he and Sparky were most effusive about Lee May's bases-loaded two-run double one night earlier which some Cincinnati fans missed on radio because it had come so late in a West Coast night game. "Beauty, beauty, beauty—it was a beautiful hit," said Pérez, who was identified by Hertzel as "May's No. 1 booster."

In terms of sheer prodigiousness, though, Pérez's blast of three nights later at Riverfront Stadium took the red-velvet cake. It was a red-seat home run into the second row down the left-field line. It stood out in part because it was a grand slam and because it ran Gary Nolan's record to 15–4, but mostly because of the "*Ahhh!*" factor. It was a towering blast, a monstrous parabola allowing for suspense to linger: *Would it or wouldn't it?* Nobody put a tape measure on it or even guessed at it, but 430 feet sounds about right.

From the on-deck circle, Bench could only marvel: "That ball kept going," he would later say. "When he hit it, I said it was gonna go. But it wasn't even close. It was gone." From his dugout vantage point, Sparky thought May's line-shot homer (number twenty-four) into the yellow seats in left-center (just below "the reds") might have gone farther than Pérez's.

Even with that homer and four RBI, Pérez was still four homers and three RBI behind Bench (thirty-five vs. thirty-nine, and 110 vs. 113, respectively). "I just let Johnny get a little cushion," Pérez said. "Now I try to catch him." Said Bench: "I may need fifty homers to win the title."

With seven weeks to go in the regular season, the Reds' "Big Three" (ninety-eight home runs) were taking aim at Mickey Mantle, Roger Maris, and Moose Skowron, who nine years earlier had blasted 143 home runs for the Yankees. If the Reds' Big Three could each average two homers a week for the final seven weeks, they could make one helluva run at the Bronx Bombers.

Two days later, when Bench hit his fortieth home run and Pérez his thirty-sixth, the Big Dog finally felt comfortable enough to declare that his slump was in the rear-view mirror: "My vacation is over," he said. "Last week, I stopped thinking and started swinging the bat again." The next night he was accidentally spiked at first base, a wound that required four stitches to close. It would slow him down again.

But through it all, Doggie remained Doggie. A reporter approached Lee May in the Riverfront clubhouse before the game of September 1. The Reds were slumping badly, losers of nine of thirteen games. "I don't know what's wrong with *those* guys," said May, nodding toward Bench and Pérez. "I've been lousy all year. Do something, Dog." To which Pérez, with the ever-present twinkle in his eye, said: "Kill somebody. I'm gonna kill somebody." Everybody cracked up.

In a 7–3 victory over the Giants at Riverfront Stadium on September 3, Concepción went 2-for-3 and raised his average to .270. Even though Sparky went with Woody Woodward most of the way after that, including in the playoffs, Concepción clearly had shown himself to be the Reds shortstop of the future.

The Venezuelan "Vitola"—the Olive Oyl-thin incarnation of Atanacio Rigal Pérez circa 1961—ended the regular season hitting .260, with six doubles, three triples, one home run, and nineteen RBIs in 265 at-bats—far better than anybody, including Concepción himself, expected. Equally important, he had ended the season with "only twenty-two errors," not bad for a rookie shortstop in 413 chances. From the time he had been benched in early June, Davey had improved his error rate from one in every seventeen chances to one in every twenty-one.

It wasn't lost on Tony that there was world news at September's end that gave many folks in the western hemisphere great pause: The United States warned the Soviets to discontinue construction of a nuclear submarine base in Cienfuegos, on Cuba's southern coast. Tony knew that tensions were still running high between Washington, Havana, and Moscow.

But his job was *baseball*. He ended the 1970 regular season with forty home runs and 129 RBIs (he batted .317, terrific for a power hitter). Bench had forty-five home runs and 148 RBIs, and May thirty-four home runs and ninety-four RBIs. The Big Three's 119 home runs were twenty-four short of Maris-Mantle-Skowron. Bench won the National League's Most Valuable Player award. Pérez finished third after the Cubs' Billy Williams.

In the postseason, the famous 3-4-5 punch of Pérez, Bench, and May sustained the Reds through the three-game sweep of the Pirates in the National League Championship Series. But in the World Series they fell victim to the other-worldly defense of Baltimore Orioles third baseman Brooks Robinson, who continually deflated them with countless great plays that robbed them of hits and killed scoring chances. The Reds fell, four games to one. Of the Big Three, only May had a good World Series (7-for-18, .389, with two home runs, two doubles, six runs, and eight RBIs). Pérez was held to one measly single (1-for-18, .056), and Bench wasn't much better (4-for-19, .211, with one home run and three RBIs).

Not even Don Santiago Torano himself ever enjoyed a cigar more than Atanacio Rigal Pérez did this one on October 5, 1970. Tony and his buddy, Pete Rose (left), had toiled long and hard in the 1960s to achieve their dream. They were headed to the World Series.

A bright spot in the World Series was Concepción, who got three hits, drove in three runs, and hit .333, including a two-out triple to score the Big Bopper in the Reds' 6–5 victory to avoid the four-game sweep. "I felt pretty good about that," Concepción told me many years later.

Concepción went home to Venezuela soon after the World Series and resumed his winter-ball career for Maracay's Tigres de Aragua. He was already a star there and would grow into a legend, just like his idol, Luis Aparicio. It was a legacy lost on his friend, the great Pérez, Man Without a Homeland. Yes, Tony was a star in his adopted land, Puerto Rico, where he headed after the Series. But there was just something about representing the country upon whose soil one first walked and ran: Land of Origin, Land That Birthed You, The Motherland.

It was a feeling the Big Dog had never known.

But, yes, "home" he went to his beloved Puerto Rico, with wife, Pituka, four-year-old Victor and thirteen-month-old Eduardo.

Tony had much to think about, and almost none of it involved baseball. ◆

CHAPTER 13

Tony and Pituka had already been sworn in as U.S. citizens by the time Tony returned home to Cuba after the 1972 season. It was the first time Tony had been home since leaving Central Violeta for the 1963 season in Macon, Georgia (Victor, left; Eduardo, right).

CHAPTER 14

Homeward

Tony had been thinking about it for years. Returning home to Cuba, that is. He had first learned in 1969 that travel restrictions between the United States and Cuba might be about to ease. He was aware that "détente"—a relaxing of the Cold War tensions between the United States and the Soviet Union initiated by President Nixon—was spilling over, in a good way, into the acrimonious U.S.-Cuba relationship.

President Nixon through his Secretary of State, Henry Kissinger, was reaching out to the Soviets in such a way as to encourage détente. Nixon wanted to go down in history for rapprochement with the Russians, and, eventually, opening up relations with China.

The left-wing student-action organization known as the Students for a Democratic Society (SDS) was organizing people-to-people trips to Cuba in this slightly more relaxed atmosphere, after what had been almost a decade-long freeze on U.S. travel to Cuba. The attention in U.S. government circles to the first two group-sized tours to Cuba was significant enough to lead U.S. Senator James Eastland of Mississippi to proclaim on the floor of Congress that "what had become a comparative trickle of persons visiting Cuba in the 1960s now threatens to become a flood."

In December 1969 came the breakthrough Tony was waiting for: His former Puerto Rican League manager-friend Preston Gómez—like Tony, a longtime Cuban exile—became one of the first of the exiles to return home. Gómez hadn't been back since the *Revolución* in 1959. That was the year Gómez had managed the Havana Sugar Kings to the Little World Series championship over the Minneapolis Millers.

When the manager of expansion San Diego Padres arrived in Havana on December 22, 1969, he immediately visited his cancer-stricken father, Pedro, in the hospital. Preston also went to see his brother, Rafael, who had been sentenced by the Cuban "judiciary" to a fifteen-year prison sentence for political activity against the State. Rafael "just happened" to be released from prison after serving three years, just in time for Preston's visit home.

One night, Castro stopped by Preston's restaurant table. "The bearded one," as *The Sporting News* was fond of referring to the Supreme Commander back in those days, asked about the Cuban players in the United States. He asked about Tony Oliva, José Cardenal, Tito Fuentes, Zoilo Versalles, and Tony Taylor. Also, the four players the Reds had flown to Douglas, Georgia, in 1954 to try out: Cookie Rojas, Mike Cuellar, Tony González, and Leo Cárdenas. Gómez told Castro everything he knew.

Preston also told him about Tani Pérez, who only two years earlier had enjoyed his breakout season, hitting the bomb off Catfish Hunter in the 15th inning of the All-Star Game. Tani had just finished a monster 1969 season, Gómez told Castro, in which he'd hit thirty-seven home runs (fourth in the league behind Willie McCovey, Henry Aaron, and his buddy Lee May) and collected a whopping 122 ribeye steaks (third in the league and fourth in major-league baseball behind Harmon Killebrew, McCovey, and Ron Santo). *And, oh my, Tani was still only twenty-seven years old!* Gómez predicted a big 1970 season for Tani.

Castro didn't ask Gómez how he had come by his American handle of "Preston." As the online sports journal, *Hardball Times*, explained it: "Gómez's actual first name was Pedro, but there were a handful of Pedro Gómezes in Cuban baseball at the time, so a sportswriter hung 'Preston' on him. Preston was the name of a sugar mill in Gómez' hometown. It'd be like naming a Detroit-area player 'Buick' McKenzie."

Gómez also visited with old friends. One was Connie Marrero, the Marianao Tigers pitching coach who in 1956 had taught Jim Bunning the slider. Another was Mike González, the famous Cuba manager to whom Ernest Hemingway referred in the *The Old Man and the Sea* —"Who is the greatest manager, really, Luque or Mike González?"

Also, remarkably still around was "Martino Ribigo, the Cuban Satchel Paige," as the beat man Jack Murphy referred to Cuba's *El Inmortal*, totally misspelling Dihigo's given name *and* his surname. A handful of years later, when the National Baseball Hall of Fame began researching "Martín Magdaleno Dihigo Llanos" for electoral consideration, it would have been easy to miss Murphy's article with its mishmash of consonants and an added vowel that smacked all too much of mortality. And when it came to the Negro Leaguers, all the Hall of Fame researchers of the 1970s had to go on were a few eyewitness reports, books, and newspapers.

The researchers would have dug up everything they could get their hands on, no matter when or where written, although with Dihigo, it wouldn't have been "Was he good enough?" It would have been more, "Who *was* he?" Researchers would have learned that *El Maestro*, as he was also known, was a Castro supporter from the start and stayed that, at least publicly, to the end. But the "was he good enough?" question would have overwhelmed everything. He was as good a hitter as he was a pitcher—Hall of Fame-quality in both. There's only one other player since World War I that could be said about: Babe Ruth.

Preston Gómez would have told anybody how good Dihigo was. Like every other Cuban player, Gómez grew up knowing how good Dihigo was. Gómez treated him accordingly on his trip to Cuba. Dihigo's reach was so deep, even the American elders of the game in the early 1960s knew it. And the reason *I* know that to be true is because the teammates of Dihigo's *son* told me of it fifty-years after playing with him. They told me that in spring training, when their coaches and managers saw Dihigo Jr., the name served to remind them of the old man's greatness, and they'd begin telling stories about him.

Even if Tony had been able to get back to Cuba following the 1970 season—a year after Gómez—he wouldn't have found Dihigo as he had remembered him: strong, hearty, and vivacious. Dihigo had been going downhill for a while.

The important thing about Gómez's trip was that he had been allowed back into his homeland in the spirit of the people-to-people tours that détente was fostering—even if Castro was conflating those tours with his own political purposes.

By the time Preston's trip home was about over on January 12, 1970, he had arranged to bring his mother, Eliah, back to San Diego with him. As the Padres manager, Gómez was *hoping* to bring a left-handed hitting outfielder back with him, too, but was told by the Cuban sports officials, *Eso no va a suceder*—"That's not going to happen."

As a result of Gómez's visit, Tony went into both the 1970 and 1971 seasons with some hope that he might soon be able to reunite with his family in Cuba. The island—"Castroland" as the sportswriters referred to it in print—had been firmly in the sphere of the Soviet Union since 1960, adopting the Kremlin's governing and economic philosophies. Cuba was clearly a part of the U.S.-USSR dynamic. Even with people-to-people tours being encouraged and facilitated by SDS, America and Cuba would still be at arm's length—the U.S.-imposed embargo was still being enforced—but it would look good and speak well for détente if the Americans and their Communist neighbor ninety miles off Key West would allow some visits.

Starting first, of course, with Americans visiting Cuba. That's just how things worked. Castro wanted to control what those on the island would see, and he wanted to control what those who came to the island *could* see.

Pérez knew he was in a tough spot, because unlike many of his fellow Cuban major leaguers who had no desire to return, he wanted to visit Cuba as Gómez had done, although not to round up family members and bring them to the States. Tony's extended family was so big and intertwined that nobody wanted to leave the others behind.

Unfortunately for Tony, what Castro *didn't* want was the Cuban professional players coming back from the States without restriction, like the Americans had been doing from the 1930s up until the *Revolución*. Castro knew the Cuban people regarded the baseball players as gods. He didn't like this image of Cuba as a playground—or even as just a place to visit family. He wanted Cuba to be regarded on its own merits, not as a stomping ground. The Supreme Leader did not want to be seen as blessing the comings-and-goings of the baseball gods.

He had made an exception for Gómez, because Gómez was a manager, not a player, and he had led the Sugar Kings to the championship. It gave credence to his return—he had brought glory and good times to Cuba. During Gómez's visit to Cuba, he conducted some clinics and watched some games, but it was never announced in the Cuban press that the much-revered Gómez was back in town.

Still, Tony was heartened by Gómez's trip. For the first time in a long time, he could actually envision himself seeing his mother and father again.

In mid-March 1970, Phillies infielder Tony Taylor—whose brother, Jorge, had played for one of the Reds' Class-D teams in Palatka, Florida, while Pérez was playing for other one in Geneva, New York—was given the day off from spring camp. He drove to the Miami airport to see his mother and sister, and his sister's family, none of whom he had seen in eleven years. They were part of the "Freedom Flights" from Cuba in the nine years covering 1965 through 1973.

Three hundred thousand refugees were transported to the States during that period, "the largest airborne refugee operation in American history," said American officials. Castro didn't want anybody who didn't want to be in Cuba to stay there. *Gusanos*—"worms"—he called them. But it created a huge drain and was part of what gutted the Cuban economy.

Pérez knew about all this. He talked to his fellow Cuban players around the National League, and many of the American League's Cuban players in spring training. He knew, for example, that in the winter before the 1971 season, Tony Oliva had found a way to bring his father and sister to Minnesota and was trying to get their visas extended so they could come to spring training. Oliva's family had never before seen him play as a major leaguer, not even in an exhibition game. Oliva had once been rebuffed in trying to secure visas in Mexico City to put his family member on the freedom road.

By March of 1971, Preston Gómez had unveiled his plan to take a team of major leaguers on a tour of Cuba after the World Series. The team would be made up of, in considerable part, Cuban players. The three players mentioned most prominently (no doubt because Gómez already had their commitment) were Pérez, Oliva, and Taylor. The "three Tony's" had never been back to Cuba since leaving in the early 1960s—nor had any other Cuban player of any consequence. "Going home" was just not something one did, unless of course one were prepared to stay.

Gómez's idea for a Cuba tour had been inspired by the U.S. Table Tennis team becoming, in April 1971, the first American sports delegation to set foot in the Chinese capital of Beijing since 1949. "Ping-pong diplomacy" was hatched in a chance meeting between an American table tennis player who accidentally boarded the Chinese team bus during a tournament in Japan—the Chinese captain befriended the American—and it led to a friendship and mutual invitation of each country's table tennis team to visit the other.

The next thing anybody knew, President Nixon was matching Chinese Prime Minister Zhou Enlai *maotai* for *maotai* ("pure gasoline," wrote *The New York Times'* Max Frankel), during the many toasts at Beijing's Great Hall of the People on Tiananmen Square. Nixon called it "the week that changed the world." And he was right. "The little ball moves the Big Ball," intoned Chairman Mao Zedong.

The times they were a-changin'—albeit *s-l-o-w-l-y*, for U.S.-Cuba relations. Far too slowly for many Cuban exiles, separated for a full decade from their families. By early May 1971, Pérez was publicly expressing his longings to return home as soon as he could, attaching those hopes to whatever slivers of optimism he could find, including Gómez's dream of touring Cuba with a mostly Latino all-star team. "Seeing my family again would be a dream come true," Pérez said.

Gómez shared with him that Baseball Commissioner Bowie Kuhn was on board with the Cuba tour proposal, but that Baseball was awaiting State Department approval. It never came. The trip was eventually canceled because of protests by Cuban exiles in Florida.

By mid-May 1971, Tony Taylor was starting to heat up in the batter's box. He had three game-winning hits in five days and told everyone—teammates, opposing players, and the media—that having his mother with him (and out of Cuba) put a bounce in his step.

On May 20, 1971, the same night the Big Dog was going 2-for-5 at Riverfront Stadium (he drove in the tying run in the seventh inning and scored the go-ahead run in a 5–4 victory), Martín Dihigo Sr.—*El Inmortal*—died five days short of his sixty-sixth birthday.

On May 28, when Tony's pal, Lee May, "single"-handedly knocked off the Houston Astros with a walk-off one-bagger in the 13th inning, Pérez was down to .215—with an on-base percentage where his batting average should have been (.279) and a slugging percentage where his on-base percentage should have been (.348). Pete Rose confided to beat writer Earl Lawson that Pérez was playing with a bad wrist that he had injured in spring training. "He's always been a hot starter," Rose said.

Meanwhile, Pérez was keeping up with the Cuba comings-and-goings. He knew that his former road roomie, Chico Ruiz, now a California Angel, was going to fly to Mexico City in early June 1971. The Angels were giving him a couple of days off, even though the team's schedule was full, to arrange for visas for his parents and mother-in-law to fly to the States.

Pérez was trying to get a read on what it might take for him to be able to visit his family. He had begun working with the office of U.S. Senator Robert Taft (Ohio) to secure a visa. Tony's father, José Manuel, was ailing, and nobody seemed to know what it was. "Something terrible...cancer or something," Pérez said.

On June 3, Pérez was down to .208, and the team was 20–32. The only position player on his way to an exceptional year was Lee May (who would finish with thirty-nine home runs and ninety-eight RBIs). Gradually, Pérez got healthy: On July 11, he drove in all the Reds runs in a 5–3 victory over the Mets at Riverfront Stadium, ripping Tom Seaver for a three-run homer in the eighth inning to wipe out a 3–2 deficit. Six days later, also at Riverfront Stadium, it was Juan Marichal's turn. The Dominican Dandy had held the vaunted Big Red Machine to one hit through eight innings, but the Reds got to him for three runs in the ninth, the last two of them on a walk-off single by Pérez.

On the final weekend of the 1971 season, with Taylor's Phillies whipping the Cubs and the Reds wrapping up a dismal fourth-place finish (73–89, eleven games back of the first-place Giants), Pérez read these words straight from the mouth of the thirty-four-year-old Taylor: "I feel like I'm twenty-one again. The whole season I have felt this way. I have one of the best gifts I ever have from God. My mother from Cuba has given me life again."

Oh, to have that feeling, thought Pérez.

In early January 1972 when beat writer Hertzel reached him in Puerto Rico, Pérez confirmed that, yes, he had signed his contract for the upcoming season, but that, no, it wasn't the paper that he had hoped to have in his billfold.

"I thought by now I would have had (the visa), that I would have already been (to Cuba)," Pérez told Hertzel. "(But) everything worked out well with my father. They (the doctors) operate on him, and he is (okay). He is home now, and much better."

Then, a few days later, *bingo*, the call came from Senator Taft's office. *We are all but positive you are going to get you a visa. Get yourself to Mexico City.*

Excited, Tony went…and got nowhere. He was marooned in Mexico City, awaiting a visa that never came. While waiting, he thought a lot about Gómez's trip to Cuba. He also thought a lot about Tony Taylor having his mother with him in the States, and about Tony Oliva being reunited with his father and sister. He thought a lot about his buddy, Chico, too. Chico didn't get anywhere in his visit to Mexico City, either. Chico never did get the visas he needed to bring his mother and mother-in-law to the States. Strange things happened in Mexico City.

Tony was eleven hundred miles from Havana, fourteen hundred miles from his family in Central Violeta. Like the singer Gene Pitney, he was twenty-four hours away from his loved one's arms. Disconsolate, he packed it in. Two dollars and fifty cents is all that it cost him twelve years earlier to get out of Cuba, but now, apparently, no amount of money could get him back in. He vowed to Pituka he would keep trying, but for now, he was returning to *her* arms in Puerto Rico.

"One of us is going to be traded."

Tony and Lee May had come to that conclusion in the waning days of the miserable 1971 campaign, and agreed to call one another right after it came down. That's how sure they were it was going to happen. Pérez had for him what was an off year (twenty-five home runs, ninety-one RBIs) and thought he might be the odd man out.

Tony received the news in late November 1971 that two of his longtime buddies, May and Helms, had been traded to Houston along with super-sub Jimmy Stewart, for Joe Morgan, Jack Billingham, Denis Menke, César Geronimo, and Ed Armbrister. On the popularity scale, the trade was as lopsided as Frank Robinson for Milt Pappas, but the Reds brain trust had its reasons. They had done the math and pulled the trigger. And here was the math as laid out for Sparky Anderson by Reds general manager Bob Howsam. Sparky sets it to paper in his autobiography, *The Main Spark,* written with then-*Dayton Daily News* columnist Si Burick: Worse-case scenario was that the May-Helms for Morgan-Menke part of the deal was a wash. The on-base percentage aspect of it clearly favored the Reds. May-Helms would walk sixty-five times a year between them, compared to Morgan-Menke's 170 times. Sparky: "Using these ratios, we knew we didn't need any more hits from (Morgan-Menke) for them to equal the times on base for both May and Helms. That kind of research opened my eyes." (Howsam, like his mentor, the late Branch Rickey, was way ahead of his time.)

Giraldo "Chico" Ruiz Sablon, December 5, 1938—February 9, 1972.

Chico was gone. Tony got the news in a chilling phone call from buddy May on February 10. Chico had been killed in a one-car accident in Anaheim, California, only a little over a month since he had become a U.S. citizen, just as Tony and Pituka had done earlier that year. The authorities believed that Chico had fallen asleep at the wheel. Chico had been traded to the Angels after the 1969 season as part of the deal in which the Reds acquired reliever Pedro Borbon, who would become an important part of the Big Red Machine bullpen.

Chico had never gotten back to Cuba, had never gotten to see his family, had never been able to share with his mother and mother-in-law Disneyland, the Land of Plenty, the United States of America.

Chico had lived life to the fullest, and yet, he was unfulfilled.

It was the story for many Cuban exiles.

Tony pressed on. He flew to California for the funeral, promising himself that he would get a visa, however long it took; *he would be fulfilled.*

"You're not going to believe Tony Pérez when you see him."

Pete Rose, never one to beat around the bush, got right to it as soon as he saw beat writer Bob Hertzel at Tampa's King Arthur Inn on March 1, 1972—the official reporting date for Reds position players.

"*What?*" asked Hertzie.

"Tony just checked in, and he's absolutely skinny," Rose said.

To say that Pérez had been eager to get to spring training would have been an understatement. It had been a buffeting winter—the trading of so many of his buddies, the failed trip home, the tragic death of Chico—but Tony had gotten into great shape, working out at the gym daily, playing game after game of handball until the sweat was just pouring off of him. Soon, the weight was just pouring off him, too: *207...205...200...198...*and the "195" that the scale registered on March 2 in Tampa.

How had he done it?

"I had to stop eating all that black beans and rice," said the Big Dog.

He had managed to play the final month of the winter-ball season with Santurce, ensuring that his stroke would be grooved in Tampa from day one. There was also the matter of bonding with his new teammates—Morgan & Company. Tony knew that Pete would take them all under his wing; that's just what Pete did. For Tony, that bonding would come in the form of busting chops.

Forty-four years later, nobody would remember exactly how that first conversation went, but knowing Tony, it would have gone something like this:

"Yoe, Yoe, welcome. Welcome to the Cincinnati Reds."

"Backatcha."

"This isn't Houston, Yoe. We don't play one hundred and forty or one hundred and fifty games here. This is the Big Red Machine. We play all hundred and sixty-two."

"!#$%! you, Tony!"

It was a low-blow humor from Tony, of course. So much baseball humor is low-blow. (With Houston, Morgan had played 157 games in 1965 and 160 in 1971, and would play 157 with the Reds in 1973.) But baseball humor, especially batting-cage humor, has its roots in finding the vulnerability and exploiting it. Morgan's prototypical season in Houston was playing 140–150 games, batting .265, belting ten-twelve homers, driving in fifty or fifty-five runs, scoring be-

From jump, the Big Dog loved being a thorn in the side of Joe Morgan, telling him that nobody would have known who he was if he hadn't been traded to the Big Red Machine.

tween ninety and a hundred, which was really good, considering that he was do-ing it in the Astrodome. In Cincinnati, with the help of his new friends, he raised the bar, not one level but two: .290, twenty to twenty-two home runs, eighty-five or ninety RBIs, 115-120 runs. (Pérez told Joe, "If you had stayed in Houston, nobody would know who you are." What made it funny is that Morgan knew it was true and couldn't do a damn thing about it; all he could do was prove Pérez right.) Those numbers don't even account for the fact that on the bases Morgan turned opposing pitchers apoplectic, and at second base took away lots of hits.

Pérez loved having a new foil; he loved agitating Morgan. He got away with it, too, thanks to Little Joe's good-natured exasperation and the enjoyment of the entire clubhouse.

Morgan, on the other hand, was denied Pérez's greatest vulnerability be-cause of the trade that Morgan himself had made possible: Pérez's reputation had been that of a less-than-stellar third baseman. The deeper numbers belie it. In Morgan's autobiography, *A Life in Baseball,* he set forth the greatest descrip-tion of Pérez as a third baseman I have ever heard or read:

"Tony put up some interesting defensive numbers (in his breakout All-Star season in) 1967," Morgan wrote. "He led the league in errors, fielding chances, double plays, and total putouts. In other words, he was quick, got to a lot of balls, had good hands, but was probably not a great thrower—he was, in other words, an ideal first baseman."

The general thread of that is true, although Pérez was not among the league leaders in any third-base fielding category in 1967. He did lead NL third base-men in errors in 1968, 1969, and 1970 (he was third in 1971). He led third base-man in putouts in 1968, and assists in 1969 and 1971. He also led third basemen in double-plays in 1968 and 1969. By 1971, his last season at the hot corner, he was truly getting the hang of it: He led third basemen in range factor and was second in fielding percentage. That right there is a third baseman coming of age.

And all those errors were a season's worth of barbs, zingers, and in-house provocations. But unfortunately for Morgan, he never got to use them. From the time Joe arrived in Cincinnati, Pérez would never play another game at third base. Fifteen more seasons, 1,520 games at first base, the ideal first baseman.

Meanwhile, Tony pressed on with his needle. There have been well-chronicled episodes over the years: The time when Morgan came to the ballpark with a 104-degree fever on a night when the Mets' tough lefthander Jerry Koosman was scheduled to pitch. When Sparky found out about Morgan's fever, he scratched Little Joe from the lineup. He called Joe into his office to tell him. By the time Joe got back to his locker, there was an unrolled sleeping bag laid out in front of it, a pillow, a glass of water, two aspirins, and a note: "Take two of these and you'll get over Koosmanitis." Morgan got two hits that night, and the Reds won. On the night Morgan made some errors in Los Angeles, there was a garbage-can lid at his locker after the game with a note that read, "Here, try this...."

Four decades later, when the host at a Big Red Machine roast asked the position players who it was that stirred up the calm in their world, they all turned in their chairs and stared at Pérez—some pointing, some even jeering.

Johnny Bench: "Tony would sidle up to you and say, 'Did you hear what Pete and 'Yoe' said about you?' And then he'd go up to Pete and Joe, and say, 'Did you hear what Yonny said about *you*?' And that's when all the screeching would start."

"It was those daily things, the little things, that made coming to the ballpark fun," Bench said. To a man, if a vote had been taken of the Big Red Machine's twenty-five-man roster on where to place Pérez in the big mosaic just inside the front gate of Great American Ball Park, it would have been 24–1 to put Pérez exactly where he is: front and center. Only Pérez would have picked somebody else, and then only out of sheer modesty. Because *he* knew who stirred the pot.

Morgan remembers an early 1972 conversation with Pérez. He wrote about it with David Falkner in *A Life in Baseball*. Joe even told it four decades later at a roast of Pérez at the ballpark.

By Morgan's recollection, he and Rose were tearing it up, batting in the mid-.350's. The team, though, was struggling, and taking heat because of the trade of the popular May and Helms.

Morgan and Rose were horsing around at the batting cage, talking loudly about how well they were doing. "Suddenly, Tony," wrote Morgan, "in that deep, broken English of his, boomed out:"

"You two guys, you think you so great or something?"

Morgan: "Yeah, what's your problem?"

"You always talking 'me and you, me and you.'"

"So what? I'm hitting .350, he's hitting .350, what are *you* hitting?"

"Yeah, okay, the Big Dog's hitting .220, but what place are we in?"

We knew exactly what he was getting at. I tried to wriggle out of it.

Morgan: "Hey, man, I was just having a private talk."

Pérez: "Yeah, it's all private with you two; you don't think about the team. When the Big Dog starts hitting, we will go to the top."

Within two weeks we were in first place and, sure enough, Tony came strolling by our lockers.

"Hey, what place are we in?"

"First place, where we belong."

"Where we two weeks ago?"

"I can't remember."

"We were in fourth place and you were hitting .350 and Rose was hitting .350."

Morgan: "Well, I'm still hitting .350."

"Yeah, but now the Big Dog is hitting .288 and look where we are!"

Tony walked off in triumph.

The problem, as so often is the case, is this: The facts don't support the memory. But there is still truth there. Joe was hitting .300, but Rose was hitting .240. And, yes, the Reds got hot beginning with Tony's six RBIs in a May 14 doubleheader, but it was Bench who carried the club for the next couple weeks while Pérez was on the bench, banged up. True, Tony did return and heat up as the Reds continued the 74–36 run that took them directly into the National League Championship Series. The moral of the story is that the front of the order set you up and the heart of the order sets you off. So sayeth the Big Dog.

Pérez no longer hit cleanup—Bench had wrested that spot away from the Big Dog after the catcher's MVP season in 1970—but injuries, not the lack of

Tony knew he had Joe right where he wanted him, not only hitting in front of him and by his side, but in his place. Joe couldn't claim he had put the Big Red Machine over the top without sounding boastful. Pérez would have had a field day with that.

opportunity, is what kept the sleek, svelte No. 24 from a better year in 1972. He hit "only" twenty-one home runs, and knocked in ninety runs again. He hit .283 (fourteen points higher than 1971), but that's not what he was paid to do.

How good was Morgan's 1972 season? His all-around "Q value"—what the objective analysts call "WAR" (wins above replacement) —was point-seven points *higher* than Bench in his 1972 MVP-winning season. Morgan had two more years just like it—1973 and 1974—and then *topped* it in 1975 and 1976, when he won back-to-back MVPs.

All the while, Tony never stopped busting Joe's chops.

"If you were still in Houston, nobody'd know your name," Doggie repeated.

"!#$%! you, Tony," Joe said.

Even long-time Reds fans forget.

They see the iconic photos and the video of Johnny Bench connecting on a game-tying, ninth-inning, opposite-field home run off Dave Giusti in the deciding Game Five of the 1972 NLCS, and they forget. In their minds' eyes, they see George Foster practically skipping across the plate with the winning run following the wild pitch by Bob Moose that slid past Pirates catcher Manny Sanguillén, and they forget. They forget how Foster got on base.

He had pinch-run for Tony Pérez! And how had Pérez gotten on base? He had singled sharply to left field, just after Bench hit the home run. Bench's home run was the explosion, but Pérez's single was the one more stick of dynamite awaiting one final spark.

"Good, old reliable Tony Pérez," Sparky Anderson calls Doggie in *Main Spark*.

After Pérez singled and Foster pinch-ran for him, Denis Menke singled Foster to third, Darrel Chaney popped out to shortstop, Hal McRae stepped up to the plate, and here came the wild pitch.

And how did Sparky rate the excitement of that Game Five?

"My absolute greatest thrill as a major league manager," Sparky wrote.

Nobody's vantage point from outside the white lines was closer than Pérez's.

Of all the games, all the great moments that I saw from 1974 through 2002 at Riverfront Stadium, I totally understand where the *Main Spark* was coming from. Bench's home run *has* to be the greatest. Greater even than Pete Rose's "4,192" thirteen years later? Yes. Rose's record-breaking hit, you knew was coming—eventually. But Bench's home run to *right* field, you could not have seen *that* coming.

Al Michaels' call from the Reds radio booth explains why:

"Giusti winds and the one-one pitch to Bench is swung on and missed. Again, a full rip on a sinker. One-and-two. Giusti, sinking fastball, slider, palm ball, good control, Tony Pérez on deck. Giusti bends in, takes the sign. The right-hander winds and the one-two pitch to Bench. Johnny swings and drills it a mile, but foul. Boy, he had all of that one, but foul by plenty, hit it up in the red seats, the upper deck, one-and-two. The wind and the pitch to Bench; change, hit in the air to deep right field, back goes Clemente, at the fences, she's gone! *(Crowd roars for thirty-four seconds.)* Johnny Bench, who hits almost every home run to left field, hits one to right. The game is tied!"

When the excellent thirty-one-year-old Cuban-born shortstop Bert Campaneris arrived in Cincinnati with his Oakland A's teammates for the 1972 World Series to take on the Reds and *their* Cuban-born star, Tony Pérez, it was yet another reminder of the contribution Cuba had made to the American game over the years. And anybody in the United States in 1972 who could read or watch the news couldn't help but notice that Cuba still out there, still only ninety miles from America's shores. Between 1968 and through the beginning of the World Series, there had been ninety skyjackings of U.S. commercial airliners to Cuba. It was so pervasive and such as threat to passenger safety that it prompted negotiations between the two countries to bring the threat under control.

Eleven years earlier—1961—Campy was in Costa Rica with Tito Fuentes playing with a young Cuban All-Star team when the CIA-backed rebels landed at *Bahía de Cochinos*—the Bay of Pigs—on April 17.

That is the day Campy and Fuentes signed U.S. baseball contracts. Ever since February 1961, when Fidel Castro told Cuba's pros that the days of their comings and goings from the U.S. to play ball were over— *If you come back next time, you won't be getting back out*—Campy knew his days in Cuba were numbered. It's all right there in the book, *Full Count: Inside Cuban Baseball*, by Milton H. Jamail. Campy and Fuentes "decided not to go home and instead pursue major league careers."

At the Major League Baseball All-Star Game "Fanfest" in July 2015 in Cincinnati, Campy told me, "The last thing I said to (my parents) before leaving Cuba was, 'When I come back, I'll be a star.' And I think I was—well, at least *we* were—stars. Because just before I went back to Cuba that winter for the first time in ten years—just like Tony—we beat the Reds in the World Series. We had the rings, so I figured we were the stars."

"One and two, Giusti, sinking fastball, slider, palm ball, good control, Tony Pérez on deck…The wind and the pitch to Bench…" The Pérez-Bench embrace tells the rest of that story from Game Five of the 1972 NLCS.

It had been a taut World Series, the Reds losing four one-run games, the A's two. The Reds had gotten off to a 3-games-to-1 deficit in the World Series, losing the first two games at home, and then winning Games Three and Five in Oakland and Game Six in Cincinnati. When Campy had come to bat late in Game Six with his team trailing 8–1, he told Bench "We haven't lost three in a row the whole season." (He was wrong—the A's had two four-game losing streaks and several three-game losing slides—but the point was well-made; the A's weren't prone to losing streaks.)

To which Bench replied: "You haven't played the Big Red Machine."

But the great comeback wasn't to be. The Reds lost in seven.

Campy hit only .179 for the Series (5-for-28); his countryman Pérez .435 (10-for-23). Tony was in the middle of a lot of the action, scoring the only run in Game Three in Oakland, slipping as he came around third and going down in a heap ("a sudden baseball bad dream," wrote Roger Angell in the *New Yorker)*, but he got to his feet in time to score. In Game Seven, Pérez doubled into the left-field corner to lead off the fifth inning against Blue Moon Odom and eventually scored on a sacrifice fly to deep center field by McRae to tie the game at 1. In the eighth, Pérez smacked a sacrifice fly to score Rose and cut the deficit to 3–2. It's as close as the Reds got.

After the game, Pérez let it sink in. Bridesmaids again.

But no Red had a bigger offseason dream than Pérez. In late August, he had received his visa. He was going home.

Not just "home," as most people know it.

He was going home...to *Cooba*. ◆

Cuba's José Vargas slides home in March 1940 in Havana in front of another future National Baseball Hall of Fame catcher (Ernie Lombardi) in a game in which Luis Tiant Sr. held the Reds to one run over seven innings. That 1940 Reds team had a slugging first baseman, too (Frank McCormick)—and Tiant Sr. shut him down just like Tiant the younger shut down Tony Pérez in the 1975 World Series.

CHAPTER 15
The Answered Prayer

The first thing Tony wanted to know was, "How much? How many?" As in how much/how many necessities and gifts could he bring for his family? The answer came back, "As much, as many, as you want."

And that is how Tony came to have seventeen—yes, *seventeen*—bags at the Mexico City airport in mid-November, 1972.

The flight to Havana is not long. The jet comes in from the south, over the Isla de la Juventud, and then a straight shot into the capital. Pérez didn't know there wouldn't be any baggage inspectors working after 5 p.m. on Fridays through the weekend, so he had to cool his heels in Havana for two-and-a-half days. His brothers, Gustavo and José, named for their father, had come in from Central Violeta to help him with his bags at the airport and load them up on the train for the three-hundred-mile ride to Central Violeta.

But first, the inspectors would have to go through all seventeen bags, piece by piece. One thing everybody in Cuba knew: You weren't allowed to bring in guns. No problem for Tony. His trove was mostly health- and comfort-related: shoes, food, medicines, everything he could think or had been told his family needed. He wasn't worried if it all passed inspection; he wasn't worried if none of it did.

Later, he would say, "I just want to see my daddy," who was ill, weak, broken down. "Tough luck if they take my bag. All I care about is getting through myself."

Two of the bags, intended for friends and neighbors in Central Violeta, were confiscated. *Sólo para la familia,* he was told—"Family only." It was Tuesday by the time Tony left the airport. It was an eight-hour train ride to Violeta. Staring at the countryside, he had plenty of time to think. He couldn't believe that he was almost home.

He arrived in Violeta in the late afternoon, unloading at the station near the sugar mill where he had worked and played shortstop for the mill team years earlier. His father, José Manuel, gave him a hug for the ages, then poked Tani in the stomach and said, *Miralo. Eres todo músculo sin grasa*—"Look at him. All muscle, no fat."

As Tani recalled that memory years later, he touched me the way his father touched him, and he used his father's words.

From the train station, Tani was taken straight to his grandparents' home. (It would have been his maternal grandparents: Tani's father, José Manuel, was already seventy-six years old. His wife, Tani's mother, Teodora, was sixteen years younger, and would live to see her Tani make the National Baseball Hall of Fame.)

"When I was young, we always used to go to my grandmother's house for Christmas and the holidays," Tony later explained. "My grandfather, he said he wanted it to be just like the old times. So, we all went there and it was...well, you just can't describe it.

"Everyone was so emotional. Everybody don't say much. For half an hour, we just sit around. Then we start talking and we start crying. They say, 'We're so happy. He's here. He's here at last.'"

After the reunion at the grandparents, the group moved on to the Pérez family home—a two-bedroom, cottage-like structure where Tani had grown up with his two brothers, three sisters, mother and father. It was eight o'clock at night; a big crowd was gathered out front.

A lot of the people were extended family. "I have a large family," Tani explained. There were friends, neighbors, townspeople he didn't know from Adam—or Eve.

"I left (Central Violeta) a long time ago," Pérez said later. He said he was confused by the presence of so many strangers, some of them carrying the Pérez name, others his mother's maiden name, Rigal, everybody welcoming him home.

They all knew about the *gran pelotero*—big leaguer—coming home: They knew he had turned thirty only six months earlier, and that he had already had played in four All-Star Games and two World Series. They knew he played alongside the fast and powerful Joe Morgan; that he received pickoff throws from the great Johnny Bench; dug low throws out of the dirt from the hardest man of them all, the barrel-chested river rat, Peter Edward Rose. They knew, because when they asked José Manuel, he would share the stories. He didn't brag on his son, but he was proud of him, and he knew people didn't have access to the information he was privy to through Tani. The Cuban newspapers, run by the state, weren't allowed to carry any baseball news from the United States, and certainly none of the names of the Cuban players, or their exploits.

"All my friends, the kids I played with when I was young, were all waiting for me," Pérez said. "They wanted to talk. They have so many arguments about baseball, and they want me to answer them."

Was Ted Williams better than Tony Oliva? That is the question Pérez remembered above all the others. He wasn't surprised by the depth of the questions. It confirmed what he always knew: The people of Central Violeta were—and always would be—sophisticated *fanaticos*.

It made him happy to know so many people were aware of the exploits of Oliva, who was from the far western part of the island, many hours away. Oliva had won back-to-back batting titles in his rookie and sophomore seasons (1964–1965); in 1971, he led the league in both batting average (.337) and slugging percentage (.546), the stuff of ol' Teddy Ballgame himself.

He heard somebody ask what time it was, and another, looking at his watch, answered that it was half-past eleven. He hadn't reached the front door of his boyhood home. The twenty days he was in Cuba passed quickly.

"Everyone was calling me," he said. "Everyone wanted to talk with me. I try to be around my mother and father and grandparents, but it was hard. Every time my grandmother saw me she started crying."

He had even seen the Supreme Commander himself, at a ballgame. "He stayed for only a few innings, and then he left," Pérez told the *Cincinnati Post* beat writer, Earl Lawson. Rest assured that Castro knew that Pérez was at that game. The Bearded One never missed an opportunity to remind people who was in charge.

The most melancholy thing about Tani's trip home—"almost tragic," wrote the *Enquirer's* beat man, Bob Hertzel—was that Tani's "lovely, ever-smiling wife, Pituka," was granted no visa, nor were their two children, Victor and Eduardo.

Tani: "It was the only thing (my mother said) she regretted. She never met my wife, and she wanted to meet her so. She never met the children. It is sad."

The entire visit home was "emotional, so emotional," that Pérez said he wouldn't be able explain everything, without breaking down. Lawson, whose nickname was "Scoops," reached Pérez in Puerto Rico, two months after Tony's Cuba homecoming. The day of their telephone conversation was January 5, 1973—the seventy-seventh birthday of Tani's father. It was also only five days after the plane carrying "The Great One," Roberto Clemente, had crashed into the sea just after takeoff from San Juan Airport.

"I talked to Clemente two days before," said Pérez, softly. "He told me he was not going to Nicaragua. But he changed his mind when he heard some of the supplies for the earthquake survivors were winding up in the wrong hands."

Hertzel chose to plumb deeper with a face-to-face interview with Pérez in Tampa—and it paid off.

Pérez said his father was sick, suffering badly from arthritis. "He can't move around," Tony said. "He can't walk right. He can't work long. He just didn't go out of the house very much (while I was there). His right hand, he can't use it and you have to help, and his left hand is getting worse."

But, observed Hertzel, "all the miracles of medicine couldn't have done for José Manuel Pérez what a visit from his son did."

Pérez: "On the second day (home), I was going to my sister's house. It is a half-mile or so away. My father, he said he wants to come. So, we walked. The people, they were surprised to see him on the street.

"They kid him. They say, 'Now you got your kid, now you can walk.' I'm the only one to make him go out. He made it. He had to stop and rest a couple of times, but he made it."

Oh, how that memory would sustain Tony through the rest of his days. "He is crazy about his father," Pituka once told me. "He talks about his father, and he concentrates so deep."

One simply cannot make up for a lost decade in three weeks. Tony had left the island at twenty years old in the spring of 1963, and had come back at thirty. That time was gone forever.

"I could have stayed longer (on my 1972 visit), but I wanted to be home with my family for Christmas," Pérez told Lawson.

Tani saw his brothers, saw them working in the sugar mill, saw what he wanted to avoid by playing baseball. He saw what he (was) missing, and he knew he had made the right choice.

"I'm not sorry I came to America and played baseball," Tani said. Other than that—and it was *lot*— Pérez told Hertzel that the visit home "choke me up; I just can't say much.

"I am satisfied," he said. "If I never get back, I am satisfied. I have seen them. I remember when I left, my mother (was) speaking to me. She was crying. But she, too, said she was satisfied. She had gotten to see me."

It was as though Tani and Teodora had been praying for the same thing. *Dear Lord, please let me see him, her, just one time before I die. It is all that I ask. And then I will be satisfied.*

Their prayer had been answered. One does not go back to the well on that one.

When Tony told writer Hertzel that his visit back home to Central Violeta "choke me up; I just can't say much," it was from the heart. As were José Manuel's words to Tani as they parted.

"I may never see you again."

By October 1975—three years after Tani's visit home—the showdown was near for the teams of Pérez and Luis Tiant Jr. and the players themselves.

One cannot fully appreciate the story of Tani and Luis without first learning the story of the fathers—*theirs* being the back story. José Manuel's story, one already knows. Luis Sr.'s story is equally compelling.

"My father was a great pitcher, but he didn't want me to play ball," Luis Jr. tells me as he autographs baseballs at FanFest at the 2015 All-Star Game in Cincinnati. "He played baseball in the U.S. for twenty-five years. He didn't want me to experience the discrimination here. Then, some of his friends saw me pitch, and they told him, 'Hey, you better go see your kid. He's good.'"

The year was 1958. Eighteen-year-old Luis Jr. was pitching for an all-star team in Havana. And so, one day, Luis Sr. decided to see if his kid was as good as everybody said. Senior tried to be as inconspicuous as possible, so that his son wouldn't see him, wouldn't know that the father was interested in his fledgling baseball career, and take that as a sign of encouragement.

"Our ballpark was near the bus station," remembers Luis Jr., his eyes brightening at the memory. "The mound faces the station. I saw my father get off the bus, saw him look around, try to blend in with the other passengers, like he wasn't there to watch the game. But what father can 'blend'? You know when your father is watching you. I saw him back in there, trying to hide. But I let him think I *didn't* see him."

From then on, Senior did all he could to help Junior learn more of the art and science of pitching. Father could see that son had the arm, the head, and—most important—the stomach for pitching. The kid literally loved the competition with the batter, just as the old man had.

In the same year, sixteen-year-old Tani was coming to the attention of scouts in the sugar mill town of Central Violeta. In 1959, Tiant tried out for the Havana Sugar Kings, the Cincinnati Reds Triple-A affiliate. The Sugar Kings' scout—whose name is lost to history, although it could not have possibly been the ultra-astute Tony Pacheco, the scout who was the Sugar Kings' "eye of eyes"—told Luis' father: "Señor Tiant, your boy will never make it. He should accept that now, and maybe get a job in the fruit market as a salesman."

Former major leaguer Bobby Avila, who was scouting Cuba for his former team, the Cleveland Indians, came to the rescue. He knew the Tiant family and had contacts in Mexico, having been born and raised and played ball there. He got Luis Jr. a job with the Mexico City Tigers. (If only the Sugar Kings had signed Luis; how close he had come to being a Red!) In 1960, scout Pacheco signed Pérez for the Reds. By this time, Tiant was 17–7 with 107 strikeouts (and a whopping 124 walks) in 180 innings for Mexico City.

Luis returned home to Cuba after the 1959 and 1960 seasons. His father told him to stay in Mexico after the 1961 season because of the Bay of Pigs invasion the previous April, and tensions with the United States were ratcheting up in Havana.

As luck would have it—and luck, as one quickly learns, is something every Cuban major leaguer of the 1960s had to have—Luis Jr.'s baseball contract was purchased after the 1961 season by the Cleveland Indians. They brought him to the States from the Mexican League. By then, 1962, Tani was in Rocky Mount, North Carolina, and Luis was at Charleston, West Virginia. Both received full doses of the segregated mid-South, and neither one, as you can well imagine, liked it.

By 1964, both were in the Pacific Coast League, Tony at San Diego, Luis at Portland. They likely would have squared off at sixty feet, six inches in late May, given the schedule, but Cleveland needed a twenty-three-old pitcher more than Cincinnati needed a twenty-year-old corner infielder. Pérez was headed for Most Valuable Player in the PCL; Luis, after a back-to-back no-hitter and one-hitter in early May, was headed for Cleveland.

While Pérez was getting a taste of Cincinnati in brief July and late-September call-ups (2-for-25), Tiant was tearing it up in Cleveland: 10–4, 127 innings, a 2.83 earned run average with nineteen appearances, sixteen of them starts. Both struggled through 1965 and 1966—Tony as a platoon first baseman, Luis as a break-even starting pitcher—but Tony broke out in 1967 with an All-Star season. Luis wasn't far behind. (His average of 9.2 strikeouts per nine innings led the American League.) And whereas Tony put himself on the national map with his game-winning home run in the 1967 All-Star Game, Luis did the same through the entire summer of 1968: On July 3 in Cleveland, he pitched a shutout and ran his record to 13–5, punching out nineteen Minnesota Twins in ten innings, getting the great Cuban hitter Tony Oliva and Venezuelan César Tovar once apiece. The bravura performance lowered Tiant's ERA to 1.11; his ERA for the season was 1.60, forgotten by history because the Cardinals' Bob Gibson posted one for the ages: 1.12 in the National League. But Tiant's 1.60 was the best in the AL since the Big Train, Walter Johnson, posted 1.49 in 1919.

Tiant's catcher in the July 3 game was fellow Cuban Joe Azcue, part of the Reds initial wave of Cuban signings back in 1956; his Cuban center fielder was José

Cardenal. A week later, Tiant started the 1968 All-Star Game, backed by Cuban Bert Campaneris at shortstop, and Oliva coming off the bench in the seventh inning (he almost tied the game with a rocket off the left-field fence). Pérez couldn't believe how good a hitter Oliva was. Pérez came off the bench that day, too, but not until the ninth inning at third base. He never got to bat because his team won 1–0. (Viewed on a game-by-game basis, Pérez's work in seven All-Star Games is not good—1-for-8 with six strikeouts and a walk—but when one wins one's first All-Star Game with an iconic home run in the 15th inning, everything else is forgotten.)

Yes, by the mid-1960s, Cuban players were a rock-solid presence in America's national pastime. In 1968, Tiant recorded a 21–9 season with a league-leading nine shutouts, four in a row (one shy of the record back to 1904). Tony's early 1970s' Reds teams had more success than Tiant's half-season in Minnesota in 1970 and Tiant's back-to-back twenty-win seasons in Boston in 1973 and 1974, but Luis was keeping himself on the marquee with his flamboyant deliveries and lots of strikeouts.

By 1974, Luis had had his fill of the decade-long, professionally schizophrenic lifestyle of wintering in Mexico City with his wife and three children, and then spending spring and summer by himself in the States during the baseball season. He decided to change all that.

Which is where our story *really* begins.

Luis Tiant Jr.'s first dedicated effort to move—and ultimately relocate—his mother and father from Cuba to the United States began in earnest a month before the start of spring training 1975.

It corroborated something I had first read in Mark Frost's excellent book, *Game Six: Cincinnati, Boston and the 1975 World Series—The Triumph of America's Pastime.*

Luis Jr.'s chosen lifestyle of everything-baseball-for-eight-months, and everything-family-for-the-other-four (and never the twain shall meet), was a mimic of the split lifestyle his famous left-handed father— pitching whiz Luis Tiant Sr.—

led in the 1930s and 1940. Senior wintered in Cuba, then spring-and-summered in the States, where he starred in the Negro Leagues.

Luis Jr. spoke with his parents by telephone in Cuba in the mid-1960s through the early 1970s, but was always concerned that Big Brother might be listening in.

"For the fortunate, light-hearted (younger) Tiant," wrote Frost in *Game Six*, "the likelihood that he would never see his parents again before they died had become a private and consuming sadness. He was haunted by the thought that if he lost them now (1975), he wouldn't even be allowed to attend their funerals."

Oh, did Tani Pérez ever know that feeling.

Heaven and earth would have to be moved to get Luis Sr. and Isabel out of Cuba. Luis Jr. had a judge-friend in Boston with connections to former Massachusetts attorney general Edward Brooke who in 1966 had become the first African-American to be elected to the U.S. Senate. Brooke was a Red Sox fan, so of course he was a Tiant fan, and took great interest in Luis' case. He brought it to the attention of Senate colleague George McGovern, who had been the Democratic nominee for president in 1972.

As serendipity would have it, Fidel Castro finally agreed to meet with McGovern in Cuba in early May 1975. McGovern had been working to repair the broken relationship between the United States and Cuba. Brooke asked McGovern if he could deliver a letter to Castro and speak with him about the Tiants. McGovern, a baseball fan, said sure.

One thing led to another, and by late August 1975—in the midst of a Boston-led pennant race—Luis Jr. and his wife, Maria, drove to Logan Airport with their three children to bring the Luis Sr. and his wife, Isabel, home with them. Luis hadn't seen his father and mother in fifteen years.

Frost: "When (Luis Sr.) stepped off the plane and into the terminal, (his son) put a hand over his eyes and wept...Luis (Jr.) had tried to prepare himself for the moment but to no avail. 'Don't cry, son,' his father whispered softly in Spanish. 'The cameras will see you.'"

Frost: "Luis Senior held out his arms to Maria and his three grandchildren, twelve-year-old Luis, seven-year-old Isabel, and one-year-old Danny, and they all crowded into his arms."

The great Cuban-born pitcher Luis Tiant Sr. (second from the right, 1935 New York Cubans, Negro National League) loved seeing and being present as the teams of his son and country-man Tony Pérez took center stage in the 1975 World Series.

The very thought of it made Tani Pérez tear up. Acutely aware of Luis Jr.'s efforts to reunite with his family, Tani immediately sent Luis a telegram, from the heart. And why did he feel moved to do that? Because he felt genuinely good for his countryman. Tony loved seeing families be reunited.

"My father never see me play—he is still very sick," Tony explained to the *Cincinnati Enquirer's* sports columnist, Tom Callahan.

A little more than a month after Luis received that telegram from Tony, their paths finally crossed on the national stage. But baseball—because of the one-through-nine batting order and the vagaries of circumstance—provides only rarely a stage that a scriptwriter would craft. In real life, the No. 8 hitter is as likely to come up to bat with the game on the line as is the cleanup man.

But behind the scenes and between the ears, other dramas play out. For the Cuban players, it is the stuff of cosmic interfaces, of transcendent imagined contests with mystical overtones, divinely steered alignment of the planets—yet on a micro scale: *mano a mano* battles that are uniquely Cuban because the participants know how narrow the needle's eye through which they have passed. Each Cuban player bears the double helixes of DNA that every family since *La Revolución* has carried in its code: "1961–1962," the years that—if you were Cuban, no matter who you were—everything changed.

Nobody on the Reds and Red Sox teams knew it firsthand except Tiant and Pérez and their families that watched them—the former's parents in the stands in Boston, and the latter's parents back home in Central Violeta working every angle they could to keep up with the action.

And for the Tiants, father and son, there was even more.

Game One. 1975 World Series, Boston.

As Luis Sr. sat in Fenway Park and watched his son mow down the Big Red Machine, he couldn't help but think back to March 1940 when he did the same. Yes, he remembered it vividly.

He remembered that he, too, had faced a Reds catcher who was a future Hall of Famer and a first baseman who might be: Ernie Lombardi and slugger Frank McCormick, respectively, along with reigning National League Most Valuable Player Bucky Walters. How good Walters must have been in 1939 to win the MVP as a *pitcher*, Tiant Sr. remembered thinking when the vaunted Reds came to Havana for that greatly ballyhooed three-game series in March 1940.

Cuban *beisbol* fans couldn't wait. They knew that their own former superstar Cincinnati Reds pitcher Dolf Luque (27–8 in 1923)—and now famed Cuban League manager—had assembled quite a team to take on the Reds, who were favored to return to the World Series in 1940. Frank Grayson, the Reds beat writer for the *Cincinnati Times-Star*, wrote that Luque had "gathered together and put in uniform about two dozen human jackrabbits" for the *Selección cubana*, a Cuban all-star team.

What the Cuban fans didn't know was that Luque, five months shy of his fiftieth birthday, was planning a one-day "comeback." Luque told his thirty-three-year-old left-handed ace, Luis E. Tiant, of the plan: If the Cuban team could win one or both of the first two games, Luque would start the final game of the series and Luis would relieve him and pitch the bulk of the game. Luque hadn't pitched in the majors in five seasons and only dabbled in it the previous few seasons on the island.

These Cuba-U.S. matchups and the Cuban Winter League were the toast of the island, the toast of young José Manuel Pérez in 1940. Later, José Manuel would begin passing the stories of these games on to his sons. For example, José Manuel would proudly tell Tani of Alejandro "Home Run" Crespo, who many said was the greatest Cuban outfielder of them all, maybe even better than the great Dihigo, best known for his pitching prowess. Crespo had smashed a mammoth grand slam off the Reds' Johnny Vander Meer in the first game of the *Selección cubana* vs. Reds series. The Cubans won that game 11–7, beating the remarkable Vandy who just two years earlier had pitched the only back-to-back no-hitters in major league baseball history.

In his formative years in Central Violeta at the knee of José Manuel, Tani would learn what American baseball fans did not likely know: that two generations before Jackie Robinson broke the color line in American baseball, integrated baseball was being played all over Cuba. In the 1930s and 1940s, during the young fatherhood of José Manuel Pérez, Cuban winter ball was a beautiful white, black, brown and mulatto stew of Latino and American players, major leaguers and Negro Leaguers, stars and soon-to-be's. No incidents, no racial epithets, just baseball.

Tani grew up knowing that Luis Sr. had pitched that day in March of 1940 in relief of Luque and had limited the Reds to one run over the final seven innings, the game ending in a 4–4 tie after 10 innings because the Reds ship was leaving for Florida in a couple of hours. The series ended in 1-1-1. Only the great Walters had beaten the Cuban all-stars.

All of this is why—when the subject in the Cincinnati clubhouse in October 1975 got around to just how old Tiant Jr. might actually be—Tani Pérez said, "I don't know, but he was already a legend in Cuba when I was growing up." That brought a laugh. But Pérez was referring to Luis E., the father, not to Luis C., the son. Luis C., the son, aka "El Tiante," allowed Pérez a line-out to deep right field in the second inning of Game One of the 1975 World Series, then struck him out twice and got him to softly fly out to short center.

Meanwhile, Luis Jr. reached base twice in Game One. He had walked in the fifth and singled in the seventh off Don Gullett to start the Bosox winning rally. All this, even though Tiant had batted only one time in the past three years. (Was there anything Tiant couldn't do? Like the old man, El Tiante was not just a pitcher; he was a *ballplayer*.)

After the Bosox victory in Game One, Luis Jr. held an impromptu party at his home for family and friends. Author Frost: "At around two (in the) morning, as the joyful celebration was winding down, Luis (Jr.) came through a door and saw his father looking up at him from a nearby easy chair, the sweetest, proud, sad smile on his face. (Luis Sr.) held out his arms, and Luis sat down beside him, and they held on to each other, without saying a word, both of them crying silently. The dream, passed down from father to son, had come all the way home."

Tani Pérez didn't like being tied in knots by Luis Jr., and he liked even less having lost, but he was proud of his persevering countryman whose story reminded him so much of his own.

The Reds won Game Two in Boston, and Game Three in Cincinnati. Luis Jr. then confounded (again) the Reds in Game Four with a series of head feints, turns and twists in a 5–4 Boston victory. But it took him 163 pitches to finish it off. He earned the complete game. At bat, he had walked in the third inning, and singled and scored in the Sox five-run fourth. Tony also was charged with an error on the ground ball from Juan Beniquez, thereby extending the inning. To make matters worse, Tony was again collared (0-for-4) by Tiant.

"I can't stay back," Doggie Pérez confided to the columnist Callahan. Tiant's quirky, off-speed slants had him all screwed up.

When Tony came up to bat to lead off the second inning of Game Five, he stood at 0-for-14 for the Series. Soon, it was 0-for-15 because Bosox starter

Reggie Cleveland struck him out. It was Pérez's sixth whiff of the Series. But the fans at sold-out Riverfront Stadium in Cincinnati stood behind their struggling slugger.

"It is true," said his wife, Pituka, equally amazed. "They hollered, 'Next time, Doggie.' 'Next time, Tony! Don't worry, baby!' There were over fifty-five thousand people there, and nobody booed!"

Almost none of the fifty-five thousand people were in the concession lines when Pérez came to bat. They prayed; some crossed themselves; those who had rosaries in their pockets clutched them. Morgan, Rose and Bench—*especially* JB—had always marveled that nobody at Riverfront Stadium ever booed the Big Dog. Lord knows, the Big Three had been booed. Even on the road, the fans seldom booed Doggie. It was as though they sensed the thorough decency of the man, felt it outside the dugout, imagined it inside the inner sanctum, the clubhouse.

"If you keep this up," Sparky had told Tony before Game Five, trying to keep the mood light, "you'll set a World Series record." Most at-bats without a hit, said Sparky, telling his sunny-dispositioned first baseman all about Gil Hodges who had gone 0-for-21 in the 1952 World Series. (Actually, it was Dal Maxvill, the St. Louis Cardinals shortstop who held the record for World Series ineptitude, going 0-for-22 in 1968, but nobody paid attention to it; everybody paid attention to the thumpers, in this case, the Brooklyn Dodgers' Hodges and his 0-for-21. Besides, Hodges was a first baseman, so the analogy fit even better.)

In October 1952, Sparky had just begun his senior year at Los Angeles' Dorsey High where he was the school's shortstop. He was drafted by the Dodgers, and was proud of their traditions and knew their history. "Your children can tell their children all about it," Sparky chided the Big Dog. Replied Pérez: "I don't want my children to remember me that way."

Most accounts say that Reggie Cleveland hung a breaking ball in the fourth inning of Game Five to Pérez, but Doggie remembered it eleven years later as a fastball that didn't move much. Either way....

Crack! Tie game, 1–1; Reds and Pérez on the board, ghost of Hodges off it.

Going into the sixth, the Reds were up 2–1. Joe Morgan led off the inning with a walk. After an off-and-on seventeen throws to first base—*seventeen!*—Cleveland re-routed a delivery to Bench, who grounded a Sunday hop to second. But second baseman Denny Doyle had broken to cover second, thinking Morgan was coming. The ball skipped through the vacated "4-hole," a gift single. On-the-move, Morgan easily reached third, and when Boston right fielder Dwight "Dewey" Evans threw wildly to the infield, Bench took second. Two men on, none out, first base open. Red Sox manager Darrell Johnson approached Cleveland on the mound.

Were they discussing walking Pérez? "We were discussing striking him out," Johnson later told the media. Pérez fouled off three pitches, giving Cleveland just enough time to think his way into a slider, believing he could spin it past the Big Dog and put him away. But as soon as the ball left Cleveland's hand, he knew he was in trouble. He had thrown a hanger.

Crack!

The Reds were up by a score of 5–1, going on to win the game 6–2. The Reds were also up three games to two and headed for Boston.

"Tony Pérez was not in a slump," Pete Rose pronounced afterward. "He just didn't get any hits. Big difference. With Doggie, that's a *big* difference."

Famed Reds' Latin America scout George Zuraw of the Big Red Machine era wept when he saw this photo the first time. "Just think if I had some players," Sparky Anderson said.

The bottom of the 12th inning of Game Six awakened the ghosts of Smoky Joe Wood, Harry Hooper, Jimmie Foxx, and Joe Cronin, even Teddy Ballgame himself. Carlton Fisk homered off the left-field foul pole for the 7–6 victory, leaving Sparky shaken. ("It was like being in an axe fight and coming in second," he said.) But none of the players, except maybe the man who gave it up, right-handed rookie Pat Darcy, were anything other than nonplussed.

"You did great out there," the sage of the Reds pitching staff, Cactus Jack Billingham, told Darcy. "Shit happens. Don't let it bother you."

Game Seven. Twelve outs to go. Reds down 3–0…

Much as Sparky tried not to think about it, Game Six kept creeping into his mind. And 1972 crept back into his mind, too, because he had convinced himself that he was responsible for that World Series loss to Oakland. He believed that in 1972 he had cost the Reds their first World Championship since 1940 when he failed to reposition shortstop Davey Concepción late in the Series. Afterward, Reds advance scout Ray Shore threw the scouting report on Sparky's desk. "Why should I even write it if you're not going to read it?" Shore snapped.

Now, here Sparky was, with his team that had never won the big one down 3–0 with twelve outs to go. Sparky worried? You're damned right. He looked like the most harried person in the world, in his usual spot at the home-plate-end of the dugout. Tony was fourth up in the inning and came to the bat rack to get his 35½-inch, 36.6-ounce Hillerich & Bradsby "R43" model, the same style bat the Bambino wielded, albeit lighter in weight. Doggie's was heavily pine-tarred from two inches above the knob right up the H&B label. It was a helluva nice-looking piece of lumber.

"What's wrong with you, Sparky?" asked Pérez in the high-pitched squeal that he uses when he's going to zing a teammate. His zinger-voice goes several octaves above his normal basso profundo.

"Damn, Doggie. We're down three to nothin'!"

"Don't worry 'bout it," the Big Dog said. "Get somebody on base. I'm going to heet one. I'm going to heet a bomb."

The Big Dog noticed right away that Sparky's eyes had come alive. The Reds skipper was back to being himself. It would take one hell of a doubting Thomas to not believe something when Doggie looks you in the eyes with those deep ebonies of his and tells you it's going to happen. Pituka de la Cantera knew. Remember that October day in 1964 in San Juan when they first met and Tani asked her, *Are you the one inquiring about my status?* Tani had her at "Are you…" Now, he had Sparky at "Don't worry…."

The skipper was on his toes now, going up and down the dugout. "Nobody panic, fellas. We got some outs left. Somebody get on base. Morgan or Bench or Doggie's gonna hit one out!"

That somebody to get on base was Rose: He singled to right off Bill Lee to open the sixth inning. Sparky rubbed his hands together in anticipation. Morgan flew out to right. From the on-deck circle, Pérez watched Bench ground one to shortstop in what appeared would be an inning-ending double play. Rick Burleson flipped it to Denny Doyle for the easy one, but Doyle knew Rose was barreling in. *If I can just get rid of it quick enough.* He leaped to avoid Rose, and with that he sailed the throw over Yaz's head at first base and into the Bosox dugout. Bench, now on second base, watched Lee carefully.

"Spaceman," as he was called for his out-there philosophies, started Pérez off with a fastball away, a *sinking* fastball—a "sinker" as it's known in the biz. Bench said to himself, "Please throw him a breaking pitch on the next one." At the plate, Doggie was thinking along those lines, but not exactly.

If you throw me that bloop pitch again, I'll be ready.

Eleven years later, in Tony and Pituka's high-rise condo overlooking the Ohio River and Riverfront Stadium, I entered a deep conversation with Tony about that at-bat. I wanted to know exactly what was in the Big Dog's head.

"Oh, yes," he said, laughing. "The bloop pitch. He (first) threw it to me (in Game Two)."

That is the part that many chroniclers miss. They mistakenly say Pérez learned all that he needed to know from the second-inning bloop pitch in Game Seven.

Definitely not, Pérez told me.

"When he threw it to me (earlier in Series), the ball bounced and I *swung* at it…It was embarrassing. I could see people laughing. But it was fun. Then, in the first time up (in Game Seven), he threw me another one. I took it. I was looking all the way. The umpire called it a strike. I remember that pitch. I said to myself, 'I *know* he's going to throw me that again.' Sure enough, he did. People ask me, 'Were you looking for that pitch?' I say, 'No, but I was ready for it. It was in the back of my mind.' It was the exact same pitch I took in my first at-bat."

Doggie watched as Spaceman came to a slight stop in his windup. That is when Doggie knew. *Here comes the floater…*

It seemed to hang in the air forever. Two teams' fates hung with it. Pérez started to move into the ball, pulled back, double-clutched, timed it.

Oh my god, Yastrzemski said to himself. *Not that pitch. Look at that hip-cock. He's gonna murder this thing.*

The ball rocketed off his bat, going high and deep. Fred Lynn in center and Bernie Carbo in left started toward the fence…then stopped. They knew.

Pérez: "As soon at the bat met the ball, I said to myself, 'We're back in the game.'"

Out in the visitor's bullpen, Will McEnaney said the same thing.

"Before he (swung)," said McEnaney, "I thought, 'I'm not going to get a ring, not going to get a (winning) World Series share.' And when he hit it, I thought, 'My god, what's our ring going to look like? How much money are we going to get?'"

The best way to describe that ball that Pérez synched up perfectly is that it is still going. It went all the way into Reds lore. I believe it to be the single greatest hit in Reds history. Without it, in my opinion, the Reds don't come back to win Game Seven. No World Championship. And with no World Championship, there is no Big Red Machine in the history books; there is a Big Red Machine in name only.

Eduardo, six, Pituka, and Victor, nine (from left), in the Reds' World Championship Parade through downtown Cincinnati. October, 1975.

The Reds were still down on the scoreboard, but only by 3–2. After Pérez's home run, there wasn't a Reds fan worth his or her salt who didn't feel the Reds were going to win this thing. In the seventh inning, Ken Griffey Sr. walked and stole second, Rose singled him in with the tying run. In the ninth, Griffey walked again—the "unsung Red," I've always called him, for his all-around fine play, uncanny knack for being in the middle of the action, and uncomplaining willingness to do whatever it took to help the team win. César Gerónimo bunted him to second, and Morgan drove him in with a soft single to center for the go-ahead run. Reliever McEnaney nailed it down from there, a 1-2-3 ninth, the final out a Yaz can of corn to center field where Gerónimo confidently gathered it in.

World Champions!

"Best feeling in the world," said Pérez.

He wasn't thinking of Luis Tiant's father at that point.

He was thinking of José Manuel.

Para ti, Papá.

For you, Papa. ◆

Pituka and Tony being feted on Tony Pérez Appreciation Day in Cincinnati, September 21, 1986.

CHAPTER 16
The Great Parting

The talk about trading Tony Pérez didn't begin a few weeks before the trade was announced on December 16, 1976. Nor did it begin immediately after the 1976 World Championship, a four-game beatdown of the New York Yankees that cemented the Reds' standing as one of the great teams of all-time, and arguably the greatest National League team ever. (The Reds were the first team since the 1922–1923 New York Giants to repeat as world champions.)

No, the talk didn't begin in 1976 or 1975, nor after the 1974 season, when the Reds won ninety-eight games and finished a disappointing four games behind the first-place Los Angeles Dodgers, against whom the Reds had won only six of their eighteen games. (Each one of those twelve losses twisted Sparky Anderson's stomach into *laugenbrezel*—a German pretzel. The Main Spark, after all, had grown up in Los Angeles and was drafted by the Dodgers out of Dorsey High School.)

No, the talk about trading Tony Pérez actually started *during* the 1974 season—more than two years before the trade itself. The Reds brass was assessing the club for the purposes of where it needed to improve, given that the most recent World Championship recognition in the glass case in the lobby at Riverfront Stadium Way was from 1940.

The consensus among the brass was that they had to get Dan Driessen off third base, because while The Kid could hit (.281/.347/.400), he was well on his way to committing twenty-four errors in only 283 chances at third. One of the things that the Reds—one of the great defensive teams of all-time—couldn't abide in their everyday lineup was any Dr. Strangegloves, no matter how many Gold Gloves the Bench-Morgan-Concepción-Gerónimo up-the-middle defense would win (four: 1974–1977).

And where was the position for Driessen, since the outfield was already stocked? First base, stomping grounds of the Big Dog.

I've never seen the trade-scape for Pérez described better than by Joe Posnanski in *The Machine*, who wrote that "every time the Reds tried to trade Pérez, something fouled up," be it for the young George Brett or Butch Hobson or Sal Bando.

"That left only one trade on the table, and it looked all but certain," wrote Poz, referring to the New York Yankees All-Star third baseman, Graig Nettles. "The trade made too much sense not to happen. The Yankees needed a quiet leader, someone who could help lift the team from a ten-year World Series drought, their longest since World War I. And Nettles would give Sparky that third baseman who could play breathtaking defense and hit long home runs. Back home in Puerto Rico, Doggie imagined himself in pinstripes. But that trade disintegrated, too."

For all of the Big Dog's popularity, most of Cincinnati would have taken Nettles after five straight seasons (1970–1974) of "The Big Red Machine and no World Championships." Most fans in Reds Country weren't any more aware of the Big Dog's value in the potentially high-strung Cincinnati clubhouse than were Sparky and the team's general manager, Bob Howsam, who admitted later they were clueless.

For sure, the Reds could have gotten Nettles after the 1974 season, had Howsam been willing to pull the trigger; the problem was, Howsam still liked Pérez's upside. He hadn't yet notched *his* first of two-straight ninety RBI seasons (1975), and he hadn't yet led the American League in homers (1976).

Toward the end of the final game of that season's Reds-Yankees' World Series, Sparky—miked-up for national TV—had exclaimed famously to his bench coach and longtime mentor, George "Sugar Bear" Scherger, "We're going to be World Champions again, Sugar Bear!" So most fans were fulfilled; they didn't want to tear things up. In the immortal words of the *Post's* Earl

Lawson the day after the Reds swept the Yankees: "If it were up to Reds fans, Pérez...still would be wearing a Cincinnati uniform, even if he had to get to first base in a wheelchair."

And besides, the Reds couldn't have gotten Nettles for Pérez by then, anyway. The Yankees could read "32 HR" and "93 RBIs" and "two years younger" as well anybody. The Reds, meanwhile, projected Nettles' value three years before the Yankees acquired him from Cleveland in 1973. They knew that Nettles' overall 1976 season was as good as anything Pérez ever put up, even 1970 (when Doggie drove in 129 runs and cracked forty home runs).

Yes, for sure, Howsam knew all this, because he had brought new thinking to the Reds as soon as he arrived in 1967. Like his mentor, Branch Rickey, Howsam was a "total player guy," factoring in defense, baserunning, position played, on-base percentage—and here's one of the big ones when it came to evaluating a player's RBI total—*opportunities.*

It was as close to today's WAR—wins above replacement—evaluation as one could get in 1976, and it was thirty years ahead of its time. Howsam evaluated the on-field value of his players and *every other clubs'* players better than anybody else in baseball. It is, in part, how one winds up watching the Big Red Machine. The point: Nettles would have made the Reds better on the field as far back as 1974; by 1976 it wasn't even close. But by 1976, Nettles' baseball-card numbers caught up with what Howsam had projected since 1970, and the Yanks kept their man.

On December 16, 1976, the trade was announced: Tony Pérez and reliever Will McEnaney to Montreal for starting pitcher Woodie Fryman and reliever Dale Murray.

The trade devastated a lot of fans in Cincinnati, but none more so than a Pérez fan normally defined as a player—Johnny Bench. He gave Pérez a huge embrace that day and couldn't even bring himself to go to the microphone at the press conference, knowing that he wouldn't be able to hold himself together. He realized it was highly unlikely the two of them would ever play together again. The trade ended not only the most productive RBI pairing since Willie Mays and Willie McCovey, it ended an incredibly close clubhouse bond of which few were aware. Bench, better than anybody, totally got Pérez's almost extraterrestrial equanimity, his disposition, his balance. The man had an ease of compatibility that was almost unparalleled in Bench's eyes. Pérez never got upset, no matter the setting, social or otherwise. Bench knew *he* didn't have that, and it's part of the reason why he admired Pérez so.

My favorite on-field story about the two of them is the one in which JB—on the last day of the regular season in 1972—took a fast pitch down Broadway on a 3–0 count with two outs and Bobby Tolan on second base and first base open in the first inning, just so Pérez would have an RBI opportunity. And why was that so important? Because Pérez stood at eighty-eight RBIs for the year and wanted to keep his streak alive of consecutive seasons of ninety or more RBIs. Sure enough, Bench walked and Pérez doubled home Tolan for RBI No. 89. In Tony's last at-bat of the regular season, he singled home Tolan in the eighth inning for No. 90.

Yes, the trade of Pérez turned out to be one of the big minuses on Howsam's overall balance sheet. The trouble wasn't that the Reds traded Tony Pérez, though; the trouble was they traded him for Woodie Fryman and Dale Murray. Both were gone by the middle of the 1978 season.

Meanwhile, Old Man River just kept rolling along.

"That he (Pérez) should eventually depart, even in the face of heavy criticism, was inevitable." Earl Lawson of the *Cincinnati Post* wrote that on January 1, 1977. The Earl of Xenia, Ohio, was widely known as a straight shooter, didn't side with the players or the owners, played it right down the middle, and was elected to the writers' wing of the National Baseball Hall of Fame in the summer of 1986. More Lawson: "Tony knew the Reds wanted to make room at first base for Driessen, and Pérez had informed the Reds brass

that he'd rather be traded than remain with the club in a platoon at first base with Driessen."

And Lawson quoted Howsam as saying, "The new reserve system made it almost imperative that we create an opening in the lineup for Driessen."

The "new reserve system" of which Howsam spoke was a reference to the 1976 Collective Bargaining Agreement. In it, every player was eligible to play out his option in 1977 if he chose. So, at best, the Reds would have had Driessen for only the 1977 season, assuming that he had decided to play out his option.

And that was exactly Lawson's conclusion: "Obviously, Driessen was assured Pérez would be traded *or he wouldn't have signed a 1977 contract with the Reds.*" Driessen agreed to a contract after Thanksgiving of 1976 and before the Pérez trade was announced on December 16. Reds scout Ray Shore had initiated contract talks with Driessen during the Puerto Rican winter league that November. Driessen closed the deal over the telephone with Reds executive Dick Wagner, who had assured Driessen that Pérez was as good as gone. Otherwise, no way would Driessen have signed.

It wasn't like it came out of the blue for Pérez. Even during the World Series, Lawson had written that Sparky Anderson said Driessen wouldn't be traded. "It's a question (Sparky) wouldn't answer with a yes or no in the case of Tony Pérez," wrote Lawson, adding that "The fans weren't calling the shots, though. Even Tony's wife, Pituka, knew that." Lawson talked to her, too. "Tony and I love Cincinnati," she said, "but I always keep suitcases packed."

Conventional wisdom has developed that Howsam cost the Reds another world championship or two after he had already designed and built two. But the *facts* say the 1977 Reds wouldn't have won the division, let alone the World Series, even with Tony Pérez-*1970* playing first base—not with *that* pitching staff's ineffectiveness and injuries. Sparky, and even Howsam himself, would later buy into the myth that they had cost the Reds more world titles. The Reds' "Great Eight" starting lineup—actually, mostly the Big Three of Rose, Bench, and Morgan—have perpetuated the myth, selling it everywhere they go.

As the newspaper reporter said in the movie, *The Man Who Shot Liberty Valance*: "This is the West, sir. When the legend becomes fact, print the legend." Well, the legend of 1977 isn't true. Yes, the 1977 Reds would have been a happier and more functional group with Pérez, but they weren't going to reach the postseason in 1977—not even if Lou Gehrig-1927 were the first baseman (though they'd have come close).

If the Reds hadn't traded Pérez, they would have lost Driessen, who was nine years younger than the Big Dog. Driessen and Pérez were basically the same player between the white lines in 1977—.300/.375/.468 vs. .283/.352/.463, respectively. But Driessen would never see any of those numbers again, except for the on-base percentage, whereas the ancient Expo/Red Sox Pérez was right on that slugging percentage for three of the next four seasons. At the time, though, the Reds didn't know how well Pérez would age. Had they kept Pérez, they would have been keeping a player who was about to turn thirty-five, and, despite his genes, was in typical player-decline since his excellent season in 1973.

In 1973, Howsam and his staff ranked Pérez—on the board Howsam kept on a wall behind his desk—as the best first baseman in the National League. In 1975 and 1976, they ranked him third or fourth. The Reds brain trust slotted every NL team's position players and pitchers on a "1" through "14" basis.

"You put a number one to fourteen by each player (and at the end, you add up all the numbers)...If your club had the lowest number you had the best team," said Sparky, explaining the Reds' player-assessment system of the 1970s to author Greg Rhodes (*Big Red Dynasty*). "If somebody else had a lower number, then you started looking at where you could catch up. It's so easy. You stop kidding yourself when you put the numbers down."

The player-assessment board in Howsam's office "had a curtain," the Big Man himself conceded, "and I would close it when somebody came in who I didn't want to see it."

Howsam knew numbers because he was trained by Branch Rickey. By 1947, Rickey was ranking players *not* by batting average—as was everybody else in baseball—but by on-base percentage. (And the Mahatma knew all about "on-base plus slugging percentage (OPS)," too, although he didn't call it that.) He was made aware of this by numbers' analyst Allan Roth, whom he had hired the same year Jackie Robinson broke the color line, 1947.

As Rickey's disciple, Howsam knew that at his peak, Pérez was as productive as any first baseman in the NL. But Howsam figured that Pérez in his thirties was unlikely to remain among the top tier of NL first basemen. Howsam had a young replacement on hand to match or improve upon Tony's performance.

Yes, Howsam was a Rickey disciple through and through. The surprise isn't that Howsam traded Pérez in December 1976; the surprise is he didn't trade him in December 1975. The Rickey disciples always traded productive players in their 30's if they had younger (and cheaper) options. One of the few exceptions was Jackie Robinson, for the obvious reasons: By the time Rickey deigned that America was remotely ready for a black man in organized baseball, Jackie was twenty-seven (his Triple-A Montreal season), and twenty-eight by the time he broke the major-league color line. He was still a highly productive player at thirty-four. By thirty-five, no surprise to Rickey, Robinson had started to slip. When Rickey traded Robinson at thirty-seven, Robinson retired rather than play for the archrival New York Giants.

Put it this way: If Branch Rickey was willing to trade Jackie Robinson, his disciple was surely willing to trade Tony Pérez.

As a player, it is human nature to want things both ways: to want the protections and freedoms guaranteed by the Basic Agreement and the precedent of court decisions backing free agency, but also to want to be protected by the club in one's waning years, despite the younger talent coming up the pipeline. In the end, the Big Dog was nothing but human, and Howsam was nothing but practical: Doggie had to go.

The Great Parting of 1977 triggered—for all Tony Pérez fans—an eight-year Big Dog Odyssey that was largely a black-and-white blur, with occasional color splashed in:

- 1977: The gratifying-from-afar extension of Doggie's consecutive ninety-RBI seasons to eleven (with the familiar ninety-one, this time in Montreal).
- 1980: Following another trade, the (Green) monster rebirth of the now thirty-eight-year-old free agent Big Dog in Fenway Park (twenty-five homers! 105 RBI!).
- 1983: The amazing—but for the fans in 1982 Redsland, with their 101 losses, *envious*—"Wheeze Kids" reunion of Pete-Joe-and-Tony in Philadelphia that took the trio back to the World Series "one last time."

In 1983, I remember thinking, "Hmmm, Tony has 43 RBIs in only 285 plate appearances—that is, one RBI for every 6.6 plate appearances, almost exactly what he averaged in his breakout season at age twenty-five: one RBI for every 6.3 PA. *Why the Big Dog is a forty-one-year-old friggin' freak of nature!* Doggie himself was impressed by 1983. "It was like April 1970—a great start," he told me. He wasn't exaggerating: .369 in April, and for the season .291/.350/.582 in "late-and-close" situations. ("Late-and-close" refers to any plate appearance from the seventh inning on in which the batting team is either in a tie game, ahead by one run or has the potential tying run on deck.)

And one of the best things about Doggie's far-flung adventures? Who he *didn't* play for. He had a chance to play for the Dodgers in April 1982—the Red Sox had arranged a trade for him there if he wanted it—but he turned it down. "They (the Dodgers) kept telling me about that blue-blue stuff," he told me. "They told me they were going to win. They said I'd get a chance to be in another pennant race." (And it really was a helluva pennant race: The Atlanta Braves beat the Dodgers by one game and the Giants by two. That was the year the Giants' Joe Morgan hit a three-run homer in the last game of the regular season to beat the Dodgers and give the Braves the pennant. But Tony was aware he wouldn't have received much playing time behind Ironman Steve Garvey at first base.)

There was so very much about Tony's away-from-Cincinnati years of which Reds fans were unaware because they were so absorbed in following their Reds.

The one I totally missed—and *none* of us would have missed had Pérez stayed in Cincinnati, because it is so heart-wrenching—occurred in Tony's "Canadian stretch" in the late 1970s. I learned of it years later while reading a piece by the *Orlando Sentinel's* Dave Hyde.

Hyde wrote that Tony was preparing for a game in Montreal when the phone call came that his father, José Manuel, had passed. Tony immediately began the paperwork to return to Cuba, even though he knew that the travel plans wouldn't work out for months, if ever.

"So Pérez closed his heart and played that day at first base," Hyde wrote. "It was the best way he knew. The baseball field was the only place to cover the hurt, just as it still is some days."

Tony confided in Hyde that his one regret was that "my father never saw me play as a pro."

Hyde noted that José Manuel had taught his son everything but baseball. Father and son worked side-by-side in the Central Violeta sugar mill, hauling sugar bags and stamping them with the company insignia and loading them for shipment. That backbreaking work reminded young Tani that he wanted to play baseball, and José Manuel was all for it.

"When I played, my family would listen to the radio every night, the Voice of America station out of Washington, because they'd run through how the Cuban players had done in that night's game," Tony recalled. "But see me play? I always regretted that my father didn't."

And then, here it came, again from David Hyde, the best sentence of the thousands I've ever read, written or spoken about Pérez in six seasons watching him play and thirty-plus years covering him:

Regret is the worst feeling. It surpasses sorrow, and includes pain, and worst of all means there are no playbacks possible.

Although Tony has never said the following to me, I believe the "no playbacks possible" is precisely why he wouldn't consent to go to Cuba with his son, Eduardo, and an ESPN film crew, to document his story. (Eduardo was working for ESPN at the time.) And I believe it's the reason Tony wouldn't consent to do this book. For Tony, talking about being deprived of the precious time with his family in Cuba wouldn't bring that time back, nor would it make the story come out any differently. To *not* talk in depth about the regret is Tony's way of giving the regret the respect it deserves. To complain is to whine; to not appreciate what one has. Complaining is wasted energy. So much complaining, so little time. If you're complaining, you aren't doing, and if you aren't doing, you're going backward. Above all else, be thankful. If there is one thing that defines how Tani Pérez was raised, that is it. *Ojo en la pelota, hijo mío.*—"Eye on the ball, my son."

Tony returned home one last time after the baseball season of 1962, before the curtain fell completely, and then—only with special permission—in 1972 when his father was sick. "That was the last time I saw him," Pérez said.

And, finally, this in Hyde's piece: "For years, (Tony) asked his mother or three sisters or two brothers to join his life here. None has. His oldest sister passed away (in 1997). You know the expression 'He gave his life to the game'? It gets thrown around a lot. But Pérez really did…"

In 1984, gloriously, the Big Dog returned to Cincinnati from Boston to finish out his career. ("I saw Willie Stargell and Carl Yastrzemski finish out their careers with their original teams," Pérez told me. "I wished I could do that, but I never thought it would happen.") Simultaneously, Dave Parker was brought back to his hometown to resurrect *his* career. Then, nine months later, Pete Rose returned. With Doggie and Pete and a revitalized Parker in town, baseball suddenly was fun again in Cincinnati.

It was all made possible the previous summer when, after a five-year sabbatical, Big Red Machine architect Bob Howsam returned to his old job and—after a five months' reassessment period—set forth to correct three perceived wrongs, and to right the Reds ship. Here was the order of business:

- In early December 1983 it was announced that Doggie was coming back to town as a pinch-hitter and occasional starter at first base.

- Followed two days later by the free-agent signing of two-time batting champion Parker, the Cobra out of Courter Tech whom the Reds had unwisely failed to draft in June, 1970, when he was ripe for the choosing.
- And, on August 17, the stunning return of Peter Edward Rose. (Two weekends earlier, the Reds had drawn 63,991 for a three-game homestand vs. the Dodgers; with Rose, the gate for the Cubs August 17–19 series skyrocketed to 105,698—a 70 percent increase of fourteen thousand fans per game. The game of August 17 had to be delayed for ten minutes to handle the rush for walk-up ticket sales.)

This made for a wonderful reunion of Pérez and Rose with their old pal Davey Concepción, now the thirty-six-year-old elder statesman, the last vestige of the Big Red Machine and the only one besides Johnny Bench (who retired in 1983) to have never left.

The reunion of Tony and Pete in 1984 with longtime shortstop Davey Concepción, and the infusion of free-agent slugger Dave Parker (not pictured), suddenly made baseball fun again in Cincinnati.

Voilá. Instant Renaissance.

Two weeks after Rose returned to rose petals and hallelujahs from an overnight-revitalized fan base, the pinch-hitting Pérez absolutely crushed an 11th-inning, two-run homer at Riverfront Stadium that had the more seasoned press box wags dusting off and reciting the ol' Dave Bristol bromide that hadn't been heard in town for sixteen years. All together now: "If a game goes long enough, Tony Pérez will find a way to win it." On base was Ron Oester, the second-base homeboy whose hard-nosed style would have meshed beautifully with the Big Red Machine. Inspired to be batting in front of Pérez in the 11th inning, he singled…and then scored on the bomb.

In the ecstatic clubhouse afterward, Oester told Pérez: "You used to do that all the time."

"I've still got some pop," answered Doggie, flashing that big grin of his. "It reminded me of the way I used to hit."

No question, the big Cuban had great genes. When Cuban-born and -raised first baseman/outfielder Bárbaro Garbey (who had come to America in the Mariel Boatlift in 1980) made his April debut for Sparky Anderson's 1984 Detroit Tigers (thus becoming the first player born and trained in Cuba to debut in the majors since Pérez twenty years earlier), the forty-one-year-old Pérez not only was still playing, he had three more full seasons to go.

And then, in 1985, there was this: the forty-three-year-old Doggie and his May birthday arrived again, this time blessed by a full season with Rose as manager: .328, thirty-three RBI in 183 at-bats. That 1985 season was the last of Pérez's resurrection years, following 1977, 1980, and 1983.

It reminded me of something Earl Weaver had said late in that glorious 1975 season when he brought his Baltimore Orioles into Fenway Park several games back and warned the Bosox faithful of how the O's blew by the Red Sox late in the 1974 season: "We've crawled out of more coffins than Bela Lugosi."

So had Bella Le Doggie.

Early May, 1985.

May 13, to be exact, a day before the Doggie's forty-third birthday. The wheels had begun turning early that night at Riverfront Stadium. The sixth inning was setting up propitiously for the big Cuban. It had been raining hard all day and Tony's wife, Pituka, decided not to go to the stadium that night.

By the sixth inning, it was a 3–3 game. Phillies right-handed starter John Denny had loaded the bases to start the bottom half of the inning (Concepción walk, Oester walk, Dave Van Gorder single). Rose forced the hand of Phillies manager John Felske by "announcing" left-handed pinch-hitter Wayne Krenchicki to bat for Reds starter John Stupor.

"I felt the game was going to be won or lost right there," Rose said.

When Felske signaled the bullpen for the left-handed reliever Dave Rucker, Rose had the match he wanted: he announced the right-handed Pérez was going to pinch-hit for the original pinch-hitter; "Chicki" was out of the game.

"When Tani came to bat, I was listening on the radio," Pituka said. "Joe Nuxhall (the Reds radio announcer) made me more hyper than if I was there!"

Joe Morgan, of course, wasn't there, either.

He'd seen it before, though.

"You can see the sparkle in Tony's eyes at moments like that," Morgan once told me about Pérez. "He feels like he has the upper hand on the pitcher there. He knows what he wants to do."

Rose figured the Big Dog might be able to do some damage. Pérez, who hadn't gotten enough at-bats early that season to stay sharp, had approached his old friend only a few days earlier, asking for a few at-bats—whatever his buddy could manage. Skipper Pete obliged, giving Doggie the start on May 12; Doggie reciprocated, smacking two singles, each knocking in a run.

Rucker worked him carefully—too carefully, as it turned out—and the count went to 3-0. "Ruck," knowing the kennel was full, pumped two strikes past Doggie. He tried to put him away, but the Big Dog fouled off two pitches. Reckoning time.

Crack!

Going, going, gone, over the left-field wall!

Pituka glanced instinctively out the window "to see the fireworks." She could only imagine the ovation. She imagined rightly.

"It was something," the Big Dog said. "The people really liked it."

Two months later, then *Enquirer* Reds beat man Greg Hoard found a fortuitous confluence: Tony Pérez on the Fourth of July weekend in Philadelphia, home of the Liberty Bell, site of the writing of the Declaration of Independence, scene of the famous answer to the question of what form of government have you given us, Doctor Franklin? ("A republic...if you can keep it.")

The circumstances were very good. The day before the Reds arrived in Philly, they had beaten the Dodgers in ten innings in Cincinnati when Pérez—pinch-hitting for first baseman Pete Rose—slammed a two-run double to right-center for the walk-off victory, scoring Oester and Kal Daniels. There it was again, that distinctive Pérez trademark that first distinguished the 138-pound Tani to scouts thirty years earlier in Cuba—the remarkable power the opposite way.

In a pregame interview, Pérez revealed a side of himself he hadn't often shown publicly. He decried the loss of freedoms in Cuba. (As a historical backdrop, only seven weeks earlier, the Cuban government had banned farmers' markets on the island. Castro had a marked distaste for anything that smacked of a market-based economy.)

The premise of the *Enquirer* article was made clear in the opening: *To Tony Pérez, the Fourth means something more than a day of fireworks and a backyard barbecue...*

The article featured an abundance of quotes from the forty-three-year-old warhorse who—clearly—was looking back at the Cuban way of life that he had escaped.

Pérez: "People here (the United States) don't know how good they have it. They really don't. It's pretty good here...Before (1961 in Cuba), you could do everything just like here. But afterward, no. When he (Castro) took over, everybody celebrated because they thought it was good. It wasn't good...It really didn't get bad until 1961, '62 and '63. Then it was bad."

Pérez talked of the flights from Cuba to America being stopped; "I would have to fly to Mexico and come from there (to spring training)."

In a land where Pérez, his wife, Pituka, and sons, Victor and Eduardo, are free to walk in any store at any time and buy anything they choose, he knows well that there are lands and people who do not have that privilege.

Pérez went on to describe the Cuba of the 1960s that was eerily similar to the Cuba I experienced fifty-five years later.

Pérez: "You cannot buy anything until it is your turn, your day, and then sometimes there is nothing to buy. You are given a book(let) and you stand in line…You don't see meat there; maybe chicken, fish and rice. But there is not much meat, maybe sometimes…The government owns everything. You may live in a house, but you don't own it. They can come in any time and tell you to get out, in the middle of the night. They can do that if they want to and you have to get out."

So, in his own way, Pérez will celebrate the Fourth of July. He knows what it is about, maybe better than most of us.

"I celebrate the Fourth of July—it is an American holiday," said Pérez.

Then, he added the words that would forever resonate. It was the Pérez Manifesto, and it would summarize his quarter century in the United States of America.

"This is my country, you know."

In a poetic (and historic) first-week unveiling in 1986, Cincinnati native Barry Larkin made his major-league debut on August 13 in front of three of his boyhood Big Red Machine heroes—Rose, Concepión, and Pérez. As a boy growing up in Silverton, Ohio, a suburb of Cincinnati, Larkin slid headfirst like Rose and played shortstop like Davey Concepción, but as a young man, he wanted to be like Tony Pérez: easygoing (even though, by nature, the driven Larkin was anything but) and yet dignified and respected, somebody who could grow into a leader. Larkin's first week was positively spooky in the way it intertwined with the final days of Rose and Pérez.

CHAPTER 16

- On August 14, Larkin witnessed Rose's final major-league hit (No. 4,256) as part of Rose's 3-for-4 day (one RBI).
- The day after that, August 15, Larkin, in his first major-league start, notched his first big-league hit (a first-inning, leadoff single to right field off Dave Dravecky), but was out-homered and out-RBI'ed by Pérez, who got the start that game at first base, and hit a two-run homer that knocked in Kurt Stillwell.
- Two days later, August 17, Larkin hit his own (first) major-league home run, a solo shot in the sixth off LaMarr Hoyt. Two innings later, Larkin watched Rose's last major-league at-bat, a mismatch of a punchout against the power-armed Goose Gossage.

Seven weeks later, on the next-to-last day of the season, both Larkin and Doggie were in the starting lineup, and each collected two hits. But one of Pérez's was especially historic, the 379th and final home run of his career, a third-inning solo shot off the San Diego Padres' Ed Whitson that tied Orlando Cepeda for the most major league home runs by a Latino.

The historic home run happened as Pérez would have scripted it, had he the opportunity: as part of a thunder-and-lightning inning that can and really did rattle the opposing pitcher. Dave Parker had led off the inning with a solo homer to tie things up at 4–4; then, two batters later, Pérez tied the Baby Bull, aka "Cha Cha," with No. 379, putting the Reds up 5–4.

"I know what it (the Latino home-run record) meant to him," said Pete Rose, the Reds skipper. "I told Dave Parker, 'Look at that smile.' You're not going to see Tony run around the bases too often with a smile like that."

And you know what the Big Dog loved more than anything? The Reds went on to win the game 10–7.

Two weeks earlier, Cepeda had played in an old-timer's game at Riverfront Stadium and stayed over an extra day to honor his buddy on Tony Pérez Day. They are best of friends, and played side-by-side many winters in the Puerto Rican League.

Pérez remembered a humorous exchange that weekend with the Baby Bull.

"He said, 'Please, just *tie* me,'" recalled Pérez, grinning.

Appropriately, Tony never did hit No. 380. The next day, in the Big Dog's first at-bat in the final game of his magnificent big-league career, he was greeted by a standing ovation. Doggie tipped his cap and pointed to the sky, signaling the fans to look heavenward for a love letter from Tony, Pituka, Victor and Eduardo.

It came right on cue...a plane flying above Riverfront Stadium, pulling a streamer bearing a message in large red letters:

Muchas gracias—Love, Tony. ◆

Tony and Johnny Bench at the 2000 Induction Ceremony in Cooperstown.

CHAPTER 17
The King at His Coronation

Cooperstown—If you are a baseball fan or player, Cooperstown (population 1,834) is the capital city where all roads lead, even though those roads get really crowded in the summertime. Cooperstown attracts three hundred thousand pilgrims a year, anywhere from twenty thousand to eighty thousand of them for one Sunday afternoon in late July. Central Violeta (where Tani Pérez grew up), and the National Baseball Hall of Fame (where Tony Pérez was headed) are 1,447 miles apart, although if one had told Tani that fact when he was growing up in Camagüey Province, he'd have pointed to the thousands of stars in the sky and said *Cúal?*—"Which one?"

Teenager Tani knew all about Martin Dihigo Sr. but couldn't have told you a thing about Cooperstown. Twenty-year-old Tani couldn't have found Cooperstown on a map even if you had spotted him Albany, Syracuse, and Leatherstocking Country. Although he spent his first two professional seasons in Geneva, New York, only 140 miles away, Cooperstown just never came up. Tani never heard of John Fenimore Cooper, the town's namesake and author of *The Leatherstocking Tales*, the collection of five novels that includes *The Deerslayer* and *The Last of the Mohicans*; never heard of "leatherstockings," a term for the leggings that were often worn by native Americans in this neck of the woods to protect them from briers and brush; never heard of Natty Bumppo, the original pathfinder.

In 1960, there were no Cubans in the National Baseball Hall of Fame. By the time Martín Dihigo became the first one—though he never played in our major leagues, barred as he was by the color line—Pérez had secured both of his World

Championship rings, logged all seven of his All-Star Game appearances, and bagged most of his 1,652 runs batted in. He wasn't even in *Cincinnati* anymore; he was in Montreal playing in his fourteenth major-league season.

The first time Pérez likely would have even heard the word "Cooperstown" was in Cincinnati in 1964, and then only if somebody had equated it with future Hall of Famer Frank Robinson. Tony would have understood it then—he considered Robinson a mentor—and yet, in another way, he wouldn't have understood it at all. Seeing Willie Mays and Henry Aaron and Roberto Clemente up close would have helped; and facing Sandy Koufax at twenty paces would have brought the concept of Higher Ground into sharper focus, no question.

But could he have dreamed back then of making it to Cooperstown himself? No way. Would it have registered with him as a possibility in the Big Red Machine Years of 1975 and 1976, when there were keen baseball observers who wondered openly whether the Reds entire infield might one day be headed for baseball's Valhalla? Absolutely.

The catcher (Johnny Bench), second baseman (Joe Morgan), and third baseman (Pete Rose, in the days before the baseball gambling rumors began to arise), were all regarded as locks. Pérez, the first baseman, wasn't far behind, and his protégé, the shortstop Dave Concepción, was only twenty-seven, so it wasn't all that difficult to imagine him going the way of Pee Wee Reese from the great Brooklyn Dodgers teams and being Cooperstown-bound, too.

Back in December, 1991, I talked with Tony for a story on his first year on the Hall of Fame ballot (and did the same thing for almost every one of the next eight until he got in). He said all the right things, but it wasn't until his Orientation Day in Cooperstown in May 2000—two months before the Induction Ceremony—that I literally saw in his eyes what the Hall of Fame meant to him. He had just entered "The Gallery," the arched ceiling with the indirect lighting that gives a golden cast to the bronzes of the two hundred-some baseball immortals. It is the most sacred spot in an American sport, because it honors the greatest of the greats of the national pastime.

Tony had first seen the plaques in 1967 when his Reds had come to town to play the Baltimore Orioles in the then-annual Hall of Fame exhibition game. But back then, he was just a kid in search of his first good season. By Orientation Day in May 2000, he was "in the club," though not yet committed to public bronze. Tony saw the plaques in a totally different light then. He knew *his* plaque would soon be among them. He shook his head, bowed it for a few seconds, raised it. *In saecula saeculorum*—Latin for "Unto the Ages of Ages." His eyes were glistening. He touched his left arm with his right hand.

"I get goosebumps," he said.

From the time Tony and his wife, Pituka, snacked on coffee and Danish at eight-thirty in the morning with the Hall of Fame staff, to the wrapup at 5:30 in the evening, Orientation Day proved to be a free-spirited, genuinely mystical, nine-hour dip into an amazing fifty-eight-year odyssey from Cuba to Cooperstown:

- Tony, seeing a huge wall-hanging photograph of fellow Cuban Sandy Amorós' great catch against the left-field fence in Yankee Stadium in Game Seven of the 1955 World Series: "I can still see it. I was watching the game on TV with my dad. I was thirteen years old, and I was a Dodgers fan. My father loved the Dodgers."
- Tony, watching a nine-minute video of his career, flashing a big grin when he saw himself in 1968 make a diving stab of a no-man's land popup as a *third* baseman—"See, I wasn't so bad at third as they say," said Tony, nudging Pituka with his elbow.
- The pleasantly surprised pilgrims on their self-guided tours, who themselves couldn't stop smiling at the unexpected bonus of stumbling upon such a down-to-earth, engaging, thankful Hall-of-Famer serendipitously materializing out-of-nowhere.

Tony knew it would be emotional for him that coming July in 2000. His mother, Tita, had shown him just how emotional when he had called her in Central Violeta, only moments after he had received the January 2000 phone call at his winter home in Puerto Rico heralding the news that he had been elected to the Hall. All those years of waiting, through all those disappointments, Tita had stood strong. Eight humbling Januarys in a row, she had told her son, "I know it's going to happen." This time, for the first time, she actually had a premonition it would. But when Tani called with the good news, it was *her* head that bowed, the tears coming instantly.

"I got emotional (then), too," Tony said. No doubt because they were thinking of José Manuel. "The greatest man I ever knew," Tani once said of his father. "All he did was work, work, work, for me and my brothers and sisters. There's an emptiness inside me a little (that he didn't live to see this). It hurts…My dad… my dad loved baseball so much."

But maybe José Manuel knew. How can we say he didn't? Maybe he was walking with Tani all along. Maybe he was walking with him now, head held high, just like on that walk they took in '72 back home in Central Violeta.

What was it the letters from José Manuel had begun saying to Tony in Macon, Georgia, way back in 1963? "Stay in the U.S. Succeed in the way we dreamed and make a good life in baseball."

Hadn't Tony exceeded that?

Well, hadn't he?

John Fay, the *Enquirer*'s then-Reds beat man, alluded to it in an article a week out from the Hall of Fame induction ceremony.

"It was hard," Pérez was quoted. "You miss your country, your mother, your father, your family. I wasn't with my father when he died, or my older sister. It was very difficult."

Fay wrote that even Pérez's son, Eduardo "didn't know the price his father had paid when he left Cuba and his life there behind."

"I didn't realize it until I went to Cuba in January of 1993, then again (in 1999)," Eduardo said. "It gave me an appreciation for what he'd gone through. Latin families are very close. It's unheard of to leave the town he came from. It had to be very traumatic."

Tony Pérez is the first (and as of 2017 only) Cuban-born major leaguer to be elected to the Hall of Fame. (Martín Dihigo played in the American Negro

Leagues.) He was also one of the last players to get out freely. If he had been born in 1945—instead of 1942—his life would have been different.

"The guys two or three years behind me didn't make it out," Pérez said. "I don't know what would have happened to me."

I believe I can tell you what Cooperstown means to Tony Pérez. I *know* what it means to me, having visited Cooperstown on at least fifteen occasions since my first time there in 1963. (I grew up in Syracuse, New York, only a two-hour drive away.) I saw my first major-league game in Cooperstown (Red Sox vs. Milwaukee Braves), ran the bases at Doubleday Field (back in the days before city fathers shut down Abner's place like it was an anti-Fidel rally in Havana), toured the museum and collected my first of four, six-inch high, plastic player-busts (no longer made). I have attended five induction ceremonies: Bench (1989), Morgan (1990), Pérez (2000), Barry Larkin (2012), and Ken Griffey Jr. (2016). I feel more at home in Cooperstown than in any baseball stadium I've ever been in, as a fan or writer. The best thing I can say about the place is from the heart: If baseball wasn't invented in Cooperstown, it should have been.

There may not be another hamlet, village or town (population: one thousand to twenty thousand) in America as recognizable as Cooperstown (without the need of a state designation). I can think of only a few possibilities.

Gettysburg (7,655) is unparalleled for gravitas, Arlington unsurpassed in solemnity, although the latter of the two is more place than town. Punxsutawney (5,934) has both the Americana of Cooperstown and the annual national genuflection from TV. But it lacks the transcendence. Woodstock (5,884) has its backers, and yes, it pulled in four hundred thousand in 1969. But it's not like it does it every year, and besides, the music festival was not even in Woodstock, it was on Max Yasgur's dairy farm in Bethel (4,255), New York, sixty miles away.

I don't think any burg combines the qualities of Cooperstown, all of which make it unique: "hallowed ground, walkable, socio-cultural transcendence." Quite simply, there is no place like it in America.

And there's one other thing of which I'm even more sure:

Besides Tony, Pituka, Victor and Eduardo Pérez, I am the only person on the planet who can tell you that Cooperstown, New York, is just as hard to find as Central Violeta, Cuba.

But *reaching* Cooperstown from Central Violeta?

Only one person on Earth can tell you about *that*.

"Sparky, on the day you're enshrined in Cooperstown, you'll see the returning Hall of Famers and you'll know who they are and what they've done. The fear of God does not hold back at that moment."

—Al Kaline to George Lee Anderson

A then-record forty-eight living members (alphabetical order: Anderson, Sparky, to Yount, Robin) of the two hundred and twenty-eight in the National Hall of Fame—ten more than the thirty-eight returnees achieved twice before—were on hand for the induction ceremony of July 23, 2000. Tony had played with or against, been managed by or against, twenty-nine of them.

In the movies, the following scene captured the essence of it. (It wasn't said about Induction Day, but it surely could have been.):

"Ray, people will come, Ray...They'll come (for) reasons they can't even fathom...They'll walk out to the bleachers; sit in shirtsleeves on a perfect afternoon. They'll find they have reserved seats somewhere along one of the baselines, where they sat when they were children and cheered their heroes...Baseball has marked the time. This field, this game: it's a part of our past, Ray. It reminds of us of all that once was good and it could be again...People will come, Ray. People will most definitely come."

—James Earl Jones in "Field of Dreams"

On July 23, 2000, the people came all right: twenty-five thousand of them. Among them, on the dais, behind that day's speakers: Bench and Morgan from the Big Red Machine. Brett and Yount from Tony's three years in the American League. Brock and Gibson from the big coming-of-age brawl in St. Louis in 1967; "sweet-swinging" Billy Williams, who for me was "the left-handed Tony Pérez," the closest to the Big Dog in temperament as any player I'd ever come across; "Yaz" from the 1975 World Series and Tony's Boston years. His Latino *simpaticos*, Cepeda and Marichal, were on hand, too. (Oh how Tony wished Roberto Clemente could have been there.) The super-tough pitchers, Bunning, Carlton, and Jenkins…"Brooksie," the incomparable Brooks Robinson and the still underwear-ad handsome Jim Palmer, Pérez adversaries in the 1970 World Series (and Palmer again in the 1983 Series). And, speaking of '83, his Phillies teammate, the incomparable "Schmidty"…and "Rollie" from the 1972 World Series. The managers Lasorda and Schoendienst. Players he respected to the utmost because they were such gamers: Eddie Mathews, Phil Niekro, Sutton, and the one-only Gaylord…the amazing "Tom Terrific," practically in a class of his own.

And, speaking of which, the three guys one doesn't even think about measuring oneself against when one is coming up, because anybody of any humility whatsoever knows instinctively the ego cannot withstand such comparison: Koufax and Mays, and yes, even though he was his teammate for a season, Frank Robinson. (Henry Aaron wasn't there this day.)

As almost everybody can tell you who has attended Induction Sunday, it isn't the electees who get you, it's those already enshrined, those who return, who get you. It is baseball's cornfield moment to be sure, when the immortals come down from the walls and the plaques come to life.

That's a lot of life flashing before anybody's eyes. But if you're a new inductee, it's beyond humbling.

Joe Morgan said it best during his enshrinement in 1990. "Now that my induction is complete," he said, "I feel like I belong here. But no matter how long I'm in the Hall of Fame, I'm always going to have problems trying to say 'Mays, Musial, and Morgan' in the same breath."

It was one of my all-time favorite baseball talks. Joe spoke of a youth living against type as a 5-foot-6, 145-pound fireplug from Oakland, the same town that gave baseball that giant of a man, Willie Stargell.

I loved what Jim Palmer said into the same microphone as Little Joe.

The Orioles great traced his success to October 15, 1945.

"I was adopted at birth," he said. "You wonder about the spiritual part of you. How does this happen that you have parents that want you, that love you, and were always there for you?"

Induction Day is a day of incredible emotion and introspection.

I remembered what Jerome Holtzman had said into that same microphone as well, as he was being inducted into the writers' wing of the Hall. He spoke of his daughter, whom he had buried the previous February. He said he had taken her to seven or eight baseball games a year, and taught her how to keep score. He was at her bedside not long before.

"She knew she was dying and said, 'I won't be in Cooperstown with you.' She's in my thoughts today," Holtzman said.

What a day of speeches that was in 1990. I wondered if Tony, Sparky, Carlton Fisk, and Marty Brennaman, who was being inducted into the broadcasters' wing of the Hall, could match it.

"All of baseball history is a river that never stops. Guys who have only one at-bat or throw only one pitch step into that river and have a part of it."
—Roger Angell, quoted in *Pete Rose: 4,192*

From the time of Tony Pérez's very first National Baseball Hall of Fame ballot in December 1991, he knew the lay of the land. I speak not of the "foothills of the Adirondacks," as the sign reads outside Cooperstown. I speak of the Big Dog's territory: Clutch Town, U.S.A.

"If people don't remember me for coming through in the clutch, the big hit to win or tie the game, I'm in trouble," said Pérez in December, 1991, on the eve of his first ballot.

His career total of 1,652 RBIs was thirteenth all-time, as of the time of that first ballot. The twelve all-time career RBIs leaders at the time of Pérez's first ballot were:

Henry Aaron 2,297

Babe Ruth 2,204

Lou Gehrig 1,990

Ty Cobb 1,960

Stan Musial 1,951

Jimmie Foxx 1,921

Willie Mays 1,903

Mel Ott 1,860

Carl Yastrzemski 1,844

Ted Williams 1,839

Al Simmons 1,827

Frank Robinson 1,812

(Tony Pérez ....1,652)

In his first year on the ballot, Doggie shared a spot with fellow first-timer Tom Seaver, whose final season as a player was also 1986. Pete Rose should have been on that ballot, too. A player goes on the ballot five years after he retires. If he's a megastar, iconic, he gets elected and is enshrined the following summer. I call it the 5+1 rule. Seaver is a perfect example—Final Year as a Player: 1986; First Ballot: December 1991; Enshrined Summer, 1992.

Rose's last year as a player was also 1986. After his gambling problems came to light in 1989, his name was in essence legislated off the ballot. Had Rose not had his gambling problems, the combined voting total of Seaver and Rose assuredly would've been the largest combined voting percentage for a duo to that point, and possibly for all-time. There are those who think Rose might have been unanimous, a hundred percenter, something nobody's ever done. Seaver received 98.84 percent.

Pérez knew that his hoped-for elevation into the Hall was staked on the voters' perception of whether he really was the man who delivered under the pressure of tight games at crunch time—"late-and-close," being the term of art used by the numbers' analysts.

Pérez's lifetime batting average was .279, but only in preparing for doing this book did I learn that he hit twenty-one points higher—.300—in what are referred to as "late-and-close" situations. (For the definition of "late-and-close," please see charts below). I asked the nonpareil objective numbers' analyst Greg Gajus, with whom I've worked closely over the years, to break down (in a similar way) Pérez's contemporaries in the National Baseball Hall of Fame, and the other seven players in the Great Eight of the Big Red Machine. I asked him to use whatever measuring tools he wanted in pursuit of baseball truth.

The Index for Late & Close and RISP (Runners in Scoring Position) represent how a hitter's OPS (On Base + Slugging) in those splits compared to his overall performance. A number greater than 100 indicates a batter performed better in a split than he did overall, a number less than 100 indicates he performed worse in that split than he did overall. Tony Pérez's 114 Index in Late & Close appearances would read as follows: "Tony Pérez's Late & Close OPS was 14% higher than his career OPS." Source: Baseball-Reference.com

OPS: The sum of On-Base and Slugging Percentage, which provides a better indicator of a hitters performance than batting average alone. OPS+ converts OPS to an index where 100 equals league average. This equalizes performance across different run environments and ballparks.

BRS%: Percentage of all baserunners who scored on the batter's play, including instances where an RBI is not awarded, such as on an error.

RISP: A runner on second or third base is considered to be in scoring position because he could presumably score on a single.

Late and Close: Any plate appearance from the 7th inning on in which the batting team is either in a tie game, ahead by one run or has the potential tying run on deck.

Tony Perez Clutch Stats Rankers (vs. Contemporary Hall of Famers)

Player Name	Career BRS	League Average	Player Name	OPS Index Late & Close	Career OPS+
Tony Perez	18%	14%	Roberto Clemente	121	130
Willie Stargell	18%	14%	Tony Perez	114	122
Hank Aaron	18%	14%	Hank Aaron	113	155
George Brett	18%	14%	Billy Williams	111	133
Roberto Clemente	18%	14%	Willie Stargell	109	147
Orlando Cepeda	18%	14%	Ron Santo	107	125
Mike Schmidt	17%	14%	Eddie Murray	107	129
Johnny Bench	17%	14%	Willie McCovey	105	147
Jim Rice	17%	15%	Harmon Killebrew	105	143
Willie McCovey	17%	14%	Johnny Bench	104	126
Dave Winfield	17%	15%	George Brett	103	135
Billy Williams	17%	14%	Willie Mays	102	156
Harmon Killebrew	17%	14%	Brooks Robinson	100	104
Eddie Murray	17%	15%	Frank Robinson	99	154
Frank Robinson	17%	14%	Carl Yastrzemski	97	130
Andre Dawson	17%	15%	Mike Schmidt	97	147
Robin Yount	17%	15%	Carlton Fisk	96	117
Willie Mays	17%	14%	Lou Brock	96	109
Al Kaline	17%	14%	Joe Morgan	94	132
Ernie Banks	17%	14%	Gary Carter	94	115
Reggie Jackson	16%	14%	Andre Dawson	93	119
Carl Yastrzemski	16%	14%	Al Kaline	93	134
Ron Santo	16%	14%	Robin Yount	92	115
Rod Carew	16%	14%	Reggie Jackson	91	139
Gary Carter	16%	14%	Rod Carew	91	131
Brooks Robinson	15%	14%	Dave Winfield	90	130
Carlton Fisk	15%	14%	Jim Rice	86	128
Lou Brock	15%	14%	Orlando Cepeda	86	133
Joe Morgan	14%	14%	Ernie Banks	81	122

Hall of Famers with 600+ RBI, 1964–1986. Source: Baseball-Reference.com

Big Red Machine Great 8, Career Averages

OPS, BRS%, Late & Close Index, RISP Index
(Index compares performance in Late and Close and RISP vs. performance for all plate appearances)
Ranked by Late & Close Index

Player Name	Career OPS	Career BRS%	Index Late & Close	Index RISP
Tony Perez	804	18%	114	108
Dave Concepcion	679	15%	113	105
Johnny Bench	817	17%	104	105
Pete Rose	784	16%	99	115
Ken Griffey	790	15%	98	100
Cesar Geronimo	693	13%	97	114
Joe Morgan	819	14%	94	96
George Foster	818	17%	87	106

Gajus: "For Pérez's career in late-and-close situations, he outperformed his overall offensive performance by 14 percent—higher than every contemporary Hall of Famer except for Roberto Clemente. These accounted for 17 percent of his career plate appearances. He scored 18 percent of the runners that were on base in all his plate appearances, a total that matches contemporaries Clemente, Willie Stargell, Hank Aaron, George Brett, and Orlando Cepeda. The league average during that era was 14 percent..."

This was the first-ever deep-drill into the Big Dog's clutch mystique. Until guru Gajus' dissection, Pérez's legendary prowess in the clutch had been talk—good talk, but all talk, nonetheless. Dave Bristol: "If the game goes long enough, Tony Pérez will find a way to win it." Joe Morgan: "I want to be up there with the game on the line, but if you put it to a vote, everybody—including me—would vote for Tony." Willie Stargell: "There's nobody better in the clutch."

There is chapter and verse now: Check out the charts. Had Gajus been able to produce these charts back in 1991, I believe the Big Dog would have reached the promised land sooner than he did. Gajus: "Regardless of whether clutch hitting is a skill or not, the evidence suggests Pérez performed well in clutch situations. He was not a better hitter than most of his contemporary Hall of Famers, but he certainly was a notable clutch hitter."

Gajus told me he'd still rather have Willie Mays at the plate than Pérez in those late-and-close situations, even if Mays didn't stand out as much as Pérez did from his/their overall performances. "(Mays) was a better hitter overall," Gajus reasoned. And I couldn't disagree. But look at the charts, and know this: Tony Pérez will *always* be humbled to see himself up there with one of his idols, The Great One, Clemente.

There are some caveats, of course. Gajus said there is some disagreement in the sabermetric community on whether driving in runs in clutch situations is a skill distinct from hitting ability. One would expect a true skill to track fairly consistently year-to-year, he said. But for most players, their performances in clutch situations such as late-and-close varies considerably by the year, and this is also true for Pérez.

Gajus cited this example: in 1970, Pérez hit .307 in late-and-close; in 1971, he hit only .210 in the same situations; in 1974 he was a monster in clutch situations (.349/.427/.614); in 1975, he hit .265/.371/.470 in those same spots. "If you believe that clutch hitting is a skill distinct from hitting ability," Gajus said, "it's hard to explain a drop like that..."

My only response is to repeat what the great Ted Williams said about bloop hits: "They average out over a career, not a year." I, like Teddy Ballgame, believe that you are what your career numbers say you are.

And there we shall rest the case.

"I doubt that a king at his coronation could feel better than me today."
—Tony Pérez

The Big Dog had them from the get-go.

"Good afternoon; hi, everybody...What a feeling!" he exclaimed, beaming as he surveyed the big crowd splayed about the grassy half-acre at the Clark Sports Center in Cooperstown. "Many thanks to my friends in Boston, Montreal, Philadelphia, everywhere, and especially in Cincinnati, a city that embraced me (and) refused to boo me any time, who at my worst times supported and loved me all the time. The feeling of love and respect is mutual, and I really mean it."

He spoke of having "three flags in my heart—one for the United States, where the best baseball is played; one for the country that adopted me, Canada, and one for the country where I was born, Cuba."

There were flags of all three countries in the sun-bathed crowd. One particularly large one, tended to by three middle-aged men and draped across a fence in the middle of the infield, is the one I noticed above the others. It was the Cuban national flag: a red equilateral triangle at the hoist, with a white, five-pointed star and blue and white alternating stripes.

On such a beautiful, warm, and invigorating day, Tony could not resist recalling the initial meteorological shock of Geneva, New York, to a young Cuban in late April of 1960: "I'd (just been) to my first spring training in Tampa, despite my mother's pleading (with me not to go) because of her love. When the season started in Geneva, the cold was so intense, I could feel it in my bones. My mother, how I missed her, the heat of my country, and the love from my family."

He spoke deeply and warmly of his siblings and "my father-in-law, Pablo de la Cantera who is watching from Puerto Rico." Tony did not discuss the political situation in Cuba. He didn't need to.

"I was born and raised in a small sugar mill (town) in Camagüey, Cuba," he continued, "where my father loved baseball, always supported me and taught me to respect and love the game...When the late (Havana Sugar Kings scout) Tony Pacheco—and his car full of Cuban sugar cane—signed me at sixteen, my father supported me...I came from a poor, hardworking family, but rich in love and respect.

It was old home week at the 2000 Induction Ceremony in Cooperstown. Sparky Anderson and Tony, with Jim Palmer in the background.

Tony, Carlton Fisk, and Sparky Anderson.

Eduardo, Victor, and Pituka, during Tony's acceptance speech at the 2000 Induction Ceremony in Cooperstown.

"My father had a tremendous admiration for Minnie Miñoso," said Tony, giving the "n" in the Cuban star's last name the hard, sharp, biting "n" of the single-syllable "nyet" in the Russian tongue. "And one day I told my mother, 'Tita, I'm going to be like (Minnie).' She said, 'Son, I wish you luck. It isn't going to be easy.' Well, it wasn't easy, Tita, but here I am!" said Tony, flashing that wonderful smile that fans came to know so well. No matter how old grows the Big Dog, one hopes, he will never lose that smile.

He talked of his visit home to Cuba in 1972 after a ten-year absence to visit his ailing father.

Think of it…Can you imagine the pride of José Manuel when the strapping thirty-year-old Tani—all filled-out with fifty pounds of muscle—stepped off the train that day, the very incarnation of the ballplayers such as the 6-foot-2, 190-pound Martín Dihigo, of whom they had talked when Tani was growing up? And, more important, consider what a success Tani was: He had made the "fine career of baseball" in America that José Manuel had encouraged; Tani was a devoted husband and father of two.

This was the Tani—the Tani who had averaged twenty-eight homers and 105 RBIs the previous six seasons, the Tani who had been to two World Series, the Tani who had played in four All-Star Games—who Tita watched get off the train that day.

"I saw my mother," reminisced Tony to the large crowd that reached as far back as the shade of the evergreen-tree line, as distant as the upper left-field red deck at Riverfront Stadium. "And I say, 'Tita, I told you'…Her eyes go with happiness."

The crowd ate it up. Tony thanked his seven big-league managers, mentioning only his first, Dave Bristol, and longest and most accomplished, Sparky: "My dear Sparky, I think they made me wait so long so that we could be inducted together."

Tony then departed his prepared remarks for fifteen seconds, before acknowledging an oh-so-worthy former adversary and teammate. "Somebody mentioned that I have a record of twenty-three years without being on the disabled list," smiled Pérez, obviously proud of that one. "But I have to mention winning the All-Star Game in 1967 was a tremendous thrill. And all the competition in the World Series, especially the final game in 1975, when my friend, Carlton Fisk, was good enough to ask Bill Lee for the blooper pitch one more time."

Fisk grinned—even though he hadn't called for the pitch.

Tony thanked all his teammates and friends, using just the right nomenclature for "my *brother* back in Cincinnati, Lee May." He acknowledged his opponents at sixty-feet six inches, personifying them into a one-and-only nemesis, adding yeast for lightness: "I know that if it weren't for Bob Gibson, I would be here earlier than today."

And then came the magic moment that brought the crowd closest to his heart. "And my wife, Pituka…*What can I say?*" He had the crowd at "say."

"I think the day I met her my career really started. She helped me so much during these years on my way here that I don't have words to thank her for this happiness in my life. I think I am not the only Hall of Famer in the family. She is the real one. She also gave me two wonderful sons, Victor, and Eduardo. No father can have two better sons than I have…These guys are wonderful, and really always respect us. I mean, especially my wife."

The crowd laughed; Tony rose to it.

"Yeah, they have to!" said the Big Dog, letting all the moms—and dads— out there know who was the disciplinarian in the Pérez house. One could see, right then and there, why Tony was never booed in his home park, not once in twenty-three seasons. He is Everyman, Joe Bag of Donuts, lunch pail in hand, headed off for another nine-hour shift. Next day, do it again, no complaints. Above all else, be thankful. That is *esencia del padre*—essence of the father. Straight José Manuel.

Then more…

"Before I finish, I want to pass along a little bit of advice to all the present and future players," Tony said.

And here you knew it was going to get serious by the Big Dog's standards, because now he was going to take you into his baseball world. Only, he didn't talk about himself. He didn't say "I"—not once. But everybody knew. Even in 2000, there were ugly rumors of performance-enhancing drugs in baseball.

"Please, respect and honor the uniform you wear. Respect your fans and more important respect the game of baseball, a national great pastime."

It was the right thing to say—and it got everybody's attention.

Tony asked "to say something in Spanish to all who are here, to all the people in all the countries" of the Caribbean and "Latin America who have supported me for so many years."

Buenas tardes. Quiero darle a mi mamá un abrazo y mis fanaticos y familiares de mi isla de Cuba y especialmente Camagüey, siempre están cuidando de mí.—"Good afternoon. I want to give my mom a hug and my friends and family from my island of Cuba and especially Camagüey, they are always looking out for me."

Un saludo sincero a todos mis fans en general ya mis amigos que me ayudaron a llegar aquí en este día …Espero que en el futuro, Dave Concepción, Luis Tiant, Tony Oliva, Minnie Miñoso y Pete Rose también puedan experimentar este honor.—"A heartfelt greeting to all my fans in general and my friends who helped me arrive here on this day…I hope in the future (these tremendous former stars) can experience this honor, too."

Then, pausing for a split-second, looking up with that great smile on this greatest of baseball days, and adding the perfect closing touch.

"Thank you very much…Merci beaucoup…*Muchas gracias.*"

The crowd erupted.

Tani was home. ◆

One for the ages.

CHAPTER 18
Curtain Call

"Let's sit here at the base of this statue before it is unveiled, and look around at what this statue is going to see for eighty-one days of the season—and the off-season and days off. Let's remember this moment."

—Eduardo Pérez to his brother, Victor.

Cincinnati, Saturday, August 22, 2015, Tony Pérez Statue Day—It was sunny and already pushing eighty degrees in Cincinnati, on the way to eighty-eight. Hard to believe that it had been fifteen years since the Big Dog had been enshrined in Cooperstown. Now he was back home again, for a curtain call, a day that promised to be like none other.

Yes, Cincinnati was definitely "home" to Doggie—not his summer home (that was in Miami where he worked for the Miami Marlins); not his winter home (that was in Puerto Rico, where the family of his wife, Pituka de la Cantera, had settled after fleeing Cuba); but his *home-home*..."Who loves ya', baby?"... the big small town, sweet home Cincinnati.

Tony had come back to sweet home Cincinnati quite a bit since Cooperstown: too many Reds Hall of Fame galas to count...the Twenty-Fifth Anniversary Big Red Machine reunion in 2000 that almost brought down Riverfront Stadium two years before the wrecking ball did...the softball game to close out Riverfront Stadium in 2002...parties built around the opening of the new ballpark in 2003...Sparky's number retirement in 2005...Davey Concepción's in 2007... Johnny Bench's statue in 2011...Barry Larkin's number retirement in 2012...Joe

ßench, Morgan, and Rose fingered the Big Dog as by far the biggest troublemaker in the club-house when it came to planting stories to get under the skin of the others—and then disappearing when the finger-pointing began. Doggie, of course, professed total innocence.

Morgan's statue in 2013…the All-Star Game in 2015. But this was a new honor for Tony. To be commemorated with a statue in your adopted hometown? It's hard to imagine anything bigger than that. Yes, it was Tony Pérez Statue Day in Cincinnati—but not in Central Violeta, where Tani was born and raised.

When Central Violetans awoke on that Saturday morning, August 22, 2015, and went about their daily rounds, there was nothing but ancient memories to serve as reminders that theirs was the birthplace of Atanacio Rigal Pérez. You'd have thought it was 1960, Tani's first season in Geneva, New York—because the only billboards in Central Violeta still had Fidel's and Che's mugs on them.

In Cincinnati, a fortunate handful who attended a private dinner at the ballpark the night before the statue dedication and paid $500 a plate to support the Reds Hall of Fame were treated to Tony and his famous teammates cracking on one another and received a preview of what the weekend promised (and delivered).

• Star-studded—The entire Great Eight was there, including Joe Morgan, who *wouldn't* be on hand (due a to health issues) a year later when Pete Rose was inducted into the Reds Hall of Fame. Morgan's presence at Pérez's statue dedication, but absence at the "14" number retirement, gave every seasoned Reds fan an ice-cold splash of Baseball Mortality right in the kisser. The Big Red Machine is as close as it was good. Not only does the Great Eight always show up for one another, so does most of the pitching staff—a classy, tight, appreciative bunch if ever there were one, led by philosopher-king and resident wise-guy, former starting pitcher Jack Billingham.

• Irreverent—"I wasn't pitching well here my first three starts," Cactus Jack recalled. "I'd lost my first three, been pulled out by Captain Hook. The fans were booing, 'Go back to Houston!' After one of the games—I'd just given up a *monstrous* home run—I'm sitting at my locker, head down, all dejected. Tony walks up and says, 'Jack, Jack! How you hold that ball?' I said, 'Wha'… what?' He said, 'Jack! Show me how you hold that ball. That guy, he hit that ball a *loooooong* way!'…You couldn't stay down long in that clubhouse. And that man right there, Doggie, that man led everybody when it came to getting you smiling again."

• Funny—Pérez had brought a large contingent of family and friends to the dinner. Johnny Bench zinged him for it. "This place'd be only half full if you didn't bring forty Cubanos with you," Bench told the honoree.

• Ribald—"When I first came over here," Morgan said, "I kept hearing about the 'Big Dog' this, and 'Big Dog' that. I'm thinking, 'What kind of dog is this? A poodle?' Before I came over here (via trade) in 1972, the *only* thing we called Tony Pérez was 'the Big Guy who couldn't play third base.'" *Ba-rump-bump.*

• "Concepcióned"—When the Big Red Machine gets together, a funnel cloud inevitably forms around Davey Concepción, the shortstop-turned-gentleman-rancher-trucking magnate. Nothing takes the BRM back—and lightens its step—quite like the first sighting of the vivacious Venezuelan; nothing brings back the good ol' days like number 13. He always wanted to be a superstar, and in reality he is. But the Big Four won't let him be that. Individually, they have campaigned for his inclusion in Cooperstown. Collectively, they're still jamming him in the clubhouse laundry dryer and flipping the "On" switch. Rose calls him "Bozo" every other sentence. What makes all this work is that Davey takes it so well. Once the foil, always the foil. Even Pérez got into the act at dinner. In a heartfelt moment in front of the crowd, Concepción said he was honored to be welcomed by the Big Cuban as a road-hotel roommate so soon after joining the Reds as a rookie in 1970. Responded Pérez, "I roomed with you because they *paid* me to room with you."

• Contextual—Pete Rose, as he is wont to do when it comes to finding singularity in Reds achievement and providing context, looked across the dais to Ken Griffey Sr. and said, "How many guys can say they batted in front of three guys who all have statues outside their ballpark?" Yes, for a guy who took five years to get through Western Hills High School, Rose certainly is good at context. "This organization has made only three big mistakes," Rose said. "The trade of Frank Robinson, getting rid of Sparky Anderson, and trading away Tony Pérez."

The statue weekend was also incredibly "warm"—and I'm not talking about temperatures. When Tony is around (and Pituka, too, of course; she elevates warmth to the heavens), it is always going to be close to the heart. Caesar Geronimo spoke eloquently of this during the dinner, referring to the way Pituka took young Reds couples under her wing early in their careers. It's not stereotyping to say that the absolute best of Latin culture is embodied in Pituka and Tony. That they would be that embodiment *together*, is nothing short of magical.

It is part of the reason, no doubt, that Pituka and Tony have been together so long—"the love of my life," Tony called her that weekend, noting they had been married fifty years. The cold and the hot, the reserved and the outgoing, the calm and the storm.

"Five months after they met, they married," son Victor said that Saturday, the marvel still in his voice.

What is it that Van Morrison wrote? "*And we'll walk down the avenue again, and we'll sing old songs from way back when…when the healing has begun…*"

That's what the Pérez statue weekend was: Singing old songs from way back when, then unveiling a statue to one of the best purveyors of baseball music a town could ever have.

Oh, the music Pérez and his family have made...

I thought back to the time Tony and Pituka first met in October 1964...their first spring training in 1965...first-born Victor in 1966...the breakout season and All-Star Game home run off Catfish in the fifteenth inning in 1967...Eduardo in 1969...the career year in 1970..."Going Home" in 1972...all the World Series and playoff games...the "Great Parting" in December 1976..."The Return"...tying Cepeda for all-time home run record for Latinos...Cooperstown... The Statue.

There were low points, of course; there are always low points. The lowest came after Tony was named Reds manager for the 1993 season. By Pérez's own admission, he never sought the job, never lobbied for it. But after Lou Piniella had moved on following his three-year stint as Reds manager—including a World Championship in his first year in Cincinnati, 1990—Reds owner Marge Schott wanted to re-stamp the team with the "Big Red Machine" brand by promoting one of its stars. At the time, she was under fire for her use of racial and ethnic slurs, which eventually led to her one-year suspension; she was serving it when Pérez was fired.

After a 2–9 start under the Big Dog, the Reds appeared to have turned things around, going 17–9 to rise above .500 at 19–18. But the loss of six of seven in Los Angeles and San Francisco (as though that had never happened before) brought things to a head. When the team returned home from the 1–6 road trip with an overall 20–24 record, Reds general manager Jim Bowden fired Pérez.

Reds players played hard for Doggie; he didn't "lose" them. There was some criticism in the media that he sometimes didn't pull the trigger quickly enough on strategic moves during games, and that the players were making too many mental errors. But the legacy is that Pérez had been set up to fail (and, really, was *expected* to fail, based upon the one-year contract he was given). Bowden hadn't allowed Pérez to place his longtime manager and mentor Dave Bristol into the bench-coach role (so Pérez made Bristol his third-base coach). Bowden saddled Pérez with a proven Triple-A veteran manager in Dave Miley as bench coach. But Miley had no major-league experience. The hiring came across as a ruse to appease baseball on the racial issue, and one that gave Pérez no tools with which to succeed.

When Bowden fired him by phone on May 24, 1993, it marked for me a low-water mark in class during my thirty years covering the club. ("Ready, Blame, Fire: Just 44 Games For Pérez," read the headline in the *New York Times*. "How do you fire a guy after forty-four games?" then-Detroit Tiger manager Sparky Anderson asked the *Times*. "I'm not smart enough to judge a guy in forty-four games.") Bowden also fired Bristol and pitching coach Larry Rothschild; to his everlasting credit, coach Ron Oester resigned on the spot. (Oester said that when Bowden asked him, "You don't want to be a part of turning this around?" he responded, "You're looking to turn it around the wrong way. Tony wasn't the problem.") The rest of the season was basically a disaster with the Reds going 53–65 after Pérez's firing. (The Reds eventually did turn it around in 1994 and 1995 under Davey Johnson, but who's to say Pérez wouldn't have done the same?)

Pérez felt he had been used, and described his hiring and the constraints put on him as "fishy." But he never lashed out and called the organization what it was at that point: low-class. Within a month, he was hired by the expansion Florida Marlins as director of international relations and special assistant to the general manager. He served as Marlins interim manager in 2001, guiding the team to a respectable 54–60 record after third-year manager John Boles was fired. At the time of the statue dedication, Pérez was still flourishing as special assistant to the Marlins president.

Even during Tony's ill-fated debut as Reds skipper, he was part of baseball's renewed Cuba connection: Cuban defector/pitcher René Arocha, who pioneered the "second-wave" of Cuban talent to the major leagues, made his major league debut for the Cardinals in St. Louis on April 9, 1993. There in the opposing dugout was the king of the true first wave, Tony Pérez.

The outpouring of affection for Pérez on Statue Weekend in August, 2015, impressed Tony's sister, Argelia, even more than the statue. She had traveled to Cincinnati from Cuba to see her brother on one of his biggest and best days. She had come representing "*La Familia*," the past and present family from Cuba— father José Manuel who had died in Cuba in the late 1970s; mother Teodora ("Tita") who had died in 2008, also in Cuba; and all the others who couldn't make it, too. All of this served to make Statue Day a monumental day for Argelia, a staggering day, really.

"I never could have imagined a day like this," Argelia told me through her translator-nephew, Eduardo. Nor could have José Manuel and Teodora imagined it. Toward the end of this magnificent day, a Reds' insider from the 1970s (who shall remain nameless) approached me. I will never forget his words. "The stature of the others (Rose, Morgan, and Bench) has remained about the same since they removed their uniforms," he said. "Tony's has kept growing."

All weekend long, Tony had the crowds wrapped around him. He singled out, among others, former teammate Don Gullett, who hadn't been a fixture at Reds events over the years, "but who came back," said Tony. "Thank you."

He was talking to not only Gullett and their former teammates, but to everybody who had ever seen them play, live or on TV, or had even listened to a Reds game on radio.

Pérez comes by his humility honestly. But then it hit me.

His greatest gift is the humility he gives others.

Rose is Rose, of course, and not a lot rubs off on him. But I like the way the Great Eight has mellowed over the years. Pérez and Rose have always been *simpatico*, baseball lifers that they are, going back to 1960 Geneva, New York. And I like that Bench has grown to see past Rose's foibles and easily praises him now for his pivotal role on those Big Red Machine teams. I like that Ken Griffey Sr. singled out Rose in his autobiography (*Big Red: Baseball, Fatherhood and My Life in the Big Red Machine*) for the way he took the Reds young players under his wing. ("Top of the list" as a mentor, wrote Griffey. "If a group of us were in a restaurant and Pete came in, he would pick up the check. For a while, Reds had us wear red jackets when we traveled; Pete bought red jackets for all the rookies.")

At a Great Eight private dinner on one of the reunion tours, the greats took their seats at the guests-of-honor table, paying no regard whatsoever to the names on the place settings. They aligned themselves pretty much as one might expect: Morgan-Rose, Concepción-Gerónimo-Griffey-Foster, with the great JB in an overseeing position. And who was the one Great Eighter moving about freely among the groups, chatting up everybody, generating peels of laughter, pulling them tight? Pérez. It was as though they were all back in the clubhouse, circa 1975. Down deep, they're all good guys. By their own admission, the Big Dog brings out the best in each of them. *Is there higher praise?*

Among the other epiphanies I had on Statue Weekend: In this country, we have had, on the daily printed sports pages, our regrettable history of stereotyping Latin players as "hot-tempered"—including in Cincinnati—all the way back to Armando Marsans and Rafael Almeida in 1911, Dolf Luque in the 1920s, and Leo Cardenas in the 1960s. Against that backdrop, I say this (and again, not to stereotype): When I consider the lengthy Reds history through a Great Eight prism, Pérez (Cuban), Concepción (Venezuelan), and Gerónimo (Dominican) are three of the classiest, best-representing, most evenly dispositioned men it has been my pleasure to cover in my four decades in the game.

Before the Cincinnati crowd arrived for the statue dedication in the late afternoon that Saturday, Tony's sons had their moment at the statue. They are close; Eduardo is three years younger. He played for the Reds (1996–1998), but is best-known as a St. Louis Cardinal (1999–2003). After his baseball career he became a broadcaster. Victor played baseball for Xavier University in Cincinnati and did a turn in the minors for the Reds' Billings, Montana, farm club. He went on to a successful career of his own in acting and real estate.

Sitting at the base of the statue—sons at the father's knee—gave them an opportunity to take it all in. It was a very big day, and it needed to be slowed down just a bit. Tony's boys aren't in Dad's shadow; he is in theirs.

Not just anybody gets a statue.

The four original statues at Great American Ball Park—Frank Robinson, Ted Kluszewski, Joe Nuxhall, and Ernie Lombardi—are located in Crosley Terrace, a name chosen because the four had graced Crosley Field, the Reds' hallowed home from 1912–1970. (Originally named Redland Field, it was renamed in 1934 when inventor and industrialist Powel Crosley Jr. bought the club that

Eduardo Pérez (a former Red, he hit 16 HR in 297 at-bats in 1997; shown here with team-mate Curtis Goodwin) and Eduardo's older brother, Victor (a former Reds' minor-league player), played an integral role in their father's enjoyment of "Tony Pérez Statue Weekend."

year. He was mostly revered by Reds fans because when the Dodgers and Giants moved west in 1958, Crosley resisted offers to move the Reds to New York. "Why would I want to go all the way to New York to watch the Reds?" Powel asked. "I want to watch them at Crosley Field.")

Just outside the main gate to Great American Ball Park, the Crosley Four represent the soul of a franchise and a whole lot of *somebody*. The Big Red Machine statues—Bench, Morgan, Pérez—situated nearby along Joe Nuxhall Way and facing outward, welcome in all of Greater Cincinnati as well as the out-of-towners.

These BRM statues have been getting the buzz since Bench came out of his crouch in 2011, throwing a seed up East Freedom Way. But the statued greats— all the work of local sculptor-with-the-international-following Tom Tsuchiya—

are one big, happy family. Tsuchiya has been effusive in his praise of Big Red Machine left fielder George Foster, all but calling him a sculptor-whisperer for his eye for artistic detail, and for being able to articulate it. Foster was especially helpful on the Pérez statue, Tsuchiya said.

Every Big Red Machine statue is different, but Pérez's seems the most heroic; the most larger than life.

To others, he was already that.

Eduardo: "There *isn't* a statue to signify what our dad means to us in the family. It (the relationship) is beyond that…His brothers and sisters never got to sit in the stands to watch him play. But he always held that deep in his heart."

I will always remember the Pérez statue dedication. I will remember the third-generation Pérezes—Eduardo's young daughters, Andreanna and Juliana—stealing the show that Saturday wherever they went. I will remember Dave "The Cobra" Parker, who grew up in Cincinnati, saying afterward with a twinkle in his eye that every time Reds announcer Marty Brennaman referenced "the 1975–1976 Reds," he clapped with "the back of my hands," because it was his Pittsburgh Pirates whom the Reds knocked out of the postseason in 1975, his first as a starter.

I will remember Tony's friend and fellow Baseball Hall of Famer Andre Dawson (2010) being there on August 22, 2015, when by no means did he have to be but by every means wanted to be, explaining his presence like this: "Remember when Tony was traded to Montreal? I was a rookie that year, and Tony took all of us young guys, including me, under his wing. And guess what my number was? Yep, twenty-four. Well, not for long."

I will remember Tony standing next to the statue and replicating "The Swing" for the TV cameras. Yes, that was *very* cool.

I once asked Tony whether his election to the National Baseball Hall of Fame in 2000 was in any way recognized or acknowledged in Cuba. He held up his right hand, his thumb and index finger an inch apart, to indicate the size of the news brief in *Granma*, the state newspaper. That was Fidel's idea—not the newspaper brief, but the lack of any widespread coverage. The name of Tony's birthplace, Central Violeta, had been changed to "Primero de Enero" (First of January) soon after the *Revolución* by "Our Comrade Fidel," as Castro was known in party circles. The Supreme Commander allowed no more official public or private recognition of Tani Pérez than that little newspaper mention. Any other town in any free society in the world would have named the local ballpark after such a favorite son, put his stamp on the grade school, his signature on the hospital, a street, something, anything—at the very least erected a sign coming into town as "Home of Tani Pérez, One of the Great Cuban-born Baseball Players Ever."

There is nothing—*nada, no hay nada*—in Central Violeta/Primero de Enero, nor anywhere else in Cuba, making any sort of genuflection to this baseball great, the son of José Manuel, the son who had played their national pastime so well and so passionately, a son who had represented their country, *his* country, like a god. Yes, Atanacio Rigal Pérez was more than a match for the Maximum Leader, who couldn't wipe the collective memory clean, who couldn't purge Tani from their souls.

José Manuel's son was their son, too.

Back home in Cincinnati, the Big Dog was getting a lot more than a "Home of Tony Pérez" sign. By god, he was getting a statue.

"It is beautiful," he would later say. "It's something I never even think about when I was playing. When you play, you don't play the game for the stats (or the awards). You play the game to win. But this is something special. It is very warm."

Winning—that egoless pursuit of the team good—truly is one of those things that makes Pérez a cut above. He is in a gang of one in baseball of whom I would describe as "egoless." Indirectly, he himself had said as much fourteen years previous in Cooperstown: "The thing I am most proud of is that I always played to win and never cared for numbers or records...My only concern was winning."

And, of course, on Statue Day he beamed that "instant connector" to the fans around him, what former Marlins player Kevin Millar once described as, "that smile that knocks your socks off."

Yes, the fans in Cincinnati love their Big Dog (truth is, the media does, too), always has, and always will. Doggie had been bestowed the third-in-a-line Big Red Machine statue. And, really, he has the best spot, his statue rising high and powerful, front and center, "standing sentinel," as Reds owner Bob Castellini phrased it perfectly that Saturday, the lead act in a show that at one time was the greatest on baseball earth.

The third-generation Pérezes—Eduardo's daughters, Andreanna and Juliana (shown here)—are understandably proud of their grandfather. How many granddads have their own statue?

The statue celebrates "The Swing," Tony's behemoth blast in the sixth inning of Game Seven of the 1975 World Series that cut the deficit to 3–2 and made Reds fans believe their team was going to win their first World Series in thirty-five years.

One of the fine touches in the Saturday ceremony at GABP came when Marty Brennaman called attention to a baseball at the end of an antenna-like wire at the top of the apartment building across the street, signifying the sphere that landed on Lansdowne Street outside Fenway Park in Boston—but in lore is still going.

Victor said he fully understood why sculptor Tsuchiya   the pro's pro who had traveled to Tony's winter home in Puerto Rico to study his subject—focused on Tony's greatest "swing."

But to Tony's sons, this was never about one swing.

"To us," said Victor, "it was seeing the hard work, day after day—*that* is what we see in the swing."

After the statue dedication, I asked Pituka whether—for her— the statue symbolized that she had been vindicated. I knew she hadn't felt good when the club traded Tony in December 1976 or when it forced his retirement as player in the summer of '86, or when, seven years later, it fired him as Reds manager after a mere forty-four games. I once called Pituka "as fine a conduit as ever there could be between a baseball legend and a city's love affair with him." And I meant it.

On Statue Day, I asked for her innermost thoughts. I wanted to hear it directly, because Pituka always speaks from the heart and never minces words.

"That we are here, after all these years, receiving so much love from the fans on this very special day, and those who traded Tani and fired him are gone," she said. "And what I say to that is, 'Ha!'"

And then, pausing, adding softly, fondly, wistfully: "Oh, how they remember my Tony. So many people, giving him their love, like it was yesterday."

That ball Tony hit deep to left in 1975?

It never really did come down. ◆

José Fernández, 2016.

EPILOGUE
To an Athlete Dying Young

I awoke on Sunday, September 25, 2016, to the terrible news that the mega-popular Miami Marlins pitcher José Fernández, along with two friends, had been killed in an overnight boating accident. I felt something leave me; I had watched him pitch only five weeks earlier in Cincinnati, and I knew full well what he meant to the game, the Marlins, and especially the large Cuban community of South Florida. I had talked with him after the game, listened to the usual give-and-take with the writers, and later asked him about his relationship with Tony Pérez, who works for the Marlins.

"I love (Tony) and what he represents; the way he carries himself. I know he's the only Cuban major leaguer in the Hall of Fame," said Fernández, then adding with a smile: "As a Marlin, how could I not know that? I look at what I do—and hopefully how I carry myself—as being an extension of him. He paved the way."

Awesome, yes? It was to me. *Respect the game*; that's what Tony said in his Cooperstown speech; that was the signature phrase, the takeaway. Fernández, himself possibly bound for Cooperstown (he was only twenty-four) *hadn't* respected the game and his talent—not when cocaine was later found in his system. But I try never to judge, especially the young, because I know what I was like when I was young. The cocaine didn't diminish the loss. Fernández was a bright light extinguished, a gifted athlete dying young.

Fernández's exile story was far more harrowing than Pérez's. Fernández had tried to flee Cuba four times, once jumping overboard to save a woman (his own mother) from drowning, and another time being jailed after he was caught. I heard him say on radio that his first few months of freedom in Florida were harder than being jailed; that he didn't understand how the faucet sensors worked in our airport bathrooms; that not knowing any English kept him from doing the simplest tasks, such as deciphering where to sign his name on a high school test.

Fernández tapped into the Cuban community far more intensely than had Pérez, mainly because when Tony began his major-league career, there wasn't as big a Cuban community to tap into, and the community didn't have anywhere near as much disposable income as it does now. Also, the community as a whole back then was as preoccupied as were the Cuban ballplayers with trying to assimilate into American culture. Besides that, there was no major-league team in Florida when Pérez was working his way up the major-league ladder in the 1960s and 1970s.

In a way, Fernández was like Jackie Robinson. Though Fernández didn't break any barriers, he was as closely followed in the Cuban community as was Robinson nationally in the African-American community.

I heard the reaction Tony Pérez had when his son, Eduardo, called his mother and father that Sunday morning in Miami to tell them the horrific news of Fernández's death. Tony let out a loud, incredulous, excruciating "NO!" as though he had just lost a son.

The writer and media personality Dan Le Batard said his Cuban-born mother wept when he called her with the news. Dan wept, too. The entire Cuban community in this country wept. That's how big Fernández was.

There are about 1.2 million Cuban-Americans in Miami. The Cuban exiles are notably proud of Tony Pérez being the only Cuban to play in our major leagues to make it to Cooperstown. But the Cuban player they were *most* connected to, past or present, was Fernández. He was the contemporary embodiment of the Cuban-exile story, the young man who risked his life to fulfill his dream. Now he had died aboard his expensive speedboat, the *Kaught Looking*, on a late-night joyride.

I liked what Fernández had stood for—youth, joy, talent, exuberance. I referred to him as the "Minnie Miñoso of the mound." That's how full his joy was.

And that's how I'll remember him. ◆

APPENDIX 1

But For Castro

A Havana Sugar King

As a teenager in the late 1950s, "Tani" Pérez played on the junior team of the Triple-A Havana Sugar Kings. As his countryman—and future friend and team-mate—Leo Cardenas said: "If you grew up in the 1950s in Cuba, you grew up wanting to play for the Sugar Kings."

Had Pérez been born four or five years earlier, putting him in the age-range of then-Cincinnati Reds farmhands Cardenas, and fellow Cubans Cookie Rojas, Tony González and Mike Cuellar, the Sugar Kings are the Triple-A team he would have played for on the way up to the Reds (the Sugar Kings' major-league affiliate).

Instead of tearing up San Diego (34 HR, 8 triples, 107 RBIs as Pacific Coast League MVP), the 22-year-old Perez would have torn up Havana and been a king there to this day.

In 1959, the year of the Sugar Kings' greatest success, they finished third in the International League at 80–73, but beat Columbus and Richmond in the playoffs to win the Governor's Cup, and upset the Minneapolis Millers (82–72) in an exciting and terrifically contested seven-game series. Two of the games were decided in the ninth inning, and two others in extra innings. In Game 7 in Havana, the Sugar scored two runs in the eighth and one in the 9th to win 3–2. The Millers had been bolstered by just-turned-20-year-old Carl Yastrzemski for the playoffs, but the Sugar Kings were feted across the island for winning the Ju-nior (or as it was known back then, "Little") World Series in the first year of the reign of the then-wildly popular Fidel Castro, who attended every home game in the Series and put on quite a show.

Those were heady times for Cuban baseball fans, including the then-17-year-old Pérez, aspiring Havana Sugar King, who signed with the Reds organization the following March.

By early July 1960 the Havana Sugar Kings were no more, having been relocated to Jersey City, New Jersey, because of tensions between the Castro regime and the U.S. government.

Here's a thumbnail of the Sugar Kings history, followed by some roster identifications.

Year	Record	Finish	Manager	Playoffs
1954	78–77	5th	Reggie Otero	—
1955	87–66	3rd	Reggie Otero	Lost in 1st round
1956	72–82	6th	Reggie Otero/Nap Reyes	—
1957	72–82	6th	Nap Reyes	—
1958	65–88	8th	Nap Reyes, Tony Pacheco	—
1959	80–73	3rd	Preston Gomez	League Champs
1960	76–77	5th	Tony Castano	—

Roster Notables

1954: Julio Becquer, Mike Guerra, Ray Noble, Ken Raffensberger, Juan Delis.

1955: Yo-Yo Davalillo, Nino Escalera, Connie Marerro, Ray Noble, Pat Scantlebury.

1956: Hal Bevan, Sandy Consuegra, Dutch Dotterer, Rudy Minarcin, Marerro.

1957: Vicente Amor, Elio Chacón, Mike Cuellar, Orlando Peña, Davalillo, Escalera.

1958: Rogelio Álvarez, Tony González, Davalillo, Escalera, Peña, Cuellar, Chacón.

1959: Leo Cardenas, Cookie Rojas, Luis Arroyo, Jesse Gonder, Cuellar, González, Alvarez.

1960: Joe Azcue, Howie Nunn, Bob Miller, Cardenas, Rojas, Arroyo, Davalillo, Peña, Dotterer. ◆

APPENDIX 2

Los Cuatro Inmortales Cubanos

Tony Pérez was born humble. By all accounts he has remained that way. In May of 2000 he visited the Gallery at the National Baseball Hall of Fame where his plaque would be installed in July of that year and displayed in perpetuity. He had no words for the company he would keep, save these: "I get goose bumps."

Six years later he got goosebumps on top of his goosebumps when a Special Committee on the Negro Leagues enshrined Pérez's fellow Cuban-borns José Méndez and Cristóbal Torriente. They joined Pérez and *"El Maestro"* (Martin

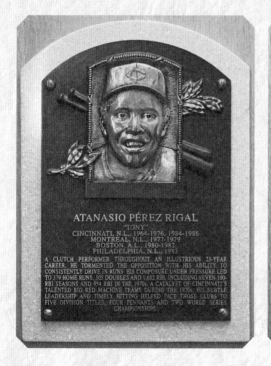

ATANASIO PÉREZ RIGAL
"TONY"
CINCINNATI, N.L., 1964-1976, 1984-1986
MONTREAL, N.L., 1977-1979
BOSTON, A.L., 1980-1982
PHILADELPHIA, N.L., 1983
A CLUTCH PERFORMER THROUGHOUT AN ILLUSTRIOUS 23-YEAR CAREER, HE TORMENTED THE OPPOSITION WITH HIS ABILITY TO CONSISTENTLY DRIVE IN RUNS. HIS COMPOSURE UNDER PRESSURE LED TO 379 HOME RUNS, 505 DOUBLES AND 1,652 RBI, INCLUDING SEVEN 100-RBI SEASONS AND 954 RBI IN THE 1970s, A CATALYST OF CINCINNATI'S TALENTED BIG RED MACHINE TEAMS DURING THE 1970s, HIS SUBTLE LEADERSHIP AND TIMELY HITTING HELPED PACE THOSE CLUBS TO FIVE DIVISION TITLES, FOUR PENNANTS AND TWO WORLD SERIES CHAMPIONSHIPS.

MARTIN DIHIGO
"EL MAESTRO"
NEGRO LEAGUES 1923-1947
MOST VERSATILE OF NEGRO LEAGUE STARS.
PLAYED IN BOTH SUMMER AND WINTER
BALL MOST OF CAREER, REGISTERED MORE
THAN 260 VICTORIES AS PITCHER. WHEN NOT
ON MOUND HE PLAYED OUTFIELD OR INFIELD,
USUALLY BATTING WELL OVER .300. ALSO
MANAGED DURING AND AFTER PLAYING DAYS.

JOSÉ DE LA CARIDAD MÉNDEZ BAEZ
"EL DIAMANTE NEGRO" "THE BLACK DIAMOND"
PRE-NEGRO LEAGUES, 1908-1919
NEGRO LEAGUES, 1920-1926
A SLENDER RIGHT-HANDED PITCHER WHO WAS ACKNOWLEDGED AS THE
FIRST CUBAN-BORN BASEBALL STAR IN THE PRE-NEGRO LEAGUES ERA.
UTILIZED A VAST ARRAY OF PITCHES, MAINLY RELYING ON A DECEPTIVE
FASTBALL AND SHARP-BREAKING CURVE TO DOMINATE OPPOSING
BATTERS. AS PLAYER-MANAGER, LED KANSAS CITY MONARCHS TO
THREE CONSECUTIVE NEGRO NATIONAL LEAGUE PENNANTS, 1923-1925.
CLINCHED 1924 NEGRO LEAGUES WORLD SERIES TITLE WITH THREE-HIT
SHUTOUT. HURLED 25 CONSECUTIVE SHUTOUT INNINGS AGAINST THE
CINCINNATI REDS DURING EXHIBITION COMPETITION IN 1908.

CRISTÓBAL TORRIENTE
"CARLOS"
PRE-NEGRO LEAGUES, 1913-1919
NEGRO LEAGUES, 1920-1928, 1932
A COMPACT AND POWERFUL FIVE-TOOL PLAYER WITH TREMENDOUS
EXTRA-BASE POWER TO ALL FIELDS. PLAYED 17 SEASONS OVERALL, AND
RANKS AMONG ALL-TIME NEGRO LEAGUES LEADERS IN DOUBLES, TRIPLES,
SLUGGING PERCENTAGE, TOTAL BASES AND RBI. LED CHICAGO AMERICAN
GIANTS TO THREE SUCCESSIVE NEGRO NATIONAL LEAGUE TITLES, 1920-
1922. EXCEPTIONAL SPEED AND RANGE ALLOWED HIM TO COVER CENTER
FIELD WITH GREAT EASE. PRIOR TO THE FORMATION OF THE NEGRO
LEAGUES, STARRED IN HIS NATIVE CUBA. FAMED FOR OUTPLAYING BABE
RUTH DURING A NINE-GAME BARNSTORMING SERIES IN 1920.

Dihigo) as the only Cuban natives in the Hall, as of 2017. (Pérez is the only one of the four to have played in the major leagues.)

Not having ever seen film footage of Dihigo, Torriente or Méndez, let alone seen them play, we can relate only the best words of those who did, as a way of providing context for *Los Cuatro Inmortales Cubanos*:

Johnny Bench on Tony Pérez: "Can we ever know what it was like to come to this country not knowing a word of English? To have gone ten years without being allowed to see his family (in Cuba)?"

Satchel Paige on Martin Dihigo: "I'm not the best; Martin Dihigo is the best."

C.I. Taylor former Negro Leagues player, manager and executive, on Cristóbal Torriente: "If I should see Torriente walking up the other side of the street, I would say 'There walks a ballclub.'"

John McGraw on José Méndez: "If Méndez was a white man, I would pay $50,000 for his release from Almendares…(He is) sort of Walter Johnson and Grover Alexander rolled into one." ◆

APPENDIX 3
Tony Pérez Career Stats

- 23 major-league years
- .279 BA/.341 OBP/.463 Slugging Pct.
- 2,777 G
- 10,861 PA
- 9,778 AB
- 1,272 Runs
- 2,732 Hits
- 505 Doubles
- 79 Triples
- 379 Home Runs
- 1,652 RBI
- 925 Walks
- 1,867 Strikeouts
- Career WAR: 53.9 (Tony Oliva, 43.0; Minnie Miñoso, 50.2; Luis Tiant Jr., 66.1)
- Career OPS+: 122 ("100" is league average. Miñoso, 130; Oliva, 131; Tiant's ERA+, 114)

- 7 All-Star teams 1967–70; 1974–76
- 7 "Top 25" MVP seasons: 1967 (8th); 1968 (19th); 1969 (10th); 1970 (3rd); 1973 (7th); 1975 (15th); 1980 (22nd)
- Awards: 1967 All-Star Game MVP; 1980 Lou Gehrig Memorial Award 11 "Top 10" seasons in RBI
- 7 "Top 10" in Extra-Base Hits
- 6 "Top 10" in HR
- 6 "Top Ten" in Total Bases
- 5 "Top Ten" in Doubles
- 2 "Top Ten" in Triples
- Defensively: 1st in "Range Factor" among NL third basemen (1971)
- Hall of Fame: 9th ballot, 2000 Elected, BBWAA, 77.2%

Year	Age	Team	G	PA	AB	R	H	2B	3B
1960	18	Geneva	104	439	384	82	107	21	4
1961	19	Geneva	121	541	460	110	160	32	7
1962	20	Rocky Mt	100	461	384	72	112	20	8
1963	21	Macon	69	285	256	44	79	19	3
1963	21	S. Diego	8	31	29	4	11	3	1
1964	22	S. Diego	124	538	479	96	148	20	8
1964	22	CIN	12	28	25	1	2	1	0
1965	23	CIN	104	307	281	40	73	14	4
1966	24	CIN	99	278	257	25	68	10	4
1967	25	CIN	156	644	600	78	174	28	7
1968	26	CIN	160	690	625	93	176	25	7
1969	27	CIN	160	704	629	103	185	31	2
1970	28	CIN	158	681	587	107	186	28	6
1971	29	CIN	158	664	609	72	164	22	3
1972	30	CIN	136	576	515	64	146	33	7
1973	31	CIN	151	647	564	73	177	33	3
1974	32	CIN	158	667	596	81	158	28	2
1975	33	CIN	137	574	511	74	144	28	3
1976	34	CIN	139	586	527	77	137	32	6
1977	35	MON	154	633	559	71	158	32	6
1978	36	MON	148	590	544	63	158	38	3
1979	37	MON	132	537	489	58	132	29	4
1980	38	BOS	151	635	585	73	161	31	3
1981	39	BOS	84	336	306	35	77	11	3
1982	40	BOS	69	215	196	18	51	14	2
1983	41	PHI	91	285	253	18	61	11	2
1984	42	CIN	71	149	137	9	33	6	1
1985	43	CIN	72	207	183	25	60	8	0
1986	44	CIN	77	228	200	14	51	12	1
		TOTALS	2777	10861	9778	1272	2732	505	79

HR	RBI	BB	SO	BA	OBP	SLG	OPS	OPS+	WAR
6	43	45	68	.279	.355	.401	.756	—	
27	132	61	86	.348	.432	.624	1.056	—	
18	74	68	61	.292	.397	.526	.923	—	
11	48	24	52	.309	.375	.535	.910	—	
1	5	2	8	.379	.419	.655	1.075	—	
34	107	45	102	.309	.374	.597	.971	—	
0	1	3	9	.080	.179	.120	.299	-15	-0.2
12	47	21	67	.260	.315	.466	.781	111	0.7
4	39	14	44	.265	.304	.381	.686	82	-0.5
26	102	33	102	.290	.328	.490	.818	121	3.2
18	92	51	92	.282	.338	.430	.769	124	5.9
37	122	63	131	.294	.357	.526	.883	140	6.0
40	129	83	134	.317	.401	.589	.990	158	7.2
25	91	51	120	.269	.325	.438	.764	120	4.1
21	90	55	121	.283	.349	.497	.846	145	4.7
27	101	74	117	.314	.393	.527	.919	159	5.3
28	101	61	112	.265	.331	.460	.791	121	2.5
20	109	54	101	.282	.350	.466	.816	124	3.1
19	91	50	88	.260	.328	.452	.779	118	2.6
19	91	63	111	.283	.352	.463	.816	121	2.8
14	78	38	104	.290	.336	.449	.785	120	3.3
13	73	38	82	.270	.322	.425	.748	104	0.5
25	105	41	93	.275	.320	.467	.786	108	0.7
9	39	27	66	.252	.310	.395	.705	98	0.4
6	31	19	48	.260	.326	.444	.769	104	0.4
6	43	28	57	.241	.316	.372	.687	91	0.3
2	15	11	21	.241	.295	.343	.638	77	-0.6
6	33	22	22	.328	.396	.470	.866	138	1.7
2	29	25	25	.255	.333	.355	.688	87	-0.1
379	1652	925	1867	.279	.341	.463	.804		

Postseasons

Series	Year	Team	Opp	G	PA	AB	R	H	2B	3B	HR	RBI	BB	SO	BA	OBP	SLG	OPS
NLCS	1970	CIN	PIT	3	13	12	1	4	2	0	1	2	1	1	.333	.385	.750	.135
WS	1970	CIN	BAL	5	21	18	2	1	0	0	0	0	3	4	.056	.190	.056	.246
NLCS	1972	CIN	PIT	5	20	20	0	4	1	0	0	2	0	7	.200	.200	.250	.450
WS	1972	CIN	OAK	7	28	23	3	10	2	0	0	2	4	4	.435	.500	.522	1.022
NLCS	1973	CIN	NYM	5	22	22	1	2	0	0	1	2	0	4	.091	.091	.227	.318
NLCS	1975	CIN	PIT	3	13	12	3	5	0	0	1	4	1	2	.417	.462	.667	1.128
WS	1975	CIN	BOS	7	31	28	4	5	0	0	3	7	3	9	.179	.258	.500	.758
NLCS	1976	CIN	PHI	3	13	10	1	2	0	0	0	4	1	2	.200	.231	.200	.431
WS	1976	CIN	NYY	4	17	16	1	5	1	0	0	2	1	2	.313	.353	.375	.728
NLCS	1983	PHI	LAD	1	1	1	0	1	0	0	0	0	0	0	1.000	1.000	1.000	2.000
WS	1983	PHI	BAL	4	10	10	0	2	0	0	0	0	0	2	.200	.200	.200	.400
TOTALS				47	189	172	16	41	6	0	6	25	14	37	.238	.291	.378	.669

Puerto Rican Winter League/Santurce Crabbers

- 7+ seasons between his first in 1964–65 and last in 1972–73
- Met future wife, Pituka in Oct. 1964 (daughter of Pablo de la Cantera and Edilia Cortina)
- Didn't play in 1968–69; played final month in 1971–72
- 70-game regular seasons (e.g. Santurce was 45–25 in 1966–67)
- League MVP in 1966–67
- Won batting crown in 1966–67 (.333)
- RBI champ in 1966–67 (63 RBIs)
- Hits leader in 1966–67 (87 hits)
- Doubles champ in 1966–67 (18); 1967–68 (20); 1969–70 (17)
- Career numbers in Puerto Rico: .303 batting average, 65 HRs, 319 RBIs

APPENDIX 4
Major League Baseball's Cuban Players

"All of baseball history is a river that never stops. Guys who have only one at-bat or throw only one pitch step into that river and have a part of it."
—Roger Angell

1. JOSÉ ABREU, Cienfuegos
January 29, 1987–
1B, DH / CHW, 2014–
Despite his late start (27), Abreu might still have a shot at being the next active Cuban major leaguer to reach Cooperstown, giving Tony Pérez some company. Excellent first year: .317/.383/.581; 36 HR 107 RBI, 35 2B; All-Star, AL ROY, fourth in MVP. Career: .301/.359/.524.

2. JOSÉ ACOSTA, La Habana
March 4, 1891–November 16, 1977
P / WSH, CHW, 1920–1922
55 G (13 starts) over three seasons: 213 1/3 IP, 4.51 ERA. Brother of Merito.

3. MERITO ACOSTA, Bauta
May 19, 1886–November 17, 1963
OF / WSH, PHIL-A, 1913–1918
He started out at 17 years old for the Senators as though he might be a force—12 G, .300/.417.400—but never approached those numbers again. Career: 180 G, .255/.354/.307.

4. RAFAEL ALMEIDA, La Habana
June 20, 1887–March 18, 1969
3B / CIN, 1911–1913

Led by business manager Frank Bancroft—an underage Civil War veteran shot by a Confederate during the Union Army's Louisiana campaign—the Reds first saw Almeida and Armando Marsans on a winter tour of Cuba in 1908. Almeida and Marsans were Alemandares teammates and under contract to a minor league club in New England when the Reds bought them out on June 11, 1911. Three weeks later they debuted on the Fourth of July in Chicago. Because of protestations around the league, the Reds defended the players as "pure Spaniards, without a trace of colored blood." In his debut, Almeida was hit by a pitch, suspected to have been racially motivated, even though it came with the bases loaded and forced in a run. History proved Marsans to be the better player, but Almeida made an indelible contribution. Died in Havana at 80. Career: .270/.335/.389.

5. LUIS ALOMA, La Habana
June 19, 1923–April 7, 1997
P / CHW, 1950-53
His 18-3 record over four seasons is the best winning pct. (.857) by a pitcher with at least 20 decisions. He was discovered in Cuba by famed superscout Joe Cambria, but Cambria's Senators let Aloma get away, and so did the Tigers. Why? Because the White Sox needed an interpreter for star shortstop Chico Carrasquel and pitcher Mike Fornieles, and were willing to trade Chico's uncle Alex to Detroit to get Aloma. (And if you need an interpreter, why not get one who can pitch?) Aloma's second season in Chicago was a doozy: 6-0 in 25 games (he pitched a shutout in his only start) with an ERA+ of 223. Chronic bursitis

ended his career (116 games, 3.44 ERA), but not his interpreting: in the 1960s, he founded an organization in Chicago to help Cuban refugees.

6. YONDER ALONSO, La Habana
April 8, 1987–
1B, OF / CIN, SDP, OAK, SEA, 2010–
Alonso left Cuba for the U.S. at nine, earning his diploma at Coral Gables (Fla.) High School. The Reds' No. 1 pick (seventh overall in the 2008 draft) debuted two years later. In December 2011, he was the top prospect in the Reds trade for San Diego pitcher Mat Latos. Alonso is finally showing the type of power (28 HR in 2017, compared to a *total* of 39 his first seven years) that his enthusiasts envisioned. Career: .268/.340/.407.

7. DARIEL ÁLVAREZ, Camaguey
November 7, 1988–
OF / BAL, 2015–
Facing the Rangers' Cole Hamels (8 IP, 2 H, 10Ks) made for a tough debut (August 28, 2015), but Álvarez gunned down Adrián Beltré at the plate on an L-9 by Elvis Andrus' to complete a 9-2 DP in the bottom of the 2nd inning at Arlington before 28,337 fans. Two seasons: 14 G, 250/.314/.406.

8. OSSIE ÁLVAREZ, Bolondon
October 19, 1933–March 8, 2008
SS, 2B / WSH, DET, 1958-59
Ossie's debut (April 19, 1958) came as a defensive replacement late in the game. He had been watching a good Cuban matchup: Boston's Mike Fornieles vs. Washington's Pedro Ramos who, no surprise, gave up a two-run bomb to Jackie Jensen in the 6th. Boston's Ted Williams stole his lone base of the season. Best of all: Alvarez was on the winning end in front of 6,649 fans at Griffith Stadium. Career: 95 G, .212/.271/.229.

9. ROGELIO ALVAREZ, Pinar del Rio
April 18, 1938–November 30, 2012
1B / CIN, 1960–62
In his debut (September 18, 1960), pinch-hitter Alvarez led off the bottom of the 9th. He was punched out by the Pirates' Vinegar Bend Mizell (9 IP, 3 H, 0 R), and watched unhappily as the Reds' Bob Purkey (17-9) lost 1-0 in front of 14,438 fans at Cincinnati's Crosley Field. Career: 17 G, .189/.211/.189.

10. VICENTE AMOR, La Habana
August 8, 1932–
P / CIN, CHC, 1955–57
Melodie D'Amor, take this song to your lover: D'Amor was the last of the seven pitchers the Cubs used on his debut day (April 16, 1955). It had to end with somebody, and did in the bottom of the 14th of an 11-11 game against Stan Musial's Cardinals. Amor managed to strand Rip Repulski after an inning-opening double in the 13th, but couldn't duplicate it. After the Cards' Bill Sarni opened the next frame with a double, Amor couldn't shoo shoo little bird, giving up the game-winner on a single to left by Wally Moon. Career: 13 G (4 starts), 33 1/3 IP, 5.67 ERA.

11. SANDY AMOROS, La Habana
January 30, 1930–June 27, 1992
OF / BRO, LAD, DET, 1952–60
Amoros will be forever remembered for his racing catch near the left-field line off Yogi Berra in Game 7 of the 1955 World Series, Brooklyn's only World Championship vs. the Yankees. When Amoros declined Castro's offer to manage a team in Cuba in the summer of '62—and instead went to Mexico City to play ball—the Supreme Commander took Amoros' ranch, car and assets. Amoros later escaped Cuba, but hard times followed: diabetes, leg amputated, died of pneumonia in a Miami hospital. Career: 517 G, .255/.361/.430.

12. ÁNGEL ARAGON, La Habana
August 2, 1890–June 27, 1992
3B, OF / NYY, 1914–17
Based upon all available records, Aragon is credited with being the Yankees' first Hispanic player. In 32 games over three seasons, he hit a buck-eighteen.

13. JACK ARAGON, La Habana
November 20, 1915–April 4, 1988
PR / NYG, 1941
The son of Ángel Aragon was a "sip espresso" player: He entered his lone big-league game as a pinch-runner for future Hall of Famer Gabby Hartnett.

14. JOSÉ ARCIA, La Habana
August 22, 1943–July 30, 2016
SS, 2B / CHC, SDP, 1968–70
In 59 games for the Cubs and 234 games with the 1969–70 expansion Padres, Arcia showed almost no power (.215/.260/.278, 1 HR in 615 AB).

15. RUDY ÁRIAS, Las Villas
June 6, 1931–
P / CHW, 1959
He made the most of one big-league season: 34 relief app (2 saves, 4.09 ERA) for the White Sox, the AL champs. He was a teammate of Jim Bunning on the '56–'57 Caribbean World Champion Marianao Tigers, and a teammate of Pete Rose on the '62 Sally League Champion Macon Peaches.

16. RENÉ AROCHA, La Habana
February 24, 1964–
P / STL, SFG, 1993–97
He was the first of the defectors, bolting from the Cuban national team at Miami airport. The government called him a "traitor"; Cuban players called him a trailblazer, equating him with Jackie Robinson. Career: 18-17, 11 SV over 124 G (36 starts).

17. ROLANDO ARROJO, Santa Clara
July 18, 1964–
P / TBAY, COL, BOS, 1998–2002
His "stunning defection" (Peter Bjarkman) from an Albany, Ga., hotel in 1998 ended the USA-Cuba "Friendly Series" for almost two decades. Career: 40-42, 158 G (105 starts).

18. ERISBEL ARRUEBARRENA, Cienfuegos
March 25, 1990–
SS / LAD, 2014–
As a 24-year-old Cuban player, he signed a five-year, $25 million contract. It proved to be a cautionary tale for major-league franchises, as in "be certain of what you're getting before opening the bank vault." Arruebarrena played only 24 big-league games (195/.241/.220) and 146 in the minors (2014-17).

19. JOE AZCUE, Cienfuegos
August 18, 1939–
C / CIN, KCA, CLE, BOS, CAL, MIL, 1960–72
One of the great throwing catchers of the 1960s. In '66, he led the AL in nailing would-be base-stealers (62% were out; 45% for his career). By comparison, Johnny Bench—rated one of the great throwing catchers of *any* era—was 43% for his career, with a career-best 57% in 1969. As a hitter, Azcue (.252/.304/.344) was no Bench, but was still quite a player.

20. DANYS BÁEZ, Pinar Del Rio
September 10, 1977–
P / CLE, TBR, LAD, ATL, BAL, PHI, 2001–11
The No. 9 pitcher on the Cuban national team's nine-man pitching staff proved to be well-worth the signing: at his peak he saved 96 games over three MLB seasons and was a 2005 All-Star.

21. ED BAUTA, Florida, Cuba
January 6, 1935–
P / STL, NYM, 1960–64
He was signed by Pittsburgh, but was traded on May 28, 1960 (with second baseman Juliàn "Hoolie" Javier) to the Cardinals for Vinegar Bend Mizell and Dick Gray. Javier went on to play in four World Series, winning two rings. Bauta went on to pitch in 97 games, all in relief (149 IP, 4.35 ERA)—and none in the World Series.

22. JULIO BECQUER, La Habana
December 20, 1931–
1B, OF, P / WSH, LAA, MIN, 1955–63
Becquer started the fireworks on the Fourth of July 1961 by smashing the Twins' first-ever pinch-hit grand slam, a two-out "walkoff" in the bottom of the 9th off the White Sox Warren Hacker. Twins owners Cal Griffith called Becquer back to the big leagues for a week in 1963 so Becquer could qualify for his pension. Career: .244/.276/.352.

23. STEVE BELLÁN, La Habana
October 1, 1849–August 8, 1932
INF, OF / Troy Haymakers, NY Mutuals, 1871-73
Esteban "Steve" Bellán was the third baseman for Troy, which took on the famous 1869 Cincinnati Red Stockings. That means the Cubans were playing both country's national pastimes all the way back to the origins of the professional game. He died in Havana at 82. Career: 60 G, 275 AB, .251/.280/.305.

24. YUNIESKY BETANCOURT, Santa Clara
January 31, 1982–
SS, 1B, 3B / SEA, KCR, MIL, 2005–13
His best season was 2007 (38 doubles, 9 HR, 67 RBI). Four years later, he hit the national stage with a good NLCS (.333/.333/.542 and 5 RBI), even though his Brewers lost to the Cardinals. Career .261/.285/.388.

25. FRANCISLEY BUENO, La Habana
March 5, 1981–
P / ATL, KCR, 2008–2014
He had a cup of coffee in Atlanta in 2008, then logged 55 games over three seasons in KC. Career 2.98 ERA.

26. JACK CALVO, La Habana
June 11, 1894–June 15, 1965
OF / WSH, 1913–20
He played in both the Negro Leagues and white major leagues, the latter stints coming seven years apart. His Washington Senators teammate both times was future Hall of Fame pitcher Walter Johnson. On the day Calvo debuted (May 9, 1913) at Comiskey Park, the Chisox starting lineup included third baseman Buck Weaver and right fielder Shano Colllins, the latter being one of only two guys from the 1919 Black Sox starting lineup *not* to wind up either in Cooperstown or banned from the game for life. The other future Black Sox to appear in the game that day was crooked Chick Gandil (ringleader of the 1919 fix), who Weaver would later wish he had never met. (Innocent Buck became a member of the "Eight Men Out" club, too). Meanwhile, Calvo—in *his* 34 career games—went on to bat a buck sixty-one.

27. BERT CAMPANERIS, Pueblo Nuevo
March 9, 1942–
SS, 3B, OF / KCA, OAK, TEX, CAL, NYY, 1964–86
Dagoberto "Campy" Campaneris was a six-time All-Star, and six times he led the league in stolen bases. He homered on his first major-league pitch (July 23, 1964) off Jim Kaat, then hit another one later that day. Although Campy struggled in his first World Series in 1972 (.179), he slashed .290/.353./.452 in his second, and .353/.389/.471 in his third, winning rings in all three (1972-74). He led the league in triples in 1965, the same year he famously became the first major leaguer to play all nine positions in one game (KC Athletics vs. the California Angels on September 8) in a box-office stunt by A's owner Charlie Finley. Campy's career: .259/.311/.342.

28. FRANK CAMPOS, La Habana
May 11, 1924–January 28, 2006
OF / WSH, 1951–53
Francisco Jose Campos knew how to make a debut (September 11, 1951). His double started a rally in the bottom of the 2nd, in which his countrymen Mike

Guerra and Connie Marrero each drove in runs. The Senators bested the great Miñoso's Chisox 7-6. Career: 71 G, 147 AB, .279/.298/.367.

29. BARBARO CANIZARES, La Habana
November 21, 1979–
1B / ATL, 2009
Canizares played seven seasons in Cuba's *Serie Nacional*, including four with Habana's *Industriales* before spending three seasons in the U.S. minors, gaining a five-game call-up to Atlanta in 2009 (.190 BA). He wrapped up his career with four seasons in Mexico and two more in Japan.

30. JOSÉ CANSECO, La Habana
July 2, 1964–
OF, DH / OAK, TEX, BOS, TOR, TBAY, NYY, CHW
Despite some fine seasons, Canseco's legacy will be that of "steroid user and whistleblower," proved largely right about the heavy use of PEDs in MLB in the 1990s. Inside and outside the game, Canseco lived a troubled but quotable life, having once memorably observed: "Every time I have ever tried to help a woman out, I have been incarcerated." 17 seasons, 462 HR, 1407 RBI, 200 SB, 1986 AL ROY, 1988 AL MVP.

31. OZZIE CANSECO, La Habana
July 2, 1964–
OF / STL, OAK, 1990–93
Jose's twin brother played 24 games over three seasons. His best stretch was brief, but exhilarating: in 29 AB in 1992, he rapped five doubles.

32. JOSÉ CARDENAL, Matanzas
October 7, 1943–
OF / SFG, CAL, CLE, STL, CHC, PHI, NYM, KCR, 1963–80
Good outfielder (strong arm) and good bat. Career: .275/.333/.395. Nice combination of speed and power: for 12 straight seasons (1965-1976), he averaged 26 SB and 11 HR. 1,913 career hits. He was creative in expressing himself: Unhappy with the Cubs front office going into the 1974 season, he refused to play the opener, claiming that one of his eyelids was stuck *open*. Second cousin of Bert Campaneris.

33. LEO CARDENAS, Matanzas
December 17, 1938–
SS, 3B / CIN, MIN, CAL, CLE, TEX, 1960–75

Cardenas was a four-time All-Star and a one-time Gold Glover, and takes his rightful place in the 50-year run of *great* Reds shortstops (Roy McMillan, Cardenas, Davey Concepción and Barry Larkin). In 1966, Leo "Chico" Cardenas delivered 20 HR, 25 doubles and 81 RBI. Career: .257/.311/.367.

34. PAUL CASANOVA, Colon
December 21, 1941–August 12, 2017
C / WSH, ATL, 1965–74
On June 12, 1967, in Washington, "Cassy" caught all 22 innings, then singled in the winning run, a "walkoff," against the White Sox. It was his personal Redemption Song, his lone time on base in nine at-bats. He had struck out three times earlier. In his first full season (1966), Casanova bombed 13 homers and five triples. He was an All-Star in 1967, the year of Tony Pérez's game-winning 15th-inning HR off Catfish Hunter in Anaheim.

35. ALBERTO CASTILLO, La Habana
July 5, 1975–
P / BAL, ARI, 2008–11
Drafted out of Miami-Dade College. Career: 60 1/3 inn, 48 Ks, 4.33 ERA.

36. RUSNEY CASTILLO, Ciego de Avila
July 9, 1987–
OF / BOS, 2014–
Castillo's hometown of Ciego de Avila is the closest big city to Tony Pérez's birthplace of Central Violeta. Castillo defected to Haiti in early 2014, triggering a bidding war that brought him a $72.5 million contract over seven years. It topped José Abreu's $68 million contract one year earlier. His ten-game debut in center field after one-and-a-half years away from the game was eye-popping: .333/.400/.528. But two-and-a-half years in the minors followed. Rawness and the need for seasoning—not to mention the Boston outfield of Betts-Bradley Jr.-and-Benintendi—has put some rust on Rusney. Career: 99 G, .262/.301/.379.

37. YOENIS CÉSPEDES, Campechuela
October 18, 1985–
OF, DH / OAK, BOS, DET, NYM, 2012–
Céspedes defected to the Dominican Republic via a 23-hour ride in a speedboat. At 26, he was second in the 2012 Rookie of the Year vote. He is the most popular slugger in Queens since (Carlos) Beltran. 2015: 35 HR, 105 RBI, Gold Glove. Career: .274/.328/.498.

38. AROLDIS CHAPMAN, Holquin
February 28, 1988–
P / CIN, NYY, CHC, 2010–
The four-time All-Star is the hardest-ever thrower on record with a pitch clocked at 105 mph. Beginning at 17, he pitched four seasons with Holquin in Cuba's *Serie Nacional* (2005-2008), striking out 367 batters in 327 2/3 innings. From 2012–17 in the majors, he averaged 34 saves, striking out 615 batters in 364 innings. He is an incredible athlete, the second fastest Red behind Billy Hamilton, the fleetest player in baseball. The "Cuban Missile" was credited with a blown save *and* the victory in Game 7 of the 2016 World Series.

39. JORGE COMELLAS, La Habana
December 7, 1916–September 13, 2001
P / CHC, 1945
He had a seven-game, five-week cup of coffee in 1945. But that's not how he's known among the old-timers in Cuba. There he's known as *El Monstruo*, the monster, being seventh all-time in the Cuban Winter League for games pitched (239). From 1980–82, Comellas coached with countryman/former major leaguer Ángel Fleitas at Caribes Baseball Academy in Florida.

40. GERARDO CONCEPCIÓN, La Habana
February 29, 1992–
P / CHC, 2016–
A Chicago Cubs drought? What Chicago Cubs drought? Concepción doesn't know a thing about it. He started his career at 18 in 2010 for Habana's *Industriales* in *Serie Nacional* (10-3 in 16 starts), then five-plus seasons in the U.S. minors. He figuratively parachuted in for The Miracle, debuting June 21, 2016, before 41,616 fans against the Cubs' archival Cardinals at Wrigley Field, beginning a three-game run with nice splash effect: 2 1/3 innings, 2 Ks, 3.86 ERA. Even for Concepción, it wasn't your run-of-the-(sugar)-mill World Championship.

41. SANDY CONSUEGRA, Potrerillos
September 3, 1920–November 16, 2005
P / WSH, CHW, BAL, NYG, 1950–57
In his rookie season, he joined countrymen Connie Marrero, Julio Moreno and Rogelio Martìnez on the

Senators staff. Career, 51-32, 3.37 ERA. He was a top "swing man" of his era: a 1954 All-Star (16-3; 39 G, 17 starts), with a devastating palm ball and sinker taught to him by manager Paul Richards.

42. JOSÉ CONTRERAS, Las Martinas
December 6, 1971–
P / NYY, CHW, COL, PHI, PIT, 2003–13
He combined with aging Orlando "El Duque" Hernandez in 2005 to bring the south side of Chicago its first World Championship in seven decades. Career, 78-67, 4.57 ERA. His defection stunned Cuban officials, because he had long been a flag-waving loyalist to *La Revolucion* and was rumored to have been among Fidel's personal favorites (Bjarkman).

43. MIKE CUELLAR, Las Villas
May 8, 1937–April 2, 2010
P / CIN, STL, HOU, BAL, CAL, 1959–77
He enlisted in the Cuban army as teenager solely to escape work in the nearby sugar mill. He was signed by the Reds in the spring of 1957. His nasty screwball, taught to him by winter-ball teammate Ruben Gomez, made him a folk hero in Baltimore. From 1969–72, he *averaged* 21 wins per year. He won the Cy Young in 1969 (149 ERA+.) He was a four-time All-Star, and won a ring in 1970. Career: 185-130, 3.14 ERA.

44. BERT CUETO, San Luis
August 14, 1937–April 2, 2010
P / MIN, 1961
He made a nice debut (June 18, 1961)—8 1/3 IP, 3 R, 8 H—in a game highly flavored with Cubania and future Hall of Famers: His shortstop was José Valdivielso; one of the opponents was Chisox Minnie Miñoso (2-for-4, 1 RBI), and there were lots of future Valhallans (teammate Killebrew, Chisox Luis Aparicio and Nellie Fox). Countryman Pedro Ramos relieved Cueto in the 9th, and gave up a walkoff bomb to Fox. Countryman Camilo Pascual pitched the nightcap. Career: 7 G, 5 starts.

45. MANUEL CUETO, Guanajay
February 8, 1892–June 29, 1942
OF, 2B, SS / STL TERRIERS, CIN, 1914–19
This Cueto was a World Champion with the Reds in 1919. In 151 games over three seasons in the 'Nati, he slashed .227/.323/.266.

46. TOMMY DE LA CRUZ, Marianao
September 18, 1911–September 6, 1958
P / CIN, 1944
His decent wartime season (9-9, 3.25 ERA) brought a better offer from Mexico, and that's the last we heard of Tomas de la Cruz north of the border. The timing of the massive heart attack that felled the *two*-time winner of the Cuba National Lottery ($120,000 in total) was fortuitous in a way: if the myocardial infarction hadn't gotten him, Fidel would have.

47. MIKE DE LA HOZ, La Habana
October 2, 1938–
3B, 2B, SS / ATL, CLE, 1960–69
His best season was 1964 as a Milwaukee Brave (.291/.346/.402 in 207 PA), when Miguel Angel de la Hoz held his own with such lumbermen as Aaron, Mathews, Torre, Carty, Felipe Alou, Ed Bailey and Ty Cline.

48. JUAN DELIS, Santiago de Cuba
February 27, 1928–July 23, 2003
3B, OF / WSH, 1955
He had a strong arm but not a strong bat (.189/.219/.227) in 54 games with the Senators. He was a member of the 1956-57 Marianao Tigers that won the Caribbean Series, led by league MVP Minnie Miñoso, and pitchers Jim Bunning and Mike Fornieles.

49. ODRISAMER DESPAIGNE, La Habana
April 4, 1987–
P / SDP, BAL, MIA, 2014–
He flourished in eight seasons with Havana's *Industriales* (58-42) and two in Mexico and the U.S. minors before grinding it out in 87 games (42 starts) in the majors, going 11-21 with a 4.72 ERA.

50. ORESTES DESTRADE, Santiago de Cuba
May 8, 1962–
1B / NYY, PIT, FLA, 1987–94
The graduate of Christopher Columbus High School in Miami had a split big-league career sandwiched around four years in Japan, where his numbers re-confirmed what everybody already knew: Saitama Prefecture is a farther from The Show than Havana, and not just geographically. From 1989–92 with the Seibu Lions, he *averaged* 39 homers per season.

51. ALEDMYS DÌAZ, Santa Clara
August 1, 1990–
SS / STL, 2016–

He was a 2016 All-Star (.300/.369/.510) and fifth in the ROY voting, despite missing six weeks with a broken thumb. It was the best rookie season by Cardinal position player since Albert Pujols. On September 27, 2016—two days after visiting the grieving family of boyhood friend Jose Fernandez, who died in a boating accident—Diaz hit a grand slam in "the most emotional game of my life" to beat the Reds in Cincinnati.

52. JUAN DÌAZ, San Jose de las Lajas
February 19, 1974–
1B, DH / BOS, 2002

Diaz graduated from Santo Domingo High School in the Dominican Republic. He logged only four major-league games, but went out in style on June 23, 2002, with a two-out, one-on, pinch-hit homer off the Dodgers' Andy Ashby in the 6th inning in LA to cut the deficit to 9-5. The Red Sox starting pitcher that day was Dìaz's countryman, Rolando Arrojo. Diaz played 14 minor-league seasons (1997-2010) with stops in 13 different cities from Nuevo Laredo, Mexico, to Winnipeg, Canada, with winter-ball stops in the Dominican, Venezuela and Mexico. His Marco Polo-like travelogue deserves a minor-league reckoning: 4377 AB, 1273 H, 280 HR, 226 doubles, 870 RBI, .291/.359/.538. Not only *could* Diaz play, he loved *playing*.

53. YANDY DIAZ, Sagua la Grande
August 8, 1991–
3B, OF / CLE, 2017–

He was the lone Cuban to make his debut in '17. Diaz played his age 16, 17 and 18 seasons for Villa Clara in *Serie Nacional*, but when he tried to defect after the 2010-11 season, he was caught and jailed for 21 days. Same thing happened again, same sentence. The third time was a charm, as Diaz departed Holquin in a motorized raft at two o'clock in morning with boyhood pal and right-handed pitcher Leandro Linares, and another friend, plus two crewmen. They landed in the Dominican 12 hours later. Diaz was signed to the Indians in late September 2013, meaning he had lost all of his age 19, 20 and 21 seasons. After three years in the minors, he showed promise in 49 games (.263/.352/.329). The Tribe signed Linares, too, who was still in the minors through 2017.

54. PEDRO DIBUT, Cienfuegos
November 18, 1892–December 4, 1979
P / CIN, 1924–25

Dibut attended the same Connecticut high school as Rob Dibble (Southington) albeit 70 years earlier. Dibut's debut (May 1, 1924) was *d'beautiful*: 2 IP, 1 H, 1 K. Overall, he had short MLB success—36 2/3 IP, 27 H, 12 BB, 1.064 WHIP—but a long life, reaching 87 in Hialeah, FL.

55. LINO DONOSO, La Habana
September 23, 1922–October 13, 1990
P / PIT, 1955–56

Donoso never forgot his debut (June 18, 1955), nor did the Reds' Wally Post, who Donoso picked off second base in the second inning at Crosley Field. Post then homered on his next at-bat on a 3-for-4 day. The incomparable Pirates rookie, 20-year-old Roberto Clemente, had a two-out RBI in the eighth inning, and Donoso (en route to a seven-inning, two-run performance), put out twice the Reds big slugger, Ted Kluszewski, who was coming off a 49-HR, 141-RBI season. Donoso died in Veracruz, Mexico, on October 13, 1990, the day after the Reds again beat his Pirates, this time in a terrific NLCS. Career: 28 G, 96 2/3 IP.

56. ROENIS ELIAS, Guantanamo
August 1, 1988–
P / SEA, BOS, 2014–

Elias had a strong rookie season, making Seattle's starting rotation out of spring training (29 starts, 163 2/3 IP; 10-12, 3.85 ERA, 143 Ks). Career: 55 G (50 GS), 15-21, 4.20 ERA, 287 IP, 244 Ks.

57. YUNEL ESCOBAR, La Habana
November 2, 1982–
SS, 3B / ATL, TOR, TBR, WSN, LAA, 2007–

Escobar was suspended for 21 games in 2004 by the Habana *Industriales* for wearing the bottom of his pants to shoetop level, ala those he idolized in the *Grandes Ligas* (major leagues). Escobar eventually fled the island in a tough, costly escape, and signed a $450,000 contract with Atlanta. Career: .282/.350/.386.

58. BOBBY ESTALELLA, Cardenas
April 25, 1911–January 6, 1991
OF, 3B / WSH, SLB, PHA, 1935–49

Robert "Tarzan" Estalella was so much fun to watch that fans would call the Senators switchboard to make sure Estalella (2,569 PA, 282/.383/.421) was in the lineup, *then* they'd head to ballpark. He is the only Cuban player in Dave Frishberg's classic all-name song, "Van Lingle Mungo."

59. ÓSCAR ESTRADA, La Habana
February 15, 1904–January 2, 1978
P / SLB, 1929
Estrada was a teammate of the much more celebrated Luis Tiant Sr. on the 1931 Cuban Stars West of the Negro Leagues. But Estrada's presence on that team made him one of only 16 Cubans who played in the Negro Leagues *and* the major leagues. The light-skinned Estrada pitched one inning in the majors (1 H, 0 R).

60. CHICO FERNANDEZ, La Habana
April 23, 1939–
SS, 2B / BAL, 1968
Fernandez played 16 seasons in the minors before finally making The Show for 24 games (2-for-18, .111). He singled in his first at-bat on April 20, 1968. Enveloped with the likes of Curt Blefary, Boog Powell, Davey Johnson, and Brooks and Frank Robinson, there weren't many outs in the Orioles lineup. For at least one day, Lorenzo Marta Fernandez fit right in.

61. CHICO FERNANDEZ, La Habana
March 2, 1932–June 11, 2016
SS / BRO, PHIL, DET, NYM, 1956–63
Humberto Fernandez broke in as teammate of Jackie Robinson. Fernandez was 0-for-4 in his debut (July 14, 1956), but knew he was in the bigs. In the lineup that day were Gilliam, Amoros, Snider, Reese, Jackie, Hodges, Furillo and Maglie. Career: .240/.292/.329.

62. JOSÉ FERNANDEZ, Santa Clara, Villa Clara
July 31, 1992–September 25, 2016
P / MIA, 2013–16
The invincible one was killed in a boat crash only two months after his 24th birthday. In only two full, major-league seasons, this favorite son of the Cuban-American community was a two-time All-Star. He was the NL's ROY in 2013, and third in the Cy Young vote. He was firmly on the early track for Cooperstown. Oh what a party it would have been. Career: 38-17, 2.58 ERA, 589 Ks in 471 1/3 innings.

63. OSVALDO FERNANDEZ, Holguin
November 4, 1966–
P / SFG, CIN, 1996–2001
He defected in Millington, Tenn., on the eve of the July 1995 U.S.-Cuba "Friendly Series." His best season (by far) was his first: 28 starts, 7-13, 4.67 ERA.

64. ÁNGEL FLEITAS, Los Abreus
November 10, 1914–July 10, 2016
SS, WSH, 1948
This "unheralded" infielder was the "offensive hero" (Bjarkman) of the 1943 Amateur World Series in Havana. Majors: 1-for-13 (.077).

65. MIKE FORNIELES, La Habana
January 18, 1932–February 11, 1998
P / WSH, CHW, BAL, BOS, MIN, 1952–63
Fornieles was one of the most polished pitchers Cuba ever produced. He was mostly a reliever, but he had starter stuff. The five-pitch craftsman was *The Sporting News*' inaugural "Fireman of the Year" in 1960, and a 1961 All-Star. As was the case with Tony Pérez, Fornieles' two brothers stayed in Cuba. Career: 63-64, 432 G, 76 GS, 55 SV.

66. TONY FOSSAS, La Habana
September 23, 1957–
P / TEX, MIL, BOS, STL, SEA, CHC, NYY, 1988–99
Fossas was educated in the States, and acclimated smoothly to pro ball. His Sisyphean rock-pushing was laborious (10 years in minors) but not futile. He debuted in the majors at 30; at 39, he signed a $750,000 contract with the Cardinals, recording 71 G, 51 1/3 IP, 3.83 ERA and 41 Ks.

67. TITO FUENTES, La Habana
September 23, 1957–
2B, SS / SFG, SDP, DET, OAK, 1965–78
Fuentes was one of the last pre-Cuban Missile Crisis signees, just before the 1962 season. Later, he was third in the 1966 NL ROY vote. Although he had four seasons in San Francisco, where he is still acclaimed, his best year was with Detroit (.309/.348/.397) in 1977.

68. BARBARO GARBEY, Santiago de Cuba
December 4, 1956–
1B, OF / DET, TEX, 1984–88
Garbey arrived in the U.S. via the 1980 Mariel Boatlift (125,000 Cubans made the passage April through

October). Upon viewing Garbey's zero-body-fat frame and excellent bat speed, Tigers manager Sparky Anderson called him "the next Roberto Clemente." Alas, Garbey's acknowledgment late in 1983 minor-league season that accusations were true about his involvement in game-fixing in Cuba, delayed his arrival in the bigs. The Marielito was the first member of the Cuba national team to sign a U.S. pro contract. 1984 World Champion the Tigers. Career: 626 AB, .267/.309/.371.

69. ADONIS GARCÌA, Ciego de Avila
April 12, 1985–
3B, LF / ATL, 2015–
The body type (5'9", 205 pounds) provided him no chance to live up to his given name, but one can't blame his parents for trying. He spent seven years in Cuba amateur ball ("*Serie Nacional*") and 4½ in the U.S. minors. Majors: .267/300/.414.

70. ONELKI GARCÌA, Guantanamo
August 2, 1989–
P / LAD, KCR 2013–
Garcia had great size (6-foot-3, 225 pounds), but was another of the "sip espresso" players: 3 G, 1 1/3 IP, 4 BB, 1 HR. He spent 2014-15 in the minors, and 2016 in Mexico.

71. RAMÓN GARCIA, La Esperanza
March 5, 1924–December 25, 2001
P / WSH, 1948
Ditto on the sip espresso: 4 G, 3 2/3 innings (7 runs, 11 hits). Garcia began and ended his big-league career vs. the Yankees. He didn't make a graceful exit (1 IP, 2 runs, 4 hits), but at least got torched by a couple of good hitters (RBI doubles by Bobby Brown and George McQuinn).

72. PRESTON GÓMEZ, Central Preston
April 20, 1923–January 13, 2009
SS, 2B / WSH, 1944
Preston Gómez managed Tony Pérez in Doggie's pivotal 1964 Puerto Rico Winter League season. Gómez was the first skipper of the 1969 expansion San Diego Padres. For his career as a manager, which is where Gómez made his bones, it was 7 seasons, 346-529 (.395).

73. VINCE GONZALES, Quivican
September 28, 1925–March 11, 1981
P / WSH, 1955

In an epic (for the Yankees) debut at Yankee Stadium on April 13, 1955, the Bronx Bombers bashed Gonzales in the final two innings of the 19-1 pasting of the Senators. Gonzales gave up six runs on six hits. At least he got outs on Mantle and Berra. Gonzales played four seasons in Mexico before his callup, and seven seasons south of the border after it. He was a pretty good hitter in the minors: .263 in 501 AB, with 25 doubles, 2 triples and 3 HR. He died in Ciudad del Carmen, Mexico ("Pearl of the Gulf" on Yucatan, known for its fishing and seafood), where only 12 years earlier he played in 23 games at 43.

74. EUSEBIO GONZÁLEZ, La Habana
July 13, 1892–February 14, 1976
3B, SS / BOS, 1918
He made the most of his appearances in three regular-season games for the 1918 World Champion Boston Red Sox, by going 2-for-5 with a triple. He began his pro career at 15, and logged six seasons in Cuba, 14 in the minors.

75. JULIO GONZÁLEZ, Banes
December 20, 1920–February 15, 1991
P / WSH, 1949
Control issues kept the stringbean (5-foot-11, 150 pounds) from achieving his fullest (34 1/3 IP, 27 walks). He ended pro career with the 1955 Crowley (La.) Millers of the Class C Evangeline League.

76. MIGUEL GONZÁLEZ, La Habana
September 23, 1983–November 23, 2017
P / PHI, 2014
Miguel was a classic "miss." He pitched eight seasons in Cuba, then needed two more years to escape. It was worth it to him—he signed a $12 million contract—but not to the Phillies. Arm problems limited him to 5 1/3 major-league innings. At 34, Gonzáles died in a car accident in Havana, where 60 years earlier the young Kentuckian Jim Bunning pitched and occasionally visited the Hotel *Nacional* casino to talk with assistant casino manager/friend Tito Carinci, the former Xavier University star linebacker.

77. MIKE GONZÁLEZ, La Habana
September 24, 1890–February 19, 1977
C, 1B / BSN, CIN, STL, NYG, CHC, 1912–32
As a catcher, his skills and handling of pitchers were so keen that at age 35 with the 1926 Cubs he split

time behind the plate with 25-year-old future Hall of Famer Gabby Hartnett. "Miguel" earned a mention in *Old Man and the Sea*. "Who is the greatest manager, González or Luque?" Along with Luque, he was "one of the two true patriarchs of baseball in Cuba" (Joseph Gerard, SABR). Miguel's "Habana Reds" and Luque's Almendares Alacranes (basically, the "Habana Blues") formed one of the great rivalries in baseball history. González won his first of 13 Cuban Winter League titles at 24. He was a prized coach with the 1934 World Champion St. Louis Cardinals (Gashouse Gang), and the first Latin manager in the bigs (Cardinals, interim basis, for the fired Frankie Frisch, 1938). Gonzo was last heard from when Preston Gomez returned from a trip to Cuba with photos of the icon's 85th birthday party showing Hemingway's favorite field general behind a big birthday cake with a beer in each hand. He is buried in Habana's famous *Cementerio de Cristóbal Colón*.

78. ORLANDO GONZÁLEZ, La Habana
November 15, 1951–
1B, OF / PHI, OAK, CLE, 1976–80
He was a good minor-league hitter (.312/.387/.401), but a total miss in the majors (182 PA, .238/.302/.250).

79. TONY GONZÁLEZ, Central Cunagua
August 28, 1936–
OF / CIN, PHI, SDP, ATL, CAL, 1960–71
He was part of the under-chronicled 1957 class of future Reds' Cuban signees. Also in that gaggle was Leo Cardenas, Cookie Rojas and Mike Cuellar. González hailed from the same province—Camagüey—as Tani Pèrez, albeit 11 miles northeast of Tani's Violeta, in a town now called "Bolivia." Bolivia's sugar mill is no longer grinding. González was part of that same Sugar Kings/Cincinnati pipeline that funneled players to Havana. But because he was six years older than Pèrez, González got to play in the pre-*Revolucion* Cuban winter league (three seasons, all with Cienfuegos, which won the Caribbean World Series in 1960) and for the Sugar Kings (1959 team MVP). Because of that, González' name is better known than Pèrez's to long-time Cuban baseball fans. "Little Dynamite" had a top-shelf career: .286/.350/.413.

80. YASMANI GRANDAL, La Habana
November 8, 1988–
C, 1B / SDP, LAD, 2012–

Grandal was the 12th overall pick by the Reds in the 2010 draft and a part of the big 2011 trade for pitcher Matt Latos. In 2012, Grandal served a 50-game suspension for testosterone use. Career: 586 G, .240/.339/.435. 2015 All-Star.

81. MIKE GUERRA, La Habana
October 11, 1912–October 9, 1992
C / WSH, PHI, BOS, 1937–51
His real first name was "Fermin," and he was the MVP of the 1949-50 Cuban Winter League. He was also initiated into the interesting *santeria* religion, a mysterious rite even on the island. He spent 20 seasons in the Winter League as one of Cuba's most sought-after catchers. He managed the 1948-49 Almendares club to the Caribbean Series title (his outfield was Al Gionfriddo, Sam Jethroe and Monte Irvin). As a resister of the Castro regime, he was sent to Camagüey to pick potatoes. Career: .242/.300/,303.

82. ÁLEX GUERRERO, Las Tunas
November 20, 1986–
OF, 3B / LAD, 2014–15
After 117 games and 232 big-league at-bats (.224/ .251/.414) and one NL Rookie of the Month (April 2015), Guerrero was released from his four-year, $28M contract in 2016, so he could take his show on the road. In 2017, he bashed 35 homers in 130 games for Chunichi.

83. YULI GURRIEL, Sancti Spiritus
June 9, 1984–
3B, DH, 1B / HOU, 2016–
Unlike the character in Chuck Berry's *Havana Moon*, Yuli's ship eventually came in. After 15 years in Cuba's *Serie Nacional*, Gurriel defected with his highly touted younger brother Lourdes in early 2016. (Everybody knew Yuli was a major leaguer in waiting when he led the 2005 World Cup with eight home runs.) The Gurriels' defections were taken as death knells by many baseball fans in Cuba. Ismael Sene, a baseball historian in Havana, told the *New York Times* in February 2016: "Yulieski is one of the most beloved (individuals) we have here, from the people to the government. It's a sad day because it means our baseball is falling apart." Yuli blew through the Astros' farm system at the end of 2016—four levels of it, with no more than 15 games and seven-to-10 plate appearances at each stop. By August 21, 2016,

he was ready to debut at iconic Camden Yards before 29,734 fans. On his first big-league a-bat, Gurriel smacked a line-drive single to center: The Gurriels' Era had begun. Big bro's 2016 was 262/.292/.385 with 3 HR and 15 RBI in 36 games. In 2017, he hit the national stage hard with a solid World Series (2 HR, 3 doubles, 4 RB) and a great postseason overall (27 hard-hit balls, topping by one his teammate and WS MVP George Springer). Career: .291/.324/466.

84. ADEINY HECHAVARRIA, Santiago de Cuba
April 15, 1989–
SS / TOR, MIA, TBR, 2012–
He defected by boat to Mexico in 2009. On May 5, 2013, he drove in seven runs off the late Phillies great, Roy Halladay, with a triple and grand slam. Adeiny's career: 717 G, .255/.291/.345.

85. GUILLERMO HEREDIA, Matanzas
January 31, 1991–
OF / SEA, 2016–
Heredia is a wide-ranging outfielder with a strong arm. 2017: 6 HR, 16 doubles in 386 AB; .322 career OBP.

86. ADRIÁN HERNÁNDEZ, La Habana
March 25, 1975–
P / NYY, MIL, 2001–04
He was originally signed by the Yankees, and almost immediately nicknamed "El Duquecito" for his pitching style so similar to Orlando Hernández's. That's where the similarity ended. El Duquecito was 0-6 in 14 games (5 starts).

87. CHICO HERNÁNDEZ, La Habana
January 3, 1916–January 3, 1986
C / CHC, 1942–43
Along with Hi Bithorn (Puerto Rico's first big leaguer), Chico and the man formed the first all-Latin battery in big-league baseball (1942). Chico's career: 90 G, .250/.309/.287.

88. EVELIO HERNÁNDEZ, Guanabacoa, La Habana
December 24, 1930–December 18, 2015
P / WSH, 1956–57
Hernández was from one of the legendary towns in Cuba: Guanabacoa was the birthplace not only of four major leaguers, but three of the greatest personalities of Cuban music: Ernesto Lecuona, Rita Montaner and Ignacio Villa. It's also famous for the practice of

the *santeria* religion, a fusion of Afro-Caribbean and Yoruba (west Africa) traditions and some Roman Catholic elements. Hernández wasn't thinking of any of that when he debuted against Al Kaline's Tigers in Detroit (September 12, 1956), giving the collar to Kaline, Harvey Kuenn and Ray Boone, leaving after 5 2/3 IP (5 hits, 2 runs) in a 2-2 game. Countryman Camilo Pascual held it there until it unraveled in the ninth. Career: 18 G, 6 GS, 1-1, 4.45 ERA.

89. JACKIE HERNÁNDEZ, Central Tinguaro
September 11, 1940–
SS, 2B / CAL, MIN, KCR, PITT, 1965–73
He played in all seven games for the 1971 World Champion Pirates, hitting .222 with 1 RBI. On the face of it, Jackie (career: .208, 12 HR, 121 RBI) subsisted barely above the Mendoza Line. But Jackie was more than this. Jackie was a jack of all trades—or should we say "Jacinto" of all trades—because he could play all nine positions including catcher (although he never did don the tools of ignorance in the majors) and parlayed that versatility into a nine-year, big-league career. Now *that's* a ballplayer.

90. LIVÁN HERNÁNDEZ, Villa Clara
February 20, 1975–
P / FLA, SFG, MON, WSN, ARI, MIN, COL, NYM, ATL, MIL, 1996–2012
Liván was a career .500 pitcher, but was brilliant at times: He was the 1997 NCLS and World Series MVP with the Marlins. He beat Greg Maddux in Game 5 of the NLCS in a game remembered as much for Eric Gregg's wide strike zone as Hernández's 15 Ks. He was 7-3 in 10 post-season starts, led the league in innings (Montreal, 2003-05), and made only one error in the last five years of career (220 G). Career: 178-177, 519 G (/474 starts), 4.44 ERA.

91. MICHEL HERNÁNDEZ, La Habana
August 12, 1978–
C / TBR, NYY, 2003–09
He attended high school in Caracas, Venezuela. In 45 big-league games, he slashed .237/.286/.305.

92. ORLANDO HERNÁNDEZ, Villa Clara
October 11, 1965–
P / NYY, CHW, ARI, NYM, 1998–2007
El Duque re-did for Cuba what "El Luque" did for it 75 years earlier: He put it back on the big-league

map. There's no better place for a rollout than NYC, and oh did Orlando Hernández deliver. Half-brother, Liván, started the fanfare with his own defection, and then El Duque took it from there. After a 10-year run in Cuba's *Serie Nacional* (126-47 (.724); Orlando burst upon the Big Apple scene in 1998 at 32 by going 12-4 (21 starts) with a 3.13 ERA (131 Ks in 141 IP). He featured a dazzling array of pitches and deliveries. Total postseason: 19 G (14 starts), 9-3, 2.55 ERA, 106 IP, 107 K. Career: 90-65, 4.13 ERA (110 ERA+); 1,314 IP, 1,086 Ks. Four rings: 1998, 1999, 2000, 2005 (Chisox).

93. MIKE HERRERA, La Habana
December 19, 1897–February 3, 1978
2B, 3B / BOS, 1925–26

Ramón "Mike" Herrera debuted on Sept. 22, 1925, at Fenway Park, going 2-for-5 with 2 RBI, sharing or topping the spotlight with the Tigers' Ty Cobb (two hits), Harry Heilmann (one hit), and Charlie Gehringer (no hits), all future Hall of Famers. Career: 84 G, 308 PA, .275/.320/.333. According to SABR's Bill Nowlin and Negro Leagues historian Todd Bolton: "(Herrera was) one of (only) 11 players who played in both the Negro Leagues and major leagues before World War II. Photographs of (him) seem to show that he could easily 'pass' for white… So did he have to 'pass for black' when he was in the Negro Leagues? Not really. There were a number of light-skinned players in the Negro Leagues and even more 'white' Cubans. These players were used to playing together in Latin America. It was only in the U.S. that they were segregated." 18 seasons in Cuba, .291 BA.

94. PANCHO HERRERA, Santiago de la Vegas, La Habana
June 16, 1934–April 28, 2005
1B, 2B, 3B / PHI, 1958–61

Pancho began his athletic career at 16 as a boxer, winning his first five bouts by knockout. He was KO'd in his sixth, whereupon his mother, who was watching from ringside, immediately proclaimed her Juan Francisco's boxing "career" to be over. The Kansas City Monarchs of the U.S Negro Leagues discovered him on a rookie team in Cuba, and teamed him up with Ernie Banks and Minnie Miñoso in KC. Pancho tore it up in 18 games at Triple-A Syracuse in 1955 (.304/.347/.478), but was demoted to Single-A Schenectady in '56 because that's where

pitcher Hank Mason was going—the Phillies' policy was to pair up blacks in the minors for traveling purposes. In '57, Pancho played with Satchel Paige for the Triple-A Miami Marlins in the International League, of which the Havana Sugar Kings were a member. Pamcho blasted 17 HR in 1960 for Phillies (finishing second in NL ROY voting). He was universally lauded as a teammate. Said Luis Tiant Jr: "He never got upset, would do anything for you, never asked for nothing in return." Career: .271/.349/.430.

95. YOSLAN HERRERA, Pinar del Rio
April 28, 1981–
P / PIT, LAA, 2008–14

In his July 7, 2008 debut before 29,387 fans at Pittsburgh's PNC Park, Herrera managed to strike out the Cards' Albert Pujols and Rick Ankiel to end a hitless first inning. However, he was on the ropes in the third, fourth and fifth (6 R/6H/4BB). That was striking distance for the new-age Lumber Company. The Bucs won 12-11 in the 10th inning on a two-run walkoff homer by Jason Michaels. Herrera's career: 25 G, 35 IP, 23 K, 6.43 ERA.

96. DALIER HINOJOSA, Isla de la Juventud
February 10, 1986–
P / BOS, PHIL, 2015–

Only two major leaguers have been born on Isla de la Juventud: Phillies reliever Dalier Hinojosa and the Reds' Raisel Iglesias. Juventud, the second biggest island in the island country of Cuba, is home to 100,000 people and is big enough to have its own team in the 16-team *Serie Nacional*. Juventud is better-known for its political prisoners than its baseball players. It used to be called "Isla de Pinos," Isle of Pines, and was the site of Cuba's internment facility. Fidel Castro, who himself had been imprisoned there in the mid-1950s, renamed it Juventud. The prison is a museum now, and that's how Hinojosa and Iglesias would have known it growing up. Career: 29 G, 35 2/3 IP, 31 Ks, 1.51 ERA.

97. JOSÉ IGLESIAS, La Habana
January 5, 1990–
SS, 3B / BOS, DET, 2011–

Everybody in the AL knew Iglesias was a good-fielding shortstop, but the national audience learned it at the 2015 All-Star Game in Cincinnati, when Iglesias took six strides to his right on a fast chopper off the bat of Yasmani Grandal, and made the classic great-SS-throw-across-the-body, falling away from any point of traction and easily knocking off Grandal. *Show-stopper.* Second in ROY vote, 2013. Career: 531 G/.270/.316/.357. GOOD

98. RAISEL IGLESIAS, Isla de la Juventud
January 4, 1990–
P / CIN, 2015–
The Cuban Bronson Arroyo will throw any pitch from any angle on any count, leaving the hitter constantly guessing. In 2015, Iglesias gave a taste of what he could do: 18 G (16 starts), 95 1/3 IP, 104 Ks, 4.15 ERA. In 2016, he was re-routed to the bullpen over concern about arm stamina. He responded with 37G, 6 SV and 83 Ks in 78 1/3 IP. Full-time closer in 2017: 28 SV, 92 K in 76 IP. Career 134 ERA+.

99. HANK IZQUIERDO, Matanzas
March 20, 1931–August 1, 2015
C / MIN, 1967
He debuted for the Twins (0-for-2) in a 20-inning loss to the Senators, 9-7. Career: 16 G, 28 PA, .269/.296/346.

100. HANSEL IZQUIERDO, La Habana
January 2, 1977–
P / MIA, 2002
Graduated from high school in Miami. Career: 20 G, 4.55 ERA 29 2/3 IP, 20 Ks. No relation to Hank.

101. GEORGE LAUZERIQUE, La Habana
July 22, 1947–
P / KCA, OAK, MIL, 1967–70
Lauzerique made a decent debut (Sept. 17, 1967) vs. a respectable Angels lineup (Aurelio Rodrìguez, Jim Fregosi, Don Mincher, Rick Reichardt), giving up only four hits and three earned runs in seven innings. Success was short-lived from there, however, as he finished at 4-8 with a 5.00 ERA in 34 games (14 starts) spread over four seasons. Graduate of George Washington High School in New York City.

102. RAUDEL LAZO, Pinar del Rio
April 12, 1989–
P / MIA, 2015–
Some folks might say the wrong Lazo left the island but Raudel is the one who rose up to take a

crack at the best competition. Raudel's career line was enough to notice—5 2/3 IP, 5H, 2 earned runs, 5 K's, 3.18 ERA—while his cousin, Pedro Luis Lazo, was rewriting the post-*Revolucion* record book with 257 victories in the *Serie Nacional*. Pedro: "I never had the dream of playing in the major leagues—it never entered my mind." He said he walked away from a $30-$35 million offer in his prime. No such woulda-coulda-shoulda for Raudel.

103. IZZY LEÓN, Cruces, Las Villas
January 4, 1911–July 25, 2002
P / PHI, 1945
Izzy wasn't dizzied by his debut (June 21, 1945) against a decent Dodgers wartime lineup (Eddie Stanky, Augie Galan, Dixie Walker Eddie Basinski et al): 7 IP, 7 H, 2 earned runs. Career: 14 G, 38 2/3 IP, 0-4, 5.35 ERA.

104. MARCELINO LÓPEZ, La Habana
September 23, 1943–November 29, 2001
P / PHIL, CAL, BAL, MIL, CLE, 1963–72
Within two months of Phillies manager Gene Mauch lauding him in spring training, 1963—"He's throwing bullets, good curve, and changeup; a natural athlete, can hit, is one of our fastest runners, can field and has a lot of poise for 19"—an elbow injury forced López's demotion to Triple-A. It was a frustrating year, capped by an incident in August: When manager Frank Lucchesi pulled him in the 2nd inning, López failed to hand the ball over per protocol; instead, he winged the sphere over the stands, drawing a $27.50 fine ("$25 for the throw, $2.50 for the ball," Lucchesi said.) López was an Angels' workhorse at ages 21 (215 IP, 14-13) and 22 (199 IP, 7-14). Arm problems forced him to the bullpen, but in 1970 he glittered for the World Champion Orioles: 25 G (3 starts) 60 IP, 49 K's, 177 ERA+.

105. RAMÓN LÓPEZ, Las Villas
May 26, 1933–September 4, 1982
P / CAL, 1966
In his debut (a start) on August 21, 1966, Ramón was rocked by countryman Paul Casanova, the Senators catcher, who crushed a two-run homer, then rapped a safety off the reliever who followed: Cuban reliever Marcelino López on a 4-for-4 day. Ramón's career: 4 G (1 start), 7 IP, 5.14 ERA.

106. DOLF LUQUE, La Habana
August 4, 1890–July 3, 1957
P / BOS-N, CIN, BRO, NYG, 1914–35
"The Pride of Havana." His 1923 season of 27-8, and a league-leading 1.93 ERA and 6 shutouts, was one of the truly great pitching seasons in history. Only 5-foot-7 and 160 pounds, Luque was remarkably durable. He logged 20-big league seasons, finishing 194-179 with a 118 ERA+ in 3,220 innings, pitching his last game at 44. There were no World Series rings in those days, just diamond-studded stick-pins. Luque collected two: his first was with the 1919 Reds; his second was with the 1933 Giants. His WS numbers: 9 1/3 IP, 3 H, 2 walks, 0 runs, 11 Ks. Every baseball fan in Cuba knows of Luque, far more than know of Pérez. It's because Luque played and managed in the Cuban Winter League. "Sure, I know of Luque," said a cabbie in early December 2015. "There are monuments to Luque and Martín Dihigo in the Estadio Latinoamericano, where my team, the *Industriales* play."

107. HÉCTOR MAESTRI, La Habana
April 19, 1935–February 21, 2014
P / WSH, 1960–61
Another "espresso drinker," but make it a "double" for Maestri: 2G, 8 IP over two seasons. Check out that 1.13 ERA. His debut vs. the Orioles on September 4, 1960, covered the waterfront: 2 IP, 1 H, 1 walk, 1 K, 1 DP (Brooks Robinson, to end the 8th).

108. CONNIE MARRERO, La Grande, Villa Clara
April 25, 1911–April 23, 2014
P / WSH, 1950–54
Connie dropped out of school as a boy to work on his father's family sugarcane plantation, and began pitching as a teenager. He was 27 by the time he joined Cuba's organized amateur baseball. He was never an overpowering pitcher, given his José Altuve-like physique. That explains how he escaped the attention of Senators famed Cuba-based scout, Joe Cambria. Marrero was four days shy of his 39th birthday when he reached the bigs with the 1950 Senators. He was an All-Star in his second season, throwing a one-hitter. From ages 39 to 42, he registered seasons of 152, 187, 184 and 145 innings, and was an 11-game winner twice. Career: 39 wins, 40 losses and 7 shutouts. One of the few former major leaguers in the post- WWII period through the Cuban Missile

Crisis in 1962 not to emigrate to the U.S. probably because his career in the States was well over by the time Castro took over on Jan 1, 1959. Why didn't he emigrate? Because "I'm Cuban—I came back to my homeland, to the place I was born," Marrero told NPR a month shy of his 101st birthday. He died in Havana two days shy of his 103rd.

109. ELI MARRERO, La Habana
November 11, 1973–
C, OF, 1B / STL, ATL, KCR, BAL, COL, NYM, 1997–2006
The grandnephew of Connie Marrero and graduate of Coral Gables (FL) High School was drafted by the Cardinals in the third round in 1993. His Cubano genes showed in his versatility: He played every position the majors except 2B, SS and P. On September 3, 2001, he caught Bud Smith's no-hitter. Eli's greatest victory, though, may have been in surviving thyroid cancer in 1998. Best season, 2004: .321/.374/.520, 2.3 WAR, 128 OPS+. Career: 243/.303/.411 (724 G).

110. ARMANDO MARSANS, Matanzas
October 3, 1887–September 3, 1960
OF, 1B / CIN, STL-TERRIERS, STLB, NYY, 1911–18
Armando the gourmando was the first Cubano of significance to hit the bigs. He had played in front of some big crowds back home, but none as big as the 26,336 that jammed brand-new Redland Field in Cincinnati for Opening Day 1912. Marsans was of "swarthy" complexion, which meant definitely white, but darkish in a Spanish or Italian sort of way. And dark enough that Reds club owner Garry Herrmann felt compelled to write a friend in Cuba and confirm to his satisfaction that Marsans didn't have any African ancestors. It was necessary that Marsans' pedigree be white, so he could play in the all-white majors. Marsans and fellow Cuban Rafael Almeida had made their debuts for the Reds the previous July 4 in Chicago, mainly because Reds business manager Frank Bancroft had vouched for them. The well-traveled "Banny" knew of the talent on the island, wanted to tap it, and had the ear of Herrmann. Marsans' best season was 1912: .317/19 doubles/7 triples (all career bests) and 35 SB. Career: .269/.325/.318. Armando caused a big stir when he jumped to Federal League (St. Louis Terriers) in 1914.

111. LEONYS MARTIN, Villa Clara
March 6, 1988–
OF / TEX, SEA, CHC, 2011–
Martin has a wild defection story, involving a 45-foot yacht, Mexico, smugglers, armed gangsters (business as usual, in other words, when it comes to Cuban baseball players defecting since the 1990s). Oh, and dueling lawsuits (just to Americanize-up the story a bit). Martin was a terrific player in his mid-20s: 3.5 WAR in 2013; 4.6 WAR in 2014. Excellent speed; good base stealer: 36 SB 2013 (80% success rate). Career: .247/.300/.360.

112. HÉCTOR MARTÌNEZ, Las Villas
May 11, 1939–12/99
OF / KCA, 1962–63
Martinez had one extra-base hit in 17 at-bats. His hometown is far better known than Héctor's lone hit, a home run. In fact, Héctor's hectares are among the most familiar in all of Cuba. The city is formally known today as Santa Clara in Villa Clara Province, but many people still call it Las Villas. It is a popular stop between Havana and the eastern provinces.

113. JOSÉ MARTÌNEZ, Cardenas, Matanzas
July 26, 1942–October 1, 2014
2B, SS, 3B / PIT, 1969–70
Martinez deserves his own Hall of Fame plaque: He introduced the Big Dog to family friend Pituka in San Juan, Puerto Rico, in October of 1964. Coached at KC and Cubs. Career: 1 HR, 16 RBI in 188 AB, .245/286/.293.

114. MARTY MARTÌNEZ, La Habana
August 21, 1941–March 8, 2007
SS, 3B, 2B / MIN, ATL, HOU, STL, OAK, TEX, 1962–72
Marty hit no HRs in 945 AB, but scored big as a scout: He discovered and signed Edgar Martínez and Omar Vizquel. Career: 436 G, .243/.296/.287.

115. ROGELIO MARTÌNEZ, Cidra
November 5, 1918–May 24, 2010
P / WSH, 1950
Martinez, one of the most revered pitchers in La Habana, was from the hometown of the great Martin Dihigo, and grew up as the fourteenth of fifteen children with baseball in his blood. His nickname was "Limonar" for the country town where he learned to play baseball. Limonar the man was a white *guajiro* ("country bumpkin") from Cuba's agricultural areas, producer of so many pitchers, wrote Roberto González Echevarría. Martinez debuted at 31 in Washington, retiring the last final two batters of the game, and a few days later got knocked out in the first inning. Those were his only two appearances in the big leagues. The culprit? A bum knee that he hadn't reported to management. The ill turn didn't affect Rogelio's stock in Cuba, and Echevarria has kept Limonar luminous in his writings. After baseball, Martínez worked in a textile factory in Cuba. He left for the U.S. in 1962, and died in New London, CT, at 91.

116. TONY MARTÌNEZ, Perico
March 18, 1940–August 24, 1991
SS / CLE, 1963–66
The 1962 International League MVP was 0-for-3 in his debut (April 9, 1963) vs. countryman Camilo Pascual. Martinez started 35 games in 1963, but hit only .156 and was returned to the minors.

117. YUNESKY MAYA, Pinar del Rio
August 28, 1981–
P / WSN, 2011–13
Maya led the *Serie Nacional* with a 1.61 ERA in 2004-05 and was second only to Aroldis Chapman's Ks in 2008-09. Career: 1-5, 5.80 ERA, 16 G (10 starts), 59 innings.

118. ORLANDO MCFARLANE, Oriente
June 28, 1938–July 18, 2007
C / PIT, DET, CAL, 1962–68
He debuted with the Pirates late in the 1962 season. His best year was 1966 with the on-the-come Tigers. In only 138 AB, he hit 5 homers, 7 doubles and had 13 RBI, slashed .254/.304/.413 and managed to look not at all conspicuous in stellar company: Al Kaline, Willie Horton, Norm Cash, Bill Freehan, Jim Northrup et al.) Career: 124 G, 292 AB, .240/.290/.332.

119. ROMÁN MEJIAS, Abreus
August 9, 1930–
OF / PIT, HOU, BOS, 1955–64
Mejias was spotted in tryout camp in 1953 Havana. Pirates scout George Sisler (Hall of Famer) signed him after a 100-mile drive to Mejías's home. Sisler: "If you've never traveled by car into the interior of

Cuba, you (cannot imagine) what kind of ride we had." Mejias was going nowhere behind Roberto Clemente in Pittsburgh, but the Houston Colt 45s plucked him from the Bucs in the 1962 expansion draft. That winter, he played in Puerto Rico, leaving his wife and nine- and 11-year-old daughters back home in Havana. He didn't see them again for more than a year. With Houston in 1962, he blasted two three-run homers on Opening Day (1962: .286/.326/.445). Career: 627 G, 254/.294/.391.

120. MINNIE MENDOZA, Ceiba del Agua
November 16, 1933–
3B, 2B / MIN, 1970
Another Hall of Famer in Doggie's eyes: Minnie took in "Tani" after "Macon 1963" when Tani's father told his son to stay put. Mendoza was originally signed by the Reds in 1954. Minnie played 16 games with Minnesota in April/May of 1970, going 3-for-16 (.188), but his two RBI were big ones, knocking the Tribe's Sudden Sam McDowell out of the game in the 9th inning of a Twins' 5-4 loss in Cleveland. And Minnie's two runs were big ones, too, because future Hall of Famers Harmon Killebrew and Rod Carew drove him in in "late and close" situations: Killebrew's RBI came after Mendoza had pinch-hit singled in the 8th inning of a 2-2 game in Baltimore off countryman Mike Cuellar, and Carew's RBI came after Mendoza had pinch-hit singled off Cuellar, in the 7th inning. At least Mendoza could later lay claim to "owning" the great Cuellar, and Miguel had the good humor and humanity to never dispute it.

121. TONY MENENDEZ, La Habana
February 20, 1965–
P / CIN, PIT, SFG, 1992–94
Menendez was signed by the Chisox, but debuted as a Red for manager Lou Piniella, and punched-out-looking the first batter he faced, Astros catcher Eddie Tucker. Menendez pitched only 29 innings over three big-league seasons, but the 20 Ks he registered were notched in an era not as redolent with whiffs as today. He graduated American High School in Miami.

122. Minnie Miñoso, La Habana
November 29, 1925–March 1, 2015
OF, 3B / CLE, CHW, STL, WSH, 1949–1980
Minnie Miñoso paved the way for Latins in postwar MLB as arguably the most exciting Cuban

ever in the majors. Three times he led AL in triples, and was a seven-time All-Star, and he has a statue at Comiskey Park. (His first Cuban Winter League manager—Marianao Tigers—was Armando Marsans, the first high-impact Cuban in the majors.) In 1951, Minnie exploded onto the big-league scene as a 25-year-old in Cleveland and Chicago. He homered in his first at bat as a Chisox, a 415-foot blast off the NY Yankees' Vic Raschi, and led the league that year with 14 triples and 31 stolen bases, finishing second in ROY and fourth in MVP. His flash was not contained to the field: The Cuban Comet "drove a green Cadillac, wore brilliantly colored silk shirts and wide-brimmed hats (and) sported an enormous diamond ring... His Caddy made the trip back and forth from Chicago to Havana for many years." (Mark Stewart, SABR). Minnie played three games as a 50-yr-old in 1976; two more in 1980. Career: 83 triples, 336 doubles, 186 HR, 1,023 RBI, 130 OPS+ (Tony Pérez's was 122) and 50.2 WAR (Pérez's was 53.9). Even given Minnie's late start because of the color line, Orestes Miñoso (.298/.389/.459) deserves enshrinement in Cooperstown.

123. ARIEL MIRANDA, La Habana
January 10, 1989–
P / BAL, SEA, 2016–
He was roughed up in the second inning of his two-inning O's debut (July 3, 2016) against the Mariners at Safeco Field. He ended his first frame on the mound by striking out (looking) his countryman Leonys Martin, the M's leadoff man. One might even say Ariel "read Martin his Miranda rights." But a Cuban pitcher who has punched out a countryman has rights, too: bragging rights, giving him the right to crow about it until las vacas (the cows) come home. Miranda's Mount Rainier-high lasted one more batter—he also punched-out-looking Seattle's 2-hole hitter, Seth Smith—but then el techo (the roof) fell in. Single, ground-rule double, two-RBI double, a quien vas a llamar? (who ya' gonna call?), el bullpen. Fortunately for Miranda, his debut line (2 IP, 4 H, 3 R, 3 ER, 0 BB, 4 K, 13.50 ERA) wasn't his career line: 13-9, 4.79 ERA, 43 G (39 starts), 218 IP, 181 Ks, 81 walks.

124. JUAN MIRANDA, Consolacion del Sur
April 25, 1983–
1B / NYY, ARI, 2008–11

A trouper, Miranda has played all over the world since 2012: Japan, Mexico and the Dominican Republic. Career: .226/.320/.420.

125. WILLY MIRANDA, Velasco
May 24, 1926–September 7, 1996
SS / WSH, CHW, STLB, NYY, BAL, 1951–59
This is the Miranda widely believed to be the fellow whose play inspired famed baseball man Joe Cambria to coin the phrase, "good field, no hit." Career: .221/.282/.271.

126. YOAN MONCADA, Abreus
May 27, 1995–
3B / BOS, CHW, 2016–
Boston backed up the Brink's truck to the Moncada barracks, signing him at 19 to a $31.5 million contract, "which may prove a test case for lavish Cuban spending" (Bjarkman). Moncada was traded to Chicago for Chris Sale in December 2016. Career: 62G, .229/.331/.399.

127. AURELIO MONTEAGUDO, Caibarien
November 19, 1943–November 10, 1990
P / KCA, HOU, CHW, KCR, CAL, 1963–73
He debuted at 19 for the Kansas City Athletics. A year after the KC Royals were formed, he was back in their bullpen (18 Ks in 27 IP, 2.96 ERA).

128. RENÉ MONTEAGUDO, La Habana
March 12, 1916–September 14, 1973
P, OF / WSH, PHI, 1938–45
The father of Aurelio Monteaqudo, René Monteagudo was only 5-foot-7 but in the tradition of the old-time Cuban game had a strong arm (100 IP, 1940) and was a good hitter (.289 BA) He returned to Cuba after his baseball career in the States had ended, but he didn't stay, passing away in Hialeah, Fla., at 57.

129. MANNY MONTEJO, Caibarien
October 16, 1935–January 19, 2000
P / DET, 1961
One of only two Cubans to have played in the majors in the early 1960s who returned home to Cuba, and since, died there. (First signed by Reds). Career: 12 G, 16 1/3 inn, 15 Ks, 3.86 ERA.

130. KENDRYS MORALES, Fomento
June 20, 1983–

DH, 1B / LAA, SEA, MIN, KCR, TOR, 2006–
In December 2004—only six months after arriving in Florida by raft—the 21-year-old Morales signed a six-year contract ($3 mil signing bonus) with the Angels. Won a ring with the Royals in 2015. Career: .270/.328/.462.

131. DANNY MOREJON, La Habana
July 21, 1930–April 27, 2009
OF / CIN, 1958
After 1956-57 with the Havana Sugar Kings, Danny (in 1958 with the Reds) batted only .192. (He had a good eye, however, judging by his .400 on-base percentage with nine walks). After five more years in the minors and nine more in Mexico, Morejon retired at 41, dying in Miami at 78.

132. JULIO MORENO, Guines
January 28, 1921–January 2, 1987
P / WSH, 1950–1953
Nicknamed "Cuban Bob Feller," the 5-foot-8, 165-pound Moreno lost his heater before his heart. (Feller, at 17, struck out 15 in his first start; Moreno, 29, struck out seven in his first *season*; 21 IP). In Moreno's debut, he recorded a complete-game, 10-4 win over Philadelphia, and struck out pinch hitter/countryman Mike Guerra to lead off the 5th. Career, 18–22.

133. CHOLLY NARANJO, La Habana
November 25, 1934–
P / PIT, 1956
Ramon Gonzalo Naranjo was treated roughly in his one-inning debut (July 8, 1956), as the NY Giants' Daryl Spencer and Wes Westrum solo-shotted him in the 9th at the Polo Grounds. Career: 17G, 1-2, 4.46 ERA in 34 1/3 IP with 26 Ks.

134. ADRIÁN NIETO, La Habana
November 12, 1989–
C / CHW, 2014
The graduate of American High School in Plantation, Fla., debuted on April 2, 2014. And how's this for a flash of youth: This backup *catcher* pinch-ran for Paul Konerko in the bottom of the 9th, scoring the first of two Chisox runs against the Twins to tie game, then caught the 10th and 11th in the 7–6 win. Try *that* at 35.

135. RAY NOBLE, Central Hatillo
March 15, 1919–May 9, 1998

C / NYG, 1951–53

It was *noblesse oblige* that Rafael Miguel Noble (he was the second black Cuban in the MLB) share a rookie year with the first. Only four years after Jackie Robinson broke baseball's color line, 25-year-old Minnie Miñoso led the AL with 14 triples and 31 SB. Noble, 32, helped the "Jints" overcome a 13½-game deficit to "Da Bums," blasting five home runs, six doubles and 26 RBI in only 141 AB.

136. VLADIMIR NÚÑEZ, La Habana
March 15, 1975–
P / MON, LAA, TEX, BAL, 1998–2009

Núñez bounced between starter and late reliever throughout his career. He was out of baseball 2005–08 before his swan song with the Braves. Career: 254 G (27 GS), 21-34, 21 SV, 4.83 ERA.

137. TONY OLIVA, Pinar del Rio
July 20, 1938–
OF, DH / MIN, 1962–78

The only rookie of the year—along with Ichiro Suzuki, who had a head start—to win a batting title in the modern era. Oliva went on to win two more. He led the AL in hits five times. In 2014, he missed election to the Baseball Hall of Fame via the Golden Era Committee by only one vote. Bad knees were the only thing that kept Oliva from being a Cooperstown lock. Had Oliva not gotten out of Cuba, what might have become of him? Answer: He'd have been another Omar Linares, also from tobacco-rich Pinar del Rio province, one of the great Cuban players of all-time (1980s/1990s) that nobody outside Cuba ever heard of. Why? Because Linares never left Cuba. Just like nobody remembers Howard Easterling, a phenomenal all-around third baseman (like Linares), who never got a shot at the white major leagues because he was African-American. The difference is Linares was an icon in Cuba. In the U.S., only the attendees of Negro League games knew how great Easterling was. The what-if stories are the saddest of all. At least Linares had Cuba, and Oliva (and Tony Pèrez) had the U.S. And at least Oliva's achy, breaky knees didn't keep him from immortality: he has a statue at the Twins' ballpark. Lifetime: .304/.353/.476.

138. HÉCTOR OLIVERA, Santiago de Cuba
April 5, 1985–
3B, LF / ATL, 2015–

Olivera signed a five-year, $62 million contract with Dodgers in May 2015. Two months later, he was traded to Atlanta as part of a three-team deal, in which the Marlins sent Matt Latos and Mike Morse to LA. In 2016, he was suspended for 82 games under MLB's domestic violence policy. He was traded to San Diego for Matt Kemp, but only as formality to save San Diego $25.5 million on Kemp's contract. The 'Pods then released Olivera. Career: 98 AB, 5 2B, 2 HR.

139. TONY ORDENANA, Guanabacoa, La Habana
October 30, 1918–September 29, 1988
SS / PIT, 1943

This one-game wonder debuted in final game of 1943 season with three RBI. Close the curtain on the aptly nicknamed "Mosquito."

140. REY ORDÓÑEZ, La Habana
January 11, 1971–
SS / NYM, TBR, CHC, 1996–2004

This spectacular, wide-ranging fielder is remembered almost as much for his punchless bat (.246/.289/.310) as his three straight Gold Gloves (1997–99). "Rey-Rey" missed the 2000 World Series with a fractured left forearm, then was traded to Tampa Bay in 2003 after the New York romance soured.

141. EDDIE OROPESA, Colon
November 23, 1971–
P / ARI, PHI, SDP, 2001–04

The sub-par middle reliever (7.34 ERA) was hired by the Dodgers to mentor and bed-check Yasiel Puig. Observed veteran LA scribe Bill Plaschke in spring training 2013: "While Puig has been celebrating the purchase of a Mercedes, Oropesa (41), was in the locker room marveling at something far more compelling, his own name on a Dodgers name plate. (Said Oropesa:) 'I'm like, oh, hey, that's me!'"

142. BILL ORTEGA, La Habana
July 24, 1975–
PH / STL, 2001

Career: 1 single, 5 AB. In his debut (Sept. 7, 2001 before 33,935 fans at Busch Stadium), Ortega flew out in the bottom of the 9th for the second-to-last out vs. the Dodgers' Terry Mulholland. Hey, at least Ortega didn't make the last out, and probably didn't mind the company, for it was good company—Albert

Pujols lined out to shortstop, dropping his batting average to .333, his OBP to .405 and his slugging percentage to .624.

143. BABY ORTIZ, Camaguey
December 5, 1919–March 27, 1984
P / WSH, 1944

The WW II fill-in was 0-2 with a 6.23 ERA, but he had a good debut (8 IP, 4 earned runs, 6 hits, and collected a hit himself). It wasn't as though the Chisox had no true major leaguers in the lineup (RF Wally Moses, leading off; 1B Hal Trosky, batting cleanup. Oliverio "Baby" Ortiz held that trio to a 1-for-7). Ortiz played for eight different minor-league teams in 10 seasons. Younger brother of Roberto; thus, "Baby."

144. ROBERTO ORTIZ, Camaguey
June 30, 1915–September 15, 1971
OF / WSH, PHA, 1941–50

Baby's big brother led the AL with eight hit-by-pitches in 1944, his only full season. His best partial season was his first (22 G, 82 PA, 329/.354/.430).

145. REGGIE OTERO, La Habana
September 7, 1915–October 21, 1988
1B / CHC, 1945

Otero played on the last Cubs team to reach the World Series before 2016 (although he didn't play in any WS games). In 14 games in the 1945 regular season, Otero was 9-for-23 (.391) with a .440 OBP, but all his hits were singles. He played eight years in the minors before he got the call-up, then eight *more* years in the minors after his send-down. He was a Reds coach (1959-65) and a big factor in Pete Rose's development at second base. Manager Otero worked Charlie Hustle like a rented *mula* in the Venezuelan Winter Season of 1964-65. That same winter, Rose's rookie-league teammate, Tony Pérez, was learning *his* craft in the Puerto Rican Winter League.

146. RAFAEL PALMEIRO, La Habana
September 24, 1964–
DH, OF / CHC, TEX, BAL, 1986–2005

Palmeiro was six years old when he came to the States on a "Freedom Flight" (250,000 Cubans emigrated to America that way, 1965-73.) The prolific slugger has been dogged by PED allegations. Prior to his 30th birthday in 1995, he had only one 30+ HR season (37 in 1993; after that, he had *nine straight*

seasons of 38+*, including 47 each at age 34 and 36 (and 43 at 37). The three-time Gold Glover (1997-1999) was one of only five players with 3000 hits and 500 HR. He played with great soul in his 20s—he led the league in hits in 1990, and doubles in 1991, and runs in 1993—before selling his soul in his 30s. Career: .288/.371/.515.

147. EMILIO PALMERO, La Habana
June 13, 1895–July 15, 1979
P / NYG, STLB, WSH, BOS-N, 1915–28

Palmero failed to get out of the 1st in his debut-start (2/3 IP, 2 H, 3 R, 3 walks, 1 HBP), but it was memorable. Behind him were Giants stars Fred Merkle, High Pockets Kelly, and "Harvard" Eddie Grant, who was killed three years later in the Argonne Forest (WWI), trying to rescue the "Lost Battalion" of his Harvard classmate Major Charles Whittlesey. On November 26, 1921—five days after Whittlesey had served as a pallbearer with fellow Medal of Honor recipients Alvin York and Samuel Woodfill at the Tomb of the Unknown Soldier, and two months after the end of Palmero's only full season in the bigs—"Whit" leaped overboard to his death from the SS Toloa, a United Fruit ship bound for Havana. At least in part, Whittlesey's depression stemmed from the horrors of what he had witnessed in France and for being unable to help out all the men of his ravaged unit after the war. Meanwhile, Palmero's baseball life spanned seven strong decades of Cuban presence in the game and four major U.S. wars. Four days before Palmero died in Toledo at 75, countryman Mike Cuellar beat the Tigers in nearby Detroit for his eleventh victory in a marvelous 24–8 season.

148. CAMILO PASCUAL, La Habana
January 20, 1934–
P / WSH, MIN, CIN, LAD, CLE, 1954–71

The "Little Potato" threw "the most feared curveball in the AL for 18 years," according to none other than Ted Williams who, as they say in NYC, "knew from curveballs." Career: 174-170, 3.63 ERA; 3 straight years led the AL in Ks (1961-63); 3 times led in complete games and shutouts; 5-time All-Star, including four straight (1959-62). Those were the same four years Fidel Castro seized and consolidated power in Pascual's hometown. Wrote Bjarkman: "Baseball was a central passion for (Camilo's father), who regularly took his two sons to *La Tropical* stadium to watch games of his favorite Almendares Alacranes, and also encouraged their early sandlot play in the capital city's San Miguel del Padrón neighborhood where they were raised."

149. CARLOS PASCUAL, La Habana
March 13, 1931–May 12, 2011
P / WSH, 1950

The "Big Potato," Carlos, was in fact small potatoes compared with his three years' younger brother, Camilo. Carlos started only two major-league games (compared to Camilo's 404), completing both in a 1-1 career. (For the record: The whole "Potato" nickname-thing resulted from a "sloppy translation of the Spanish," wrote Bjarkman, who surmises that the original nickname was meant to be "Shorty," which would have fit Carlos, who was 5-foot-6. Either way, "Big Potato," "Little Shorty" or "The Big Short," the younger brother eclipsed the older on the sports field, which is not at all unusual when brothers are close in age and the younger has an innate desire to surpass a sibling rival. For *that*, Carlos is owed a great debt: He helped "produce" one of the greatest Cuban pitchers ever.

150. CARLOS PAULA, La Habana
November 28, 1927–April 25, 1983
OF / WSH, 1954–56

Across three seasons, Paula put together a solid year 157 G, 457 AB, 23 doubles, 8 triples, 9 HR and 60 RBI (.271/.311/.416). A major reason for the late start (27) is contained in a fascinating piece on the National Baseball Hall of Fame's web site, "Carlos Paula, The Man Who Integrated the Washington Senators." The Senators were interested in signing Cuban players, largely because they could be had on the cheap. But cheap and black was a different matter. Ossie Bluege, the Senators former star third baseman became the team's first farm director in 1947 (SABR), the year Jackie Robinson broke the color line. Bluege is quoted in the Hall piece as writing to his scouts that if a player is "white, (it's) all go and well, if not, he stays home." That letter would have been written "AJ" (After Jackie), maybe even years after, because not until 1952 is Paula in the Senators farm system. Angel Scull, also a Cuban, who was supposed to be the Senators' first black player, doesn't appear in their minors until 1951. Until the Reds came along in the mid-1950s, Washington was the dominant force on the island. It is further evidence that had the scrawny Tony Pèrez come along seven years earlier or three years later, he likely wouldn't have gotten off the island.

151. CHICK PEDROES, La Habana
October 27, 1869–August 6, 1927
OF / CHC, 1902

Some call Pedroes the first Cuban-born player to perform in the modern game, because Havana-born Esteban "Steve" Bellán played in the pioneer era. Pedroes' career: 6 AB, 2 G, 0 hits.

152. BRAYAN PEÑA, La Habana
January 7, 1982–
C / ATL, KCR, DET, CIN, STL, 2005–16

Peña was highly regarded as a back-up catcher, much in demand for his clubhouse influence and on-field presence. It was a neat day in Cuba-rich Reds history when on August 1, 2015—in a 4–3 win over the Pirates at Great American Ball Park in Cincinnati—starting pitcher Raisel Iglesias earned the win and Aroldis Chapman the save, and Pena caught them both, while going 2-for-4. Peña, who had defected from Cuba at 17, returned in early winter 2015 as part of MLB goodwill group. "I was very excited, but at the same time very scared," he told MLB.com. "They follow their own rules down there. I let (Yaisel) Puig and (José) Abreu go in front. (I told them) 'If something happens, I'm going back (to the U.S.) because I'm an American citizen.' (*Peña smiled as he said it.*) For me to (see my family and friends) and touch Cuba land, I'm blessed." Career: 638 G, .259/.299/.351.

153. ORLANDO PEÑA, Victoria de las Tunas
November 17, 1933–
P / CIN, KCA, DET, CLE, PIT, BALT, STL, CAL, 1958–75

He lost 20 games for Kansas City in 1963, despite a 106 ERA+. As stated in "20-Game Losers" (SABR) by editors Bill and Emmet Nowlin: "You have to be a very good pitcher to lose 20 games in one season. (Six Hall of Famers did.) Why would a manager keep putting you out there... if you didn't have a chance to win that game?" True that. Peña had 140 ERA+'s twice ('62 in KC, '65 in Detroit) and a 137+ in Cincinnati in '60. Career: 56-77. Three seasons with the Havana Sugar Kings.

154. TONY PÉREZ, Central Violeta, Camagüey
May 14, 1942–
1B, 3B / CIN, MON, BOS, PHIL, 1964–86

In Cuba, he is known as "Tani," in Cincinnati as "The Big Dog," aka "Doggie." He is the only Cuban major leaguer in the National Baseball Hall of Fame. (There are three other Cubans in the Hall, but they weren't big-leaguers. They were barred by the color line: Martìn Dihigo, Cristòbal Torriente and Josè Mèndez.) Pèrez was a fierce competitor who grew only more fierce with the game on the line. His two-run bomb off Boston's Bill Lee at Fenway Park in the 6th inning of Game 7 of 1975 World Series was the most important hit in Reds history. He is a seven-time All-Star who rates his 1967 All-Star Game home run in the 15th inning off Catfish Hunter to be his top individual highlight. (He won the ASG MVP that year.) He is arguably the most popular player in the Reds modern era. Part of an extremely rare and historic duo: Pete Rose was his teammate on the rookie-league Geneva (N.Y.) Redlegs; they played the same position (second base). The Big Dog was a clubhouse equalizer and agitator of the celebrated Big Four (Pèrez, Rose, Joe Morgan and Johnny Bench) and fellow starting position players, Davey Concepciòn, George Foster, Ken Griffey Sr. and Cèsar Gerònimo, who together comprised the Great Eight of the Big Red Machine, arguably the greatest starting lineup ever. Married 50+ years to Pituka de la Cantera, also a Cuba native and "the love of my life," said Tony at his statue dedication at Great American Ball Park. Career: 379 HR, 1,652 RBI, 505 doubles, 2,732 hits; .279/.341/.463; 122 OPS+.

155. LEO POSADA, La Habana
April 15, 1936–
OF / KCA, 1960–62
Limited action in majors, but five seasons in Cuba with Habana and Alemndares. Uncle of former Yankees star Jorge Posada.

156. ARIEL PRIETO, La Habana
October 22, 1969–
P / OAK, TBAY, 1995–2001
He started 60 games over six-plus years, sitting out 1999 with an arm injury from which he never recovered. Career: 15-24, 352 1/3 IP, 4.85 ERA.

157. YASIEL PUIG, Cienfuegos
December 7, 1990–
OF / LAD, 2013–
He exploded onto the big-league scene with 4 HR/ 10 RBIs in first five games in June, both numbers tying modern-era rookie records. His 44 hits in the first

month were second only to rookie Joe DiMaggio's 48. Puig finished second to fellow Cuban José Fernandez in the 2013 ROY vote. Puig was a 2014 All-Star, who has been plagued by chronic hamstring, weight and personal issues. But by 2017 he was definitely earning that $42.5 million, seven-year contract, as the Dodgers made it to the World Series for the first time in 29 years. His defection from Cuba (on the 13th try) is the stuff of Hollywood: he was smuggled by boat to Mexico by a notorious narco kingpin, and held for weeks while his "rescuers" offered his services to the highest bidder. Career: .281/.357/.475. His two home runs in the 2017 World Series both occurred in games that became instant classics: his long blast to open the bottom of the 10th inning in Game 2 cut a 5–3 deficit to 5–4 (the Astros went on to win 7–6 in 11 innings), and his epic two-run bomb in the 9th inning of Game 5 closed a 12–9 deficit to 12–11 (the Astros went on to win 13–12 in 10 innings). Puig said he greatly admired fellow Cuban and Astros' strongman Yuli Gurriel, who blasted a 4th-inning, three-run homer off LA's Clayton Kershaw in Game 5 to tie the score at 4.

158. ALEXEI RAMÌREZ, Pinar del Rio
September 22, 1981–
SS, 2B / CHW, SDP, TBay, 2008–2016
He has had a very good career, beginning with his runnerup finish in the 2008 ROY vote, when at age 28 he hit .290 with 21 homers, including a rookie record *four* grand slams. (To quote the line from *Hamilton*: "Let's get this guy in front of a crowd!") He won the Silver Slugger in 2010 and 2014, and was a 2014 All-Star. Ramirez was "the first successful modern-era position player among his countrymen to strike paydirt" in the major leagues (Bjarkman). Ramirez, who won the HR title in his final year of the *Serie Nacional* (2007), is a classic late-bloomer who "blossomed beyond all expectations" (Bjarkman). He wowed scouts and fellow players with his acrobatic infield play—which by itself didn't distinguish him from a lot of Cuban shortstops. What distinguished him was his bat. Basically, he was a Rey Ordonez who *raked*.

159. BOBBY RAMOS, Calabazar de Sagua
November 5, 1955–
C / MON, 1978–84
Ramos grew up in Miami and is a good example of the way catchers can craft a "career" on defense

alone. Ramos played in 103 games over six seasons despite batting only .190.

160. PEDRO RAMOS, Pinar del Rio
April 28, 1935–
P / WSH, MIN, CLE, NYY, PHIL, PITT, CIN, 1955–70
"The Cuban Cowboy." His rural upbringing in Cuba's westernmost province may have had something to do with his fascination with America's Wild West. In Washington, Cleveland and New York, the handsome pitcher "loved to dress in lace-trimmed black cowboy duds, taking on striking resemblance to his movie-screen idols, the Lone Ranger and Hopalong Cassidy" (Bjarkman.) Ramos took it a little too far, however, when his playing days were over, getting involved in Miami's wild drug-trafficking scene of the late 1970s and early 1980s, doing three years in federal prison on drug and weapons charges. He worked both sides of the long-ball aisle, giving up some all-time, tape-measure shots (Mickey Mantle hit 12 career homers off him, one of which came within 18 inches of leaving Yankee Stadium *completely*, which would have been a first), and also hitting some of his own (Ramos had 15 career homers, including highs of three in three straight years, 1961-63). He was a 1959 All-Star and a workhorse. He started 30 or more games from 1957-61 (leading the AL in losses in four straight seasons), and averaged 244 innings per year from 1957–1962.

161. NAP REYES, Santiago de Cuba
November 24, 1919–September 15, 1995
P / NYG, 1943–50
Reyes' seven seasons as a player in Cuba were overshadowed by his managerial career: six years with Marianao (three Caribbean Series); two seasons with the Havana Cubans and four with the Sugar Kings. He loved the game and wanted his players to love it the way he did. He was positively unparallelled as a tobacco-chewer: *Everybody* who ever played for the man said a river ran down it, i.e. a perpetual brown stream down his chin. Career big-league batting average: .284.

162. ARMANDO ROCHE, La Habana
December 7, 1926–June 26, 1997
P / WSH, 1945
Armando (Baez) Roche died at age 70 in Maywood, Ill. (hometown of Dennis "Andy Sipowicz" Franz)

during the heart of NYPD Blue's phenomenal 12-year run. Roche was a handsome right-hander of regal bearing (6-foot, 190 pounds), who would not have been caught dead in a "Sipowicz," the short-sleeved-shirt-and-tie "look" favored by the hard-boiled, heart-of-gold TV detective. At 18, Roche pitched in two games (no decisions) for the wartime Washington Senators. In his two-inning debut (May 10, 1945) he got touched up by one of the best: Vern Stephens, the Browns' cleanup hitter and seven-time All-Star and three-time RBI champ, ripped him for a double on a 2-for-4 night at St. Louis' Sportsman's Park.

163. EDDY RODRÌGUEZ, Villa Clara
December 1, 1985–
C / SDP, 2012
Unbeknownst to anybody including himself, E-Rod began his homeric odyssey when he was drafted by the Reds out of "The U" (Miami) in 2006. He was released by the Reds in April 2009, and played two seasons of independent ball, before signing with the Padres as a free agent in February 2011. He worked his way to the majors after two years in the minors with five different teams. On August 2, 2012, he debuted against the team that signed him six years earlier. In his first a-bat in The Show, he homered to deep left-center off Reds ace Johnny Cueto in Cincinnati. Career: 2 MLB games, 1-for-5; .200/.429/.800.

164. FREDDY RODRÌGUEZ, La Habana
April 29, 1924–June 11, 2009
P / CHC, PHI, 1958–59
Rodriguez pitched nine innings over two years in the bigs, but more importantly, played seven seasons in the Cuban Winter League, four with Havana Cubans.

165. HÉCTOR RODRÌGUEZ, Alquizar
June 13, 1920–September 1, 2003
3B / CHW, 1952
He is the "Pete Rose of Cuban Winter League," its all-time hits leader and the only player to reach the summit of the 1000-hit mountain. He made his big-league debut on April 15, 1952, before 25,037 fans at Comiskey Park, going 1-for-3 (doubled, stole third) against Early Wynn. Rodriguez "two-upped" Cuba's main man and Chisox teammate Minnie Miñoso (single in 2 trips, caught stealing). Career: 124 G, 462 PA; .265/.346/.307 (1 HR). He played 19 seasons in Cuba, and was the Winter League's ROY in 1942–43.

166. JOSÈ RODRÌGUEZ, La Habana
February 23, 1894–December 1, 1953
2B, 1B / NYG, 1916–18
He was Cuba's Keith Hernandez as a slick-fielding first baseman. He had only three years with the Giants (58G), but is fifth on the all-time list in the Cuban Winter League for "years played" (20). Cuba Baseball Hall of Fame, 1951.

167. COOKIE ROJAS, La Habana
March 6, 1939–
2B, OF / CIN, PHI, STL, KCR, 1962–77
He was the keystone corner-mate of shortstop Leo Cardenas' for the 1959 Sugar Kings, and a five-time MLB All-Star (1NL, 4 AL). Originally signed at 17 by the Reds in 1956. He was a very good all-around player (career .263 with 54 HR ad 593 RBI). With Philly shortstop Bobby Wine, he formed the exquisitely named "The Days of Wine and Rojas," the team's mid-1960s' DP combo. In 1967 with Philly, he played all nine positions (giving up only one hit and no runs in his one frame on the mound). Coach, manager, and the Marlins' Spanish-language TV analyst.

168. MINNIE ROJAS, Remedios
November 26, 1933–March 23, 2002
P / CAL, 1966–68
Like Tony Pèrez, Rojas never played organized ball in Cuba. After a year of compulsory military service in Cuba, Rojas left the country to play semi-pro ball in Mexico. After that, he put himself on the *all*-pro track, working his way north out of Mexico. Retroactively, he led the AL in saves with 27 in 1967, when he also led the league in games finished (53) with a 124 ERA+.

169. CHICO RUIZ, Santo Domingo
December 5, 1938–February 9, 1972
2B, 3B, SS / CIN, CAL, 1964–71
His steal of home with Frank Robinson at plate started the 1964 Phillies on the 10-game losing slide that ended their pennant hopes. Ruiz "signed with the Reds in 1958 (as part of the pipeline of Cuban talent that Cincinnati enjoyed in the 1950s, thanks to the friendship between Reds general manager Gabe Paul and Bobby Maduro, the Cuban baseball man." (Rory Costello, SABR). *The New Bill James Historical Abstract:* "'Tony Pacheco was scouring the island on behalf of the Sugar Kings. Pacheco put together a team of about (15) young players who traveled Cuba. On that team were Diego Seguí, Tony González, Chico Ruiz, José Tartabull, and Tony Pérez.'" It's likely that Ruiz played with those other young men, but not Pérez, who was between three to six years younger than the others. There's also confusion over the real name of the colorful Ruiz. In Cuba, it is Giraldo Sablón Ruiz. (In the Hispanic tradition, the father's family name is second; the mother's maiden name is last.) In today's U.S., Chico's name would be Giraldo (Ruiz) Sablón. In 1950s and 1960s U.S.—even if he had been Chico Sablón. But by any name, Giraldo "Bench Me or Trade Me" Sablón was one of a kind. Career: 565 G, .240/.279/.295.

170. ÁLEX SÁNCHEZ, La Habana
August 26, 1976–
OF / MIL, DET, TBAY, SFG, 2001–05
Sánchez played at Miami-Dade Community College, and was signed by the Marlins in 1996. On April 3, 2005, he became the first player suspended for violating MLB's then-new drug enforcement policy. Career: .296, 21 triples, 122 stolen bases. He was rangy, but with a stiff glove: He led the AL in errors by a center-fielder in 2003 and 2004.

171. ISRAEL SÁNCHEZ, Falcon Lasvias
August 20, 1963–
P / KCR, 1988–90
Sánchez grew up in Chicago. He had a short career (30 G, 1 start, 45 1/3 IP, 5.36 ERA) but his debut (July 7, 1988) was star-filled: He gave up a leadoff single to Paul Molitor to begin the 8th inning at Royals Stadium, and two batters later, gave up a run-scoring groundout to Robin Yount, followed by a run-*allowing* error by George Brett—Hall of Famers all.

172. RAÚL SÁNCHEZ, Marianao
December 12, 1930–June 20, 2002
P / WSH, CIN, 1952–1960
Sánchez was 5-3 in three years in the majors. He played 10 seasons in the Cuban Winter League, and also played for the Havana Cubans and Sugar Kings. He was a major factor in the Sugar Kings' success in the 1959 regular season (11-5, 41 G, 14 GS, 145 IP, 3.10 ERA) and postseason (seven-game Junior World Series victory over Minneapolis Millers). Career: 49 G, 2 GS, 5 SV, 4.62 ERA.

173. AMAURI SANIT, La Habana
July 4, 1979–
P / NYY, 2011
4 games, no decisions, 12.86 ERA. That's Amauri.

174. NELSON SANTOVENIA, Pinar del Rio
July 27, 1961–
C / MON, CHW, KCR, 1987–93
Santovenia was born only three months after the Bay of Pigs. He grew up in Miami, and was the first-round draft pick of the Expos in 1982, having made the all-tournament team when Miami won the College World Series. On July 28, 1989, he threw out the Cardinals' Vince Coleman attempting to steal, ending Coleman's MLB record 50 consecutive SBs. (Santovenia himself was thrown out 7 times in 11 attempts during his career.). As a batter: .233 career, 22 HR.

175. DIEGO SEGUI, Holquin
August 17, 1937–
P / KCA, WSH, OAK, SEA, STL, BOS, 1962–1977
Diego was a Cincinnati Redlegs' signee in 1958. In 1970, he led the AL with a 2.56 ERA. One of his trivia claims-to-fame is that he pitched in the first game of each Seattle franchise: the Pilots in 1969, and the Mariners in 1977. In the latter, he was dubbed, at age 39, "The Ancient Mariner." Apologies to Coleridge, but had Nostradamus been domiciled in the Great Northwest in the spring of 1969, he would have prognosticated: "Ancient Mariner-To-Be Will Winneth Two of Three." (Diego's best W-L mark was 12-6, .667, for the Pilots, 1969). Career: 15 seasons, 92-111, 3.81 ERA.

176. ALAY SOLER, Pinar del Rio
October 9, 1979–
P / NYM, 2006
Alay "The Sun Will Come Up Tomorrow" Soler. Career 2-3.

177. JORGE SOLER, La Habana
February 25, 1992–
OF / CHC, KCR, 2014–
Soler made a nice rookie splash in 2014: 24G, 97 PA, .292/.330/.573 (5 HRs, 8 doubles, 20 RBIs). He was a part-time outfielder on the 2016 World Champions. In December 2016, he was traded to Kansas City for Wade Davis. Career: .244/.318/.412.

178. LUIS SUAREZ, Alto Songo
August 24, 1916–June 5, 1991
3B / WSH, 1944
After playing one game (two at-bats), he returned to Cuba to play four seasons with Clark Griffith's Havana Cubans.

179. LEO SUTHERLAND, Santiago de Cuba
April 6, 1958–
OF / CHW, 1980–81
Southerland was born during the heart of *La Revolucion*. His hometown is 114 miles east of where Castro and his rebels shipwrecked-ashore south of Niquero on December 2, 1956. When Sutherland arrived on the scene in Santiago de Cuba, a general strike organized by Castro's 26th of July movement was only three days away; a month later, Batista sent 10,000 troops into the Sierra Maestra mountains to destroy Fidel's 300 armed guerillas. Sutherland fled Cuba at a young age and grew up in California, where he was drafted in the first round. He singled in his first big-league at bat on a 2-for-3 day with a stolen base. Career: 45 G, .248/.274/.277.

180. JOSÉ TARTABULL, Cienfuegos
November 27, 1938–
OF / KCA, BOS, OAK, 1962–70
Tartabull was signed by the Giants prior to the 1958 season. His greatest baseball moment occurred nine years later, on Sunday, August 27, 1967, at Fenway Park. Tartabull's Red Sox were a half-game up on the Twins, and one game up on Tigers and White Sox in a wild AL pennant race. (Typical of Carl Yastrzemski that "Impossible Dream" season, Yaz had hit two homers to give Boston a 4-3 lead going into the 9th.) With speedy Chisox Ken Berry on third base and one out, pinch-hitter Duane Josephson lifted a soft line drive to right field. The weak-armed Tartabull charged, and threw hard but high to Bosox catcher Elston Howard, who reached for it and kept his left foot planted to keep Berry off the plate. *Out!* Red Sox win! Still in first place! "Tartabull's Throw" ranked No. 59 in "The 100 Greatest Moments in Red Sox History" by the *Boston Herald* in 2001. Said Tartabull to Peter Gammons in 1992: "Who would have thought in 1961 (when he was last in Cuba) that I'd still never have been back or seen my family?" Career: .261 /.303/.320.

181. TONY TAYLOR, Central Alava
December 19, 1935–
2B, 3B / CHC, PHIL, DET, 1958–76
Taylor was "the Philllies' Ernie Banks," a huge fan favorite. The 1960 All-Star had his best season in 1963, .281/.330/.367: 700 PA, 20 2B, 23 SB, career highs of 102 R, 180 H and 10 triples. Career: .261/.321/.352.

182. MICHAEL TEJERA, La Habana
October 18, 1976–
P / FLA, TEX, 1999–2005
Tejera's national face time came for the Marlins in the 2003 NLCS vs. the Cubs, as he pitched a scoreless inning in Game 2 and took the loss in Game 3 (11th-inning single to Kenny Lofton, triple by Doug Glanville). But his team won the World Championship. Career: 11-13.

183. LUIS TIANT JR., La Habana
November 23, 1940–
P / CLE, MIN, BOS, NYY, PIT, CAL, 1964–82
Greatest of the post-Jackie Robinson Cuban pitchers, and owner of one of the best narratives that span Cuba and the major leagues. Tremendous leader, great teammate. 19 seasons, 3-time All-Star. Memorable 1975 World Series, shut down Big Red Machine for two victories. (His father, Luis Sr., the great Cuban and Negro Leagues lefthanded pitcher, watched the first of those from the stands at Fenway Park.) Junior's 1.60 ERA in 1968 was the best in the AL since 1919. Career: 229-172, 3.30 ERA, 2,416 Ks. Postseason: 3-0, 2.86 ERA. Which all begs the question: How is Tiant *not* in the National Baseball Hall of Fame? The writers clearly got this one wrong. Will the Hall's veterans committee one day right it?

184. JORGE TOCA, Remedios
January 7, 1971–
1B, OF / NYM, 1999–2001
27 at-bats over three seasons and a .259 batting average.

185. YASMANY TOMÁS, La Habana.
November 14, 1990–
OF, 3B / AZ, 2015–
Arizona landed him in November 2014 for an "astounding $68.5 million-dollar deal... So rapidly had the market already elevated, based upon pure speculation, that Tomás (was) paid more than twice what

the Reds had paid Aroldis Chapman four years earlier, and twice what the Dodgers had gambled on Yasiel Puig...and even more than the White Sox handed out for newly crowned (AL ROY) José Abreu" (Bjarkman). Tomás' 2016 was good, with 31 HR and .272/.313/.508. He's still a work-in-progress, especially defensively. Career: .268/307/.462.

186. GIL TORRES, Regla
August 23, 1915–January 10, 1983
SS, 3B / WSH, 1940–46
Upon Gil's debut (April 25, 1940), he and father Ricardo became the first Cuban father-son to play in the majors. Career: 346 G, .252 batting average.

187. RICARDO TORRES, Regla
April 16, 1891–April 17, 1960
C, 1B / WSH, 1920-22
Thirteen seasons in Cuba. 39 plate appearances in the majors, .297 batting average. Father of Gil Torres.

188. ÓSCAR TUERO, La Habana.
December 1, 1893–October 21, 1960
P / STL, 1918–20
Arguably the most persevering of the Cubans, because he notably pitched for 28 seasons, starting in Jersey City when the great Dihigo was hitting stones with a stick as an eight-year-old in Matanzas, and finishing at age 47 only a few months before Pearl Harbor. Tuero knew all the Cuban and American greats, which in one case were one and the same: Dolf Luque, a contemporary. In the late teens just after the Great War, Luque went 29–15 while Tuero went 6–9 in 58 games (19 of them starts) with a 2.88 ERA. Tuero pitched two minor-league no-hitters. One against Shreveport, La.—which explains, in part anyway, how he came to buried in Pythian Cemetery in Bunkie, La., six months before the Bay of Pigs.

189. SANDY ULLRICH, La Habana
July 25, 1921–April 21, 2001
P / WSH, 1944-45
Carlos Santiago Ullrich was 3-3 over two seasons. He played 10 seasons in Cuba with Almendares and Cienfuegos.

190. HENRY URRUTIA, Las Tunas
February 13, 1987–
DH, OF / BALT / 2013-15

Urrutia had five seasons in *Serie Nacional* with *Leñadores de Las Tunas*, before signing with the Orioles in 2012. Career: 272/.287/.337.

191. RAÚL VALDÉS, La Habana
November 27, 1977–
P / NYM, STL, NYY, PHIL, HOU, 2010–2014
Valdés had five seasons in *Serie Nacional* with *Vaqueros de La Habana*, before signing with the Cubs in 2004. Career: 103 G (3 starts); 140 1/3 IP, 7-7, 5.13 ERA.

192. RENÉ VALDÉS, Guanabacoa
June 2, 1929–March 15, 2008
P / BROOKLYN, 1957
In his debut in the first game of a doubleheader vs. the Pirates at Ebbets Field on April 21, 1957, the 6-foot-3, 175-pound Valdes—*El Látigo,* "The Whip"—went 3 2/3 innings, sandwiched between veteran Don Newcombe and 21-year-old Sandy Koufax; Valdés' line: 0 H, 0 R, 1 walk, 1 K. He twice apiece retired future Hall of Famers Roberto Clemente and Bill Mazeroski. Career: 5 G (1 start) 13 IP, 1-1, 5.54 ERA. *El Látigo* just kept whipping it: After his big-league taste, he pitched five more years in the minors, and three in Mexico.

193. ROY VALDÉS, La Habana
February 23, 1920–January 3, 2005
C, PH / WSH, 1944
Valdés barely even *smelled* the coffee. On May 3, 1944—a month and three days before the D-Day Invasion—the Red Sox beat the Senators 12-11 at Fenway Park (Bosox player-manager Joe Cronin was 3-for-5, with 3 RBI). Roy made his debut, pinch-batting (a groundout to the pitcher) in his one career at-bat. Bye-bye, Rogelio Lazaro (Rojas) Valdés. He played five more years in the minors after his send-down. Played for Marianao in the Cuban Winter League.

194. SANDY VALDESPINO, San Jose de las Lajas
January 24, 1939–
OF / MIN, ATL, HOU, SEA, MIL, KCR, 1965–71
Valdespino was signed by the Senators' Joe Cambria before the 1957 season, and spent the next eight years in the minors. But he gloriously made it to the 1965 World Series as a Twins rookie, going 3-for-11 (.273) with one double. Career: 382 G, 839 PA, .230/.286/.295.

195. JOSÉ VALDIVIELSO, Matanzas
May 22, 1934–
SS / WSH, MIN, 1955–61
Valdivielso caught Joe Cambria's eye playing for Almendares in the 1952–53 Cuban Winter League. "Valdie" spent three seasons in the minors before his debut (June 21, 1955) at Washington's Griffith Stadium. He went 0-for-3, but watched proudly as the great Minnie Miñoso drove in two runs in the Chisox 6-1 victory. Valdivielso was a smooth fielder, but not much with the stick: lifetime .219 batting average in 401 games. Like teammate Jim Bunning, Valdivielso cherished his Caribbean World Series' Championship on the 1956-57 Marianao Tigers.

196. ZOILO VERSALLES, La Habana
December 18, 1939 June 9, 1995
SS / WSH, MIN, LAD, CLE, ATL, 1959–71
Versalles spent one year in the minors, before being called up at 19. He is Cuba's first MLB MVP (1965). The two-time All-Star also won two Gold Gloves. Versalles' MVP-season was 7.2 WAR—4.6 better than his next-best season (1963). His 1961 Topps baseball card lists him as "Zorro." After 12 years in the bigs (.242/.290/.367), Versalles finished up in Japan and Mexico. Four days after Versalles was born, the University of Havana Caribes football team was beaten 71-0 by Rollins College in an exhibition game, which included a spectacular 94-yard, 6-lateral TD romp.

197. DAYAN VICIEDO, Remedios
March 10, 1989–
OF, DH / CHW, 2010–14
Dayan "The Tank" Viciedo—all 5-foot-11 and 240 pounds of him—rolled through 2012 with 25 HR. Career: 483 G, 1798 PA, .254/.298/.424. 2016–17, Japan.

198. ADRIÁN ZABALA, San Antonio de los Banos
August 26, 1916–January 4, 2002
P / NYG, 1945, 1949
Zabala's two seasons with the Giants (4-7) don't provide a full picture of his overall career. He played 17 seasons in the Cuban Winter League, and is first on its all-time list in games pitched (330), tied for third for most games won (90) and tops as the all-time winningest left-hander.

199. ÓSCAR ZAMORA, Camagüey
September 23, 1944–

P / CHC, HOU, 1974–78
September 23, 1944–
Zamora was originally an Indians signee. He grew up in Miami. Career: 158 G (2 starts), 13-14, 4.53 ERA.

200. JOSÉ "TONY" ZARDON, La Habana
May 20, 1923–March 21, 2017
OF / WSH, 1945
With Connie Marrero's death in 2014, Zardon became the oldest living big-leaguer born in Cuba. And upon Zardon's death three years later, he became the last of the pre-VJ Day Washington Senators to cross over. Famously told SABR: "I really did not apply myself to baseball as much as I should have. There were just too many temptations for a young player. Like 'Ladies Day' at Gran Stadium." Zardon would have taken part in the Bay of Pigs invasion, if not for a training injury. (*La Revolucion* got personal for Zardon when Castro's agents broke into his Havana apartment and stole his trophies; he was also upset with poor treatment accorded his father, who was anti-Castro.) "I joined the Special Forces," Zardon told SABR's Rory Costello and Lou Hernandez in 2014. In a practice jump in Guatemala, his chute didn't open properly. "My fall was broken by the thick branches of a ceiba tree. It took me 2½ years to fully recover. Our photos were leaked and I was recognized by Castro, who decreed that there were certain 'mercenaries' who were not punished for their acts in the invasion and that if they ever stepped foot on Cuban soil, they would be incarcerated…I can never go back."

SOURCES: Baseball-Reference; Retrosheet; Society for American Baseball Research (SABR); "A History of Cuban Baseball: 1864-2006", by Peter Bjarkman; "Cuba's Baseball Defectors: The Inside Story" (2016; Bjarkman); "The Pride of Havana: A History of Cuban Baseball" (2001; Robert González Echevarria); "Cuban Baseball Legends: Baseball's Alternative Universe," by Peter Bjarkman and Bill Nowlin (2016); *New York Times* obituaries; selected articles by John Erardi, Cincinnati Enquirer.

WRITERS: John Erardi, Greg Gajus and Larry Phillips, all of SABR; Ron Lanham and Tim VonderBrink.

EDITORS: Gajus, Denny Dressman, David Lowery and Greg Erardi.

Acknowledgments

As Yogi Berra once said, "In baseball you don't know nothing."

At least not until it happens.

So here's my place-by-place genuflections in the order things happened.

For starters, it was quite a coincidence (to me, anyway) that the Erardi nuclear family of the early 1960s was traversing Central New York roads at the same time in the same make and model white Chevy station wagon with red interiors and three bench seats, the last of them facing backward, as the newly arrived "Tani" Pérez from Cuba.

I thank…

Marty Brennaman, who got me thinking about the possibilities when he mentioned many years ago that four months into the 1974 Reds season a WLW-AM call of Pérez's two-run walkoff home run off the Giants' Randy Moffitt to cap a Reds' five-run ninth (14–13) at Riverfront Stadium finally warmed Reds fans to a rookie Reds play-by-play man.

Joel Luckhaupt, for suggesting a Pérez—Cuba book in late 2014. Greg Rhodes, who convinced me I had the memories, experiences and Pérez trove of interviews to produce it. Greg Gajus, the indefatigable analyst of Pérez's numbers and co-producer of the two-hundred "Major League Baseball's Cuban Players" of Appendix Four.

The late Jim Bunning who in early December 2015, regaled me with memories of playing Cuban Winter Ball with league MVP Minnie Miñoso in 1956–57 pre-Castro Havana, while—three hundred miles away in the sugar mill town of Central Violeta in Camagüey province—fourteen-year-old "Tani" Pérez listened to the exploits of his idol on radio. Five days after meeting with Bunning, I was flying off to Cuba with my friends and former co-workers, Tim VonderBrink, and Ron Lanham, and three days after that I was in Violeta, walking the streets that Tani walked, talking to the people "who knew him when."

Bob Hertzel, whose heart-tugging piece about Tony's visit home in 1972 made me feel as though I walking those very streets with Tony and his dad. No way that trip and this book happens without Ron and Tim's help, and that of Clem Paredes Rodriguez, a Cuba-born Canadian who my friend, Larry Phillips, directed me to; Larry was instrumental throughout. Pure serendipity upon our arrival at Havana's José Marti Airport brought us cabdriver Daniel Maiza Valdés, our first real contact "in country" and—as it turned out—our best. In Vedado, our urban nest north of the airport, we hooked up with tour guide Sergio Torres and then local guide Yusbel Pérez Ruiz, who grew up in Tony's hometown. Yusbel got us safely from Cruces to Ciego de Avila in good humor under harrowing circumstances.

Luis Zayas, for his insights into the Havana Sugar Kings; Martin Dihigo Jr., for his memories of his father, *El Inmortal*; Chuck Davis, my plebe baseball coach at the U.S. Naval Academy, whose anecdotes about pitching against the Cuban national team in 1959 helped me understand the transition period between the professional and all-amateur eras in Cuba. My fellow scribes, the *Finger Lakes Times* Mike Cutillo and Alan Brignall in Geneva, New York, for opening their arms and archives. Cutillo tipped me to Tom Tryniski's amazing free-of-charge website fultonhistory.com, which has digitized over 37 million pages of newspapers in the U.S. and Canada, thus allowing me to re-create Tony's fledgling seasons in the New York-Penn League.

In lovely Geneva itself, Chuck Agonito, John "Johnny O" Oughterson and Bill Kohlberger, for keeping the fire burning for minor-league baseball at McDonough Park. My late high school pal, Dave Schardt, for his inspiration; his brother, Tom, a heck of an athlete at Hobart College in Geneva, for acclimating me to the town. My friend, Mark Pfeiffer, who spent summers in Geneva as a youth and reminisced about Tani, Pete and Cesar Tovar at Shuron Field.

In Andrews, North Carolina, where I hooked up with the one and only Dave Bristol, Tony's manager in Macon (Georgia), San Diego and Cincinnati. It took a crazy trip to reach Bristol via "The Tail of the Dragon," an eleven-mile stretch of two-lane on US 129 with 318 curves that hugged the North Carolina-Tennessee line along the southwestern edge of Great Smoky Mountains National Park, but it was worth it.

Tom Dotterer, who was one of Tony's teammates in Macon (and whose brother, Dutch, played for the Havana Sugar Kings), still has baseball in his blood (he coaches baseball at my high school alma mater in Syracuse, where Buddy Wleklinski also proved helpful).

In the Macon of today: sports columnist Bobby Pope, and former prep all sports star/Dodgers farmhand and major league scout Tommy Mixon, and long-time resident Leon Simmons. In Cincinnati of today: Reds scout Cam Bonifay and former Macon Peach Dan Neville. In Coconut Grove, Florida, Sue Mac-Donald and Viani Navarette, for their friendship and soulfulness and for letting me use their home as a staging ground for the Little Havana/Fort Myers portion of the trip. "Suemac" is also a confidante, and Viani a gifted Spanish translator with a Cuban's touch. Viani introduced me to Little Havana's Domino Park, where we stumbled upon the 80-year-old baseball savant, Gabriel Iglesias.

My translator-niece, too, Megan Sheehan; my long-ago Annapolis roomie, Brian Corcoran, for chauffeuring me from Fort Lauderdale to the Everglades and Key West and back in his 1985 Volkswagen Vanagon tintop. Tony Oliva in Fort Myers for the interview—and to Dustin Morse of the Minnesota Twins for setting it up.

In Cincinnati over four decades, Tony and Pituka Pérez, and their sons, Victor and Eduardo; the late Tony Pacheco and Lee May, Frank Robinson, Tommy Helms, Joe Morgan, Pete Rose, Johnny Bench, Davey Concepción, Jack Billingham, Don Gullett, Gary Nolan, Jim Maloney, Leo Cardenas, Ron Flender, and the late Sparky Anderson, Bob Howsam, Ted Kluszewski, Jim O'Toole and Bernie Stowe. César Gerònimo, George Foster, Ken Griffey Sr., Bill Plummer, Will McEnaney, Pedro Borbon, Mario Soto, Dave Parker, Ron Oester, Buddy Bell, Barry Larkin, Eric Davis, Tom Browning, Marty Brennaman, Bob Uecker and Chris Welsh. Mike Schmidt, Steve Garvey, Fred McGriff, Will Clark, Dwight Gooden, Don Sutton. Lou Piniella, Dusty Baker and Joe Torre.

In Cincinnati, specifically in 2015, 2016 and 2017, Davey Concepción, Cèsar Gerònimo, Tommy Helms, Luis Tiant, Tony Oliva, Bert Campaneris, Aledmys Diaz, Brayan Peña, Aroldis Chapman, Raisel Iglesias and the late José Fernandez. sculptor Tom Tsuchiya and his brother, Steve. The Big Dog himself, who though too humble to want this book, gave me as close to his blessing as I could have hoped when he told me at Pete Rose's statue dedication in June 2017: "I can't stop you, John—go ahead."

My friend and mentor Denny Dressman, whose direction, inspiration and hands-on shepherding of the material was indispensable. John Baskin, editor at Orange Frazer Press, was incredibly patient, supportive and challenging of me to make the writing better in certain places—and invariably proved to be right. Everybody at OFP, especially publisher Marcy and Sarah Hawley (champion of Appendix Four's inclusion). Baskin—Hawley—Hawley—and (designer Alyson) Rua are my Bench—Morgan—Concepción—and Geronimo, Gold Glovers all.

Charles Sotto, my counselor. Bob Crotty and Jeff Smith, for their counsel. Roberto Gonzàlez Echevarría and Peter C. Bjarkman, for their writings, and Rogério Manzano, for his Cuban baseball website, desdemipalcodefanatico. wordpress.com. Baseball-reference.com, and the historical biographies from the Society for American Baseball Research. In Cooperstown, New York, at the National Baseball Hall of Fame and Museum, Craig Muder and John Horne, and the visiting ex-Red, ex-Met, ex-Geneva Redleg, ex-Macon Peach and ex-Triple-A San Diego Padre Art Shamsky. Deeper in New York, as deep as it goes—Syracuse, Watertown and New York City—Greg and Frank Erardi, Joanne and Matt DeNinno, and Nancy and John O'Connor, for the generous use of their home on the St. Lawrence River, where a substantial portion of the manuscript was generated. My new friends, Chris Sprague and Ann Walsh, of Key West, for the newspaper articles on Cuban baseball. Big Daddy, for all the nuances.

As training ground for assimilating vast amounts of material into one coherent publication, I give homage to the coffee-chugging all-nighters at *The Cincinnati Enquirer* with Greg Noble, Mike "Flea" Ball and Rory Glynn et al, on our Reds' Opening Day sections. I hearkened back often to those moonup-to-sunrise sessions while writing this book. The photo-finders of those days and especially to my friend and fellow Rickey Henderson admirer Jeff Suess, who carries on in the best and brightest legacy of *Enquirer* librarians. The same to my friend and former *Enquirer* photo-journalist Gary Landers, for bringing out the best in the Cuba photos I forwarded him. Photographer Bill Renken; Rick Walls and Chris Eckes of the Reds Hall of Fame and Museum, who gave me access to the wonderful Jack Klumpe photo files from the late 1950s through mid- 1970s.

My daily sounding boards, John Eckberg and David Lowery. My weekly sounding boards, Cliff Radel and Bill Koch. Cliff's wife, Debbie, intrepid gold-sifter of a historical researcher who found for me Tony's Geneva teammates in 1960 and/or 1961: Dan Neville, Dan Paul, Sal Minetta, Stanley Proffitt, Bruce Montgomery and Calvin Newton. The staffs at the Public Library of Cincinnati and Hamilton County and the Erlanger branch of the Kenton County (Kentucky) library.

My wife, Barb, who allowed me to spread my papers and books all over the house, and to go where I needed to go in pursuit of the story (she did the same over my forty years of newspaper work), all because she knows this is what I love to do. Our son, Chris, who from 2,400 miles away extricated me from one computer dilemma after another; our daughter Gina, who supplied that same vivid imagination for the Cuba map-illustration in Chapter Four (and to Gina's lazy but loveable Milkshake, who during this project I renamed "Milkshakespeare"; she never left my side, and also never complained—well, except to bark at the UPS man).

Lastly, to the unnamed sisters outside the coffee house in Havana who for no other reason than that we were Americanos, waved Tim, Ron and me over on our final day in Cuba, and brought us gifts of hot espresso with cubes of raw brown sugar, and made us feel instantly welcome, at ease and hopeful. I think of you often and wonder how you're faring.

"*Amor, salud y felicidad.*"

Love, health and happiness.

—*John Erardi*
Cincinnati
January 2018

Selected Bibliography

BOOKS

Adelman, Tom, *The Long Ball: The Summer of '75 —Spaceman, Catfish, Charlie Hustle, and the Greatest World Series Ever Played*. Boston: Little, Brown, 2003.

Anderson, Jon Lee. *Che: A Revolutionary Life*. New York: Grove Press, 1997.

Anderson, Sparky, with Dan Ewald. *They Call Me Sparky*. Chelsea, MI: Sleeping Bear Press, 1998.

Anderson, Sparky, and Si Burick. *The Main Spark: Sparky Anderson & the Cincinnati Reds*. Garden City, NY: Doubleday, 1978.

Angell, Roger, *The Summer Game*. New York: Viking, 1972.

Angell, Roger, *Five Seasons: A Baseball Companion*. New York: Simon and Schuster, 1977.

Bench, Johnny, and William Brashler. *Catch You Later*. New York: Harper & Row, 1979.

Bjarkman, Peter C. *A History of Cuban Baseball: 1864-2006*. Jefferson, NC: McFarland, 2007.

Bjarkman, Peter C. *Cuba's Baseball Defectors: The Inside Story*. Lanham, MD: Rowman & Littlefield, 2016.

Brock, Darryl. *Havana Heat*. Lincoln, NE: University of Nebraska Press, 2011.

Burgos, Adrian Jr. *Cuban Star: How One Negro-League Owner Changed the Face of Baseball*. New York: Hill and Wang, 2011.

Callahan, Tom. *The Bases Were Loaded (And So Was I)*. New York: Crown Publishers, 2004.

Cardenas, Leonardo with George Guckenberger. *Cuba's Campo Corto*. Cincinnati, OH: The Mott Studio, 2015.

Collett, Ritter. *Men of the Machine: An Inside Look at Baseball's Team of the '70s*. Dayton, OH: Landfall Press, 1977.

Corbett, Warren. *The Wizard of Waxachachie: Paul Richards and the End of Baseball as We Knew It*. Dallas: Southern University Press, 2009.

DePalma, Anthony. *The Man Who Invented Fidel: Castro, Cuba, and Herbert L. Matthews of the New York Times*. New York: PublicAffairs, CQ 2006.

Detroit Free Press and Cincinnati Enquirer. *Sparky Anderson: The Life of a Baseball Legend*. Chicago: Triumph, 2010.

English, T.J. *Havana Nocturne: How the Mob Owned Cuba and Then Lost It to the Revolution*. New York: William Morrow, 2008.

Erardi, John. *Pete Rose 4192: Baseball's All-Time Hit Leader*. Cincinnati, OH: The Cincinnati Enquirer, 1986.

Erardi, John, and Greg Rhodes. *Opening Day: Celebrating Cincinnati's Baseball Holiday*, Cincinnati, OH: Road West Publishing, 2004.

Fainaru, Steve, and Ray Sánchez. *The Duke of Havana: Baseball, Cuba, and the Search for the American Dream*. New York: Villard Books, 2001.

Frost, Mark. *Game Six: Cincinnati, Boston, and the 1975 World Series—The Triumph of America's Pastime*. New York: Hyperion, 2009.

Gammons, Peter. *Beyond the Sixth Game: What's Happened to Baseball Since the Greatest Game in World Series History*. Boston: Houghton Mifflin, 1985.

Gibson, Bob, with Lonnie Wheeler. *Stranger to the Game: The Autobiography of Bob Gibson*. New York: Viking, 1994.

Gjelten, Tom. *Bacardi and the Long Fight for Cuba: The Biography of a Cause*. New York: Viking, 2008.

Gonzàlez Echevarría, Roberto. *The Pride of Havana: A History of Cuban Baseball*. New York: Oxford University Press, 2001.

Guillermoprieto, Alma. *Dancing with Cuba: A Memoir of the Revolution*. New York: Pantheon, 2004.

Henninger, Thom. *Tony Oliva: The Life and Times of a Minnesota Twins Legend*. Minneapolis, MN: University of Minnesota Press, 2015.

Hernández, Lou. *Memories of Winter Ball: Interviews with Players in the Latin American Winter Leagues of the 1950s*. Jefferson, NC: McFarland, 2013.

Hertzel, Bob. *Big Red Machine*. Englewood Cliffs, NJ: Prentice-Hall, 1976.

Honig, Donald. *The All-Star Game*. St. Louis, MO: The Sporting News, 1987.

Hyning, Thomas E. *The Santurce Crabbers: Sixty Seasons of Puerto Rican Winter League Baseball*. Jefferson, NC: McFarland, 1999.

Irvin, Monte, with Phil Pepe. *Few and Chosen: A Legend Ranks the Greatest Players of All-Time*. Chicago: Triumph, 2007.

Jamail, Milton H. *Full Count: Inside Cuban Baseball*. Carbondale, IL: Southern Illinois University Press, 2000.

James, Bill. *The New Bill James Historical Baseball Abstract*. New York: The Free Press, 2003.

Kaat, Jim, with Phil Pepe. *Still Pitching: Musings from the Mound and the Microphone*. Chicago: Triumph, 2003.

Kennedy, Robert F., and Arthur M. Schlesinger. *Thirteen Days: A Memoir of the Cuban Missile Crisis*. New York: W.W. Norton, 1999.

Lawson, Earl. *My 34 Years with the Reds*. South Bend, IN: Diamond Communications, 1987.

Leahy, Michael, *The Last Innocents: The Los Angeles Dodgers of the 1960s*. New York: HarperCollins, 2016.

Luckhaupt, Joel. *100 Things Reds Fans Should Know and Do Before They Die*. Chicago: Triumph, 2013.

Madden, Bill. *1954: The Year Willie Mays and the First Generation of Black Superstars Changed Major League Baseball Forever*. Boston: Da Capo Press, 2014.

Maraniss, David. *Clemente: The Passion and Grace of Baseball's Last Hero*. New York: Simon & Schuster, 2006.

McCoy, Hal. *The Relentless Reds*. Shelbyville, KY: PressCo, CQ 1976.

McCoy, Hal. *The Royal Reds*. Shelbyville, KY: PressCo, CQ 1977.

Miñoso, Minnie, with Herb Fagen. *Just Call Me Minnie: My Six Decades in Baseball*. Champaign, IL: Sagamore Publishing, 1994.

Morgan, Joe, and David Falkner. *Joe Morgan: A Life in Baseball*. New York: W.W. Norton, 1993.

Moruzzi, Peter. *Havana Before Castro: When Cuba was a Tropical Playground*. Layton, UT: Gibbs Smith, 2008.

National Baseball Hall of Fame and Museum. *The Hall: A Celebration of Baseball Greats*. New York: Little, Brown, 2014.

Posnanski, Joe. *The Machine: A Hot Team, a Legendary Season, and a Heart-stopping World Series—The Story of the 1975 Cincinnati Reds*. New York: HarperCollins, 2009.

Price, S.L. *Pitching Around Fidel: A Journey into the Heart of Cuban Sports*. New York: Ecco, 2000.

Quirk, Robert E. *Fidel Castro*. New York: Norton, 1993.

Regalado, Samuel O. *Viva Baseball! Latin Major Leaguers and Their Special Hunger*. Urbana IL: University of Illinois Press, 1998.

Rhodes, Greg, and John Erardi. *Big Red Dynasty: How Bob Howsam and Sparky Anderson Built the Big Red Machine*. Cincinnati, OH: Road West Publishing, 1997.

Rhodes, Greg, and John Snyder. *Redleg Journal: Year by Year and Day by Day with the Cincinnati Reds Since 1866.* Cincinnati OH: Road West Publishing, 2000.

Rose, Pete. *The Pete Rose Story: An Autobiography.* New York: World Publishing Company, 1970.

Rose, Pete, with Bob Hertzel. *Charlie Hustle.* Englewood Cliffs, NJ: Prentice-Hall, 1975.

Rucker, Mark, and Bjarkman, Peter C. *Smoke: The Romance and Lore of Cuban Baseball.* New York: Total/Sports Illustrated, 1999.

Ryan, Alan (edited by). *The Reader's Guide to Cuba.* San Diego: Harcourt, Brace & Co., 1997.

Sallah, Michael, and Mitch Weiss. *The Yankee Commandante: The Untold Story of Courage, Passion and One American's Fight to Liberate Cuba.* Guilford, CT: Lyons Press, 2015.

Szulc, Tad. *Fidel: A Critical Portrait.* New York: William Morrow, 1986.

Smith, Daryl. *Making the Big Red Machine: Bob Howsam and the Cincinnati Reds of the 1970s.* Jefferson, NC: McFarland, 2009.

Tiant, Luis, and Joe Fitzgerald. *El Tiante: The Luis Tiant Story.* Garden City, NY: Doubleday, 1976.

Van Riper, Tom, *Cincinnati Red and Dodger Blue: Baseball's Greatest Forgotten Rivalry*, Lanham, MD: Rowman & Littlefield, 2017.

Walker, Robert Harris. *Cincinnati and the Big Red Machine.* Bloomington, IN: Indiana University Press, 1988.

Wheeler, Lonnie, and John Baskin. *The Cincinnati Game.* Wilmington, OH: Orange Frazer Press, 1988.

Zanetti, Oscar, and Alejandro Garcìa. *Sugar and Railroads: A Cuban History, 1837-1959.* Translated by Franklin W. Knight and Mary Todd. New York: Grove Press, 2006.

MAGAZINES

Anderson, Jon Lee. "A New Cuba." *New Yorker*, October 3, 2016.

Blount, Roy Jr. "Beware the Dudes in the Red Hats." *Sports Illustrated*, June 24, 1974.

Deford, Frank. "Watch on the Ohio: Cincinnati and Its Baseball Team." Sports Illustrated, September 19 1975.

Dowling, Tom. "Tony Perez, Silent Cog in the Big Red Machine." *Sport*, October 1970.

Fimrite, Ron. "Seeing Red in Dodger Stadium: Cincinnati vs. Los Angeles." *Sports Illustrated,* August 19, 1974.

Fimrite, Ron. "Stormy Days for the Series." *Sports Illustrated*, October 27, 1975.

Fimrite, Ron. "Reaching Out for the Series." *Sports Illustrated*, October 20, 1975.

Fimrite, Ron. "Ah, How Great It Is." *Sports Illustrated*, November 1, 1976.

Fimrite, Ron. "The Reds Are Singing the Blues." *Sports Illustrated*, August 22, 1977.

Guillermoprieto, Alma. "Cuba: The Big Change." *New York Review of Books*, May 12, 2016.

Hertzel, Bob. "Tony Perez, the Biggest Bargain of Them All." *Baseball Digest*, December 1975.

Hertzel, Bob. "Why the Reds Call Tony Perez 'The Big Dog.'" *Baseball Digest*, August 1973.

Lawson, Earl. "Coming Home." Editors, Jim Ferguson and Jon Braude. *Cincinnati Reds 1984 Yearbook Magazine*, 1984

McHugh, Roy. "Is Perez Burning?" *Sport*, October 1967.

Leggett, William. "Hottest Team in Baseball: Cincinnati Reds." *Sports Illustrated*, August 22, 1966.

Leggett, William. "Reds Menace From Cincy." *Sports Ilustrated*, April 20, 1970.

Leggett, Wiliam. "Behind the Bold Red Rising in Cincinnati." *Sports Illustrated*, May 22, 1967.

Leggett, William. "Cincy Cannonball: Leader in National League West." *Sports Illustrated*, July 13, 1970, 12-17.

McNulty, Pat. "Why the Reds Hit So Well." *Sport*, October, 1969.

Padwe, Sandy. "Tony Perez: Baseball's Little-Known Superstar." *Baseball Digest*, September 1970.

Perez, Atanasio (sic) R. ("Tony"). "The Game I'll Never Forget," *Baseball Digest*, August 1974.

Price, S.L. "Baseball Diplomacy: How a Changing World Will Change The Game." *Sports Illustrated*, March 21, 2016.

Reed, William F. "Seeing Red in Cincinnati." *Sports Illustrated*, June 7, 1993.

Richman. Milton. "Tony Perez: He's Still a Baseball Favorite." *Baseball Digest*, July 1979.

Ryerson, Tom. "The Big Red Machine Rolls Again." *Baseball Digest*, October 1972.

Verschoth, A. "Tony Perez." *Sports Ilustrated*, June 30, 1986.

Ward, Robert. "Pete Rose & Joe Morgan Will Defend Their Championship to the Death." *Sport*, August, 1976.

Index

X

Xavier University, 24, 252

Y

Yankee Stadium, viii, 54, 227
Yasgur, Max, 229
Yastrzemski, Carl, xii, 63, 140, 143,
    203–205, 216, 231, 233, 235, 261
YMCA, 99
Yount, Robin, 230–231, 235
Yuro Ravine, battle of, 40

Z

zafra, 58
Zarza, Lazaro, *16*
Zayas, Luis, *xiii*, 63
Zedong, Mao, 172
Zimmer, Don, 77
Zuraw, George, 201

About the Author

JOHN ERARDI covered Tony Pérez through four decades, from his playing and managerial days to his Hall of Fame Induction and statue dedication. Erardi is the author or co-author of seven other books, two of them—*Crosley Field* and *Big Red Dynasty*—named Top Ten finalists by *Spitball* literary magazine as the best baseball books of the year, the latter of them a Top Five finalist for the Seymour Medal for best baseball history. His piece on high school basketball player Nick Mosley won a national first-place feature-writing award from the Associated Press Sports Editors, and his story on "Cincinnati and the Negro Leagues" was named the best feature in a state newspaper, all departments, by the Ohio Associated Press. He and wife, Barb, make their home in Crescent Springs, Kentucky, with their beloved rat terrier, Milkshake, now that their two grown children, Christopher and Gina, have moved on.